WORDSWORTH LIT

General Editor: Keit... ...abine

❧

GEORGE BERNARD SHAW

George Bernard Shaw

AN UNAUTHORISED BIOGRAPHY BASED
ON FIRSTHAND INFORMATION

FRANK HARRIS

Introduction by
J. H. STAPE

WORDSWORTH EDITIONS

In loving memory of
MICHAEL TRAYLER
the founder of Wordsworth Editions

I

Readers who are interested in other titles from
Wordsworth Editions are invited to visit our website at
www.wordsworth-editions.com

For our latest list and a full mail-order service, contact
Bibliophile Books, 5 Datapoint, South Crescent, London E16 4TL
TEL: +44 (0)20 7474 2474 FAX: +44 (0)20 7474 8589
ORDERS: orders@bibliophilebooks.com
WEBSITE: www.bibliophilebooks.com

First published in 2008 by Wordsworth Editions Limited
8B East Street, Ware, Hertfordshire SG12 9HJ

ISBN 978 1 84022 566 2

Typeset in Great Britain by Antony Gray
Printed and bound by Clays Ltd, St Ives plc

Contents

Introduction

Written during the last full year of his life, Frank Harris's biography of George Bernard Shaw was published in November 1931, two months after Harris's death. The biography of the day's most famous playwright and one of its pre-eminent social critics is of a piece with Harris's other works in the genre: an idiosyncratic would-be biography of Shakespeare (1909); a highly readable, if notoriously unreliable portrait of his friend Oscar Wilde (1916); *Contemporary Portraits* (1915–23), sketches of the day's lions – 'the usual Harrisian mixture of insight and hogwash', according to a commentator; and his own tell-all and unabashedly lascivious autobiography, *My Life and Loves* (1922–7).

In the 1880s, when he cut his teeth on literary journalism and editing, there was no one quite like Harris on the literary scene, nor was there when he died impoverished in the South of France in late August 1931. His unconventional behaviour was the stuff of legend. His lack of polish was often calculated, as he played the stage Irishman or the bluff American by turns and at his convenience, and the snooks he cocked at middle-class mores were almost unerringly well aimed and just as invariably ill received. These qualities link him most closely to his fellow Irishman, firebrand and wilful outsider, George Bernard Shaw (1856–1950), with whom his friendship dated from Harris's editorship of the *Saturday Review* in the 1880s. Although intermittent and often epistolary thereafter, it lasted until Harris's death.

The present volume's full title, *George Bernard Shaw: An Unauthorised Biography Based on Firsthand Information*, has a slight, if unmistakably, pugnacious character. Its dedication to the American journalist Frank Scully (1892–1964), Harris's literary secretary, 'who goaded me into undertaking it and then wouldn't let me have a minute's peace till it was completed', further sets the tone: one of intimacy in which the vernacular and irreverent intermingle. But just as one looks forward to beginning the life of the age's paramount playwright, another element of book-making, 'Credentials by Bernard Shaw' (four letters from

Shaw to Harris about this biographical project) intervenes to frustrate an eminently reasonable expectation.

Shaw at first pointedly denied his friend permission to write about him: 'I won't have you write my life on any terms.' Wary of his friend's penchant for invention and exaggeration, and probably fearful that their temperamental differences would result in an unsympathetic or unbalanced account, Shaw had, moreover, already appointed a biographer. Mockingly described by Harris as 'Archibald Henderson, Ph.D., Dc.L., Ll.D.', the American mathematics professor had already published *Bernard Shaw: His Life and Works* (1911) and would produce two more full-length lives of Shaw, in addition to some hundred newspaper and magazine articles. But Harris, proved hard to hold back, and in due course Shaw at first relented gracefully, and, then, under persistent assault, threw in the towel: 'I will see you through with plenty to quote.' The reader sighs with a relief that proves short-lived, for there is yet more prefatory matter in the form of an 'Introduction by Frank Harris'. The feeling that the author is donning a suit of armour for a fray proves justified, for Harris typically wades into territory where others might feel squeamish. The end is no less odd than the book's beginning, for Shaw gets the last word in 'A Postscript by the Subject of this Memoir'. If ever a biography insisted on interactivity and post-modernity *avant la lettre*, this one vies for the palm.

It is even more radical than that, however, for although not formally announced as such, it was, in fact, a collaboration. In addition to Harris's, no less than three other names ought to have graced its title-page: that of its subject, Shaw himself; that of Frank Scully, its dedicatee; and that of a figure behind the scenes, Alexander Berkman (1870–1936), an anarchist leader perhaps now best remembered as the lifelong friend of 'Red' Emma Goldman. Scully, an American with a penchant for exaggeration and self-publicity, later retailed gossip for *Variety*, becoming famous in 1950 for a controversy involving flying-saucers. He announced in the August 1936 issue of *Esquire*, and repeated in his autobiography, *Rogues' Gallery: Profiles of My Eminent Contemporaries* (1943), that he had ghostwritten this biography for Harris. His specific claims are that he wrote its preface and massively expanded Harris's portrait of Shaw in *Contemporary Portraits, Second Series* (1919).

Scully, who scented an opportunity, did, in fact, play an important role in bringing the biography to completion when Harris, beset by advancing age and illness, proved incapable of seeing the effort through.

Precisely who was responsible for what remains difficult to sort out. According to several reports, Harris himself had drafted a rudimentary manuscript, but the book's tone and style tend to suggest that Scully kick-started Harris into reminiscence and that he took down his words, later organising, amplifying and re-composing them.

Shaw sniffed out the American journalist's involvement in the book, noting in a letter to Victor Gollancz, its publisher, that: 'The book falls off badly at the end. There are two chapters (one of them commercially libellous) so bad that I think he [Harris] must have left them to Scully to write' (cited in Sheila Hodges, *Gollancz: The Story of a Publishing House*, London, Gollancz, 1978, p. 82). Documentary evidence in the diary of Nellie Harris, Harris's third wife, identifies the involvement of still another hand: she records that, with the book foundering, Scully also came to rely upon 'a competent man who knows how to write' (entry of 31 January 1931). This person, later revealed to be Alexander Berkman, made somewhat exaggerated claims about his role in a private letter, but also offers valuable testimony about the history of the book's writing:

> Now and then I also do some 'ghosting' which means writing a story or book for someone who can't do it himself. Thus it may interest you that the book on Shaw, published by Frank Harris after his death last year, had also my hand in it. It was the secretary of Harris, one Frank Scully, an American journalist, who was to help Harris write the book. Harris wrote about 40,000 words and could not go on. His memory failed and he repeated himself. So Frank Scully took the book in hand and invited me to help him, as he himself is no author, just a journalist. Some of the chapters in the book have been written by me from beginning to end. Later on Bernard Shaw read the proofs and made some changes. [To Max Nettlau, 21 December 1932, International Institute for Social History, Amsterdam]

The other collaborator – Shaw himself – revealed the extent of his involvement in letters and modestly commented on his role in the book's 'Postscript'. Another witness whose testimony must be added is George W(alter) Bishop (1887–1965), a theatre critic and book reviewer for the *Daily Telegraph* and a friend of Shaw's, who recollected in his memoirs, *My Betters* (1957):

> If it existed, one of the most interesting and valuable pieces of Shaviana would be that proof copy of *Bernard Shaw* by Frank Harris.

At Shaw's request, Victor Gollancz had a page-proof bound up with blank sheets interleaved and he let me look at it with Shaw's corrections and revisions. Page after page had been entirely rewritten by G. B. S. [. . .] Shortly after the Frank Harris book was published, G. B. S. strode into his [Gollancz's] office in Henrietta Street and asked to see him. Shaw was shown into his room and he said he wanted the proof back. 'I went to the safe, where it was kept, and handed it to him to take away and destroy,' Victor Gollancz said, somewhat ruefully.

Publishers rarely possess safes so capacious, and Bishop's assertion – colourful and calculatedly tantalising – would ordinarily set off alarmbells were it not for Shaw's statements that corroborate Bishop. To Nellie Harris, the playwright wrote: 'I have had to fill in the prosaic facts in Frank's best style, and fit them to his comments as best I could; for I have most scrupulously preserved his sallies at my expense' (17 October 1931). And to his friend the playwright and critic St John Ervine (1883–1971), he revealed: 'In Frank Harris's book, all the facts, of which he knew nothing, are by me. Its account of my mother's family and of my marriage are not to be found elsewhere' (28 April 1936, *The Collected Letters, 1926–1950*, edited by Dan H. Laurence). As a comparison with its original demonstrates, he also revised his letter to Harris of 24 June 1930, cited in the 'Sex Credo' chapter.

How, then, can one gauge the contributions of Shaw, Scully and Berkman in the making of this book? Given the absence of evidence, the question of authorship is unlikely ever to be satisfactorily resolved. This mystery need not, however, spoil the reader's pleasure, even if it may determine a final assessment of how successfully this book handles its subject. Remarkably, its style betrays little of its higgledy-piggledy compilation by various hands. Scully, a journalist to his fingertips, was able to imitate Harris's breezy style convincingly and to mask his contributions. But are there really pages 'entirely rewritten' by Shaw, an accomplished stylist with an almost unmistakable voice?

Knowing the book's complex and odd history illuminates its opening acts of self-justification. Harris's subject, then in his vigorous mid-seventies, wanted, like so many subjects of biography, to exert some control over what was revealed to the public; Harris, even if largely insouciant to it, could not have been unaware of the charges of inaccuracy and invention made about his life of Oscar Wilde;

moreover, aged seventy-five and in failing health, he must have contemplated his literary legacy, perhaps sensing that this would be his last book. The final chapter on Shaw, 'Future', a clear-eyed assessment unflinchingly contemplates eras that neither Harris nor Shaw would see, although Shaw had a further twenty years to dazzle and fulminate against the world. ('Harris' proves a name of convenience here, for this chapter is possibly by Scully, no lover of Shaw, just as Shaw, who deemed Scully a man 'constitutionally incapable of making any precisely accurate statement whatever' [to Nellie Harris, 17 October 1931], was no lover of him.)

Given Shaw's initial hostility to Harris, why did Harris persist in writing about him? Scully probably goaded Harris once he had broached it, with Harris, terribly short of money, undoubtedly welcoming its commercial possibilities. It must have appeared to promise easy income. Harris was an experienced biographer and a writer of singular facility; he had to hand Shaw's correspondence and a store of memories, although these became increasingly uncertain and difficult to call up; and he had managed to wrench out of Shaw facts otherwise unavailable about his early years and family background. Harris also had a precedent in his biography of Wilde of turning a friendship into saleable copy, and Shaw, from this perspective, was 'bankable', a figure of importance on several scenes – literary, social, political – about whom a number of books had been written and by whose colourful character the public was intrigued.

Harris was, moreover, being offered a final chance to talk about his favourite and inexhaustible subject – himself. This double thread runs throughout this biography as it does through his other biographical writings, with Shaw used as a fulcrum for Harris's own ideas, prejudices and sentiments. One example will suffice. Speaking of Shaw's unconventional upbringing and childhood, Harris typically takes the occasion to state his ideas about moulding children's characters: 'For my part I prefer to throw the emphasis on child play rather than on child work. More parks for children and no idea of labour till they are old enough to vote for the jobs they will take – if there are any' (Chapter 6, Boyhood in Dublin). The sideswipe at the economy is typical: tagged on, conversational and unashamedly opinionated, it reveals the man himself, but as it does so the ostensible subject recedes momentarily. But these moments accumulate, tend to stretch and have irritated more than one reader.

Dictation (obviously the method for at least some of the book) famously lends itself to looseness and prolixity, as the cases of Henry James and Joseph Conrad famously demonstrate. There is necessarily as well a greater consciousness of the speaking self. This example vividly demonstrates all these tendencies:

> I did not know London at its worst, as I came there in 1882, by way of Galway, Liverpool, New York, Chicago, Kansas, Athens, Heidelberg, Plevna, and Paris, a journey that took about fifteen years. Up to that time I had been an under-river worker, hotel manager, cowboy, college student, lawyer (I had retired from the Kansas Bar before I was twenty-five), and master at Brighton College. Afterwards I studied at two German universities and had stopped at Paris before going to London.   [Chapter 8, Lean Years in London]

Already calling for the editor's proverbial 'red pencil' (what has this to do with Bernard Shaw?), the passage goes on and on, the section quoted being only part of it. Harris's contemporaries would little have expected an author to establish his or her qualifications. Simply to write upon a topic was to assert one's authority to do so.

The passage reveals a speaking voice deeply in love with itself. In some of Harris's writing this self-regarding style can attain a certain charm; here, it too often tends to simple garrulity, the voice of the inveterate *raconteur*, an updated version of the Ancient Mariner, unable to stop talking and incapable of letting his auditor go. The words tumble out, some more or less obvious padding to fill up the tale required for a full-length book. The catalogue, a literary device as old as Homer, has not, in the main, survived well in literary Modernism, with the possible exception of James Joyce (not incidentally, perhaps, another Irish writer prone to it). In Harris's hand it is, as another instance makes even clearer, a blunt instrument:

> He [Shaw] has kept up a newspaper knowledge of contemporary America, but his literary interest died out with Mark Twain and Henry James. Before that he knew a bit of Poe, Whitman, Emerson, Longfellow, Hawthorne, and Cooper, but of Edith Wharton, Willa Cather, Zona Gale, James Branch Cabell, Sherwood Anderson, Theodore Dreiser, and such writers he hasn't the remotest idea. O. Henry he knows; Mencken, O'Neill, Upton Sinclair, too, and a bit of Sinclair Lewis.   [Chapter 24, Attitude towards America]

This reveals 'the courage of the cornered rat', as Joseph Conrad called it when faced with the blank page and the necessity to fill it, for Harris had to hand few documents and only a small library upon which to draw, a situation that neither hindered his writing a life of Wilde nor his willingness to write on Shaw. The final product is, however, less a 'biography' than a highly impressionistic portrait, only partly completed, and with its shades and shadows. The title boasts, not inaccurately, of 'first-hand information', but 'hard' facts are few, dates rarer still and documentation scant. It would not be exaggerating to speak of an almost complete contempt for normal biographical protocols as regards evidence and its use. Shaw's letters are quoted in full or in extract, but dates are rarely supplied, and where and when he said the words put into his mouth is not a concern for Harris, never a man much inclined to show his cards and generally disposed to run as he wrote.

His hotchpotch method none the less suits his idiosyncratic voice, even if it lays him open to several obvious charges. For example, his portrait of Ireland in the 1860s, mainly a feat of memory listing names and partly relying upon a pastiche of quotations from Shaw, is seemingly intended more to amuse than to inform, a display of knowledge (not 'first-hand', given Harris's birth in 1856) that also helps him unburden himself about his own and Shaw's cultural heritage. Harris recalls the extreme poverty caused by 'an intolerable landlord system'; the 'primitive' trains linking the principal cities; the lack of employment that justified poaching, 'the last blasphemy to English minds'; the 'Augustan' English Shaw learned at his mother's breast. He covers the terrain rapidly, and with a certain professional deftness but in a style so intimate at times as to disconcert the reader, who is more often than not too startled to protest. Harris's sketch, decidedly unsociological, largely resists psychologising as well. Thus, Harris merely states that Shaw seems to have imbibed much from his mother and from mid-nineteenth century Dublin and lets things go at that. The inclination not to delve ensures that Harris's portrait remains mostly on the surface, with the result that the essential man either eludes or mystifies him.

Even the appeal to truth turns out mainly to be window-dressing. Harris (thus to call the multiple author) covers his tracks so thoroughly that the reader is uninvited to challenge him, and a vigorously self-confident style, tottering on mere breeziness, supplies bravado. Under it, the pretence to documentary evidence is lost, although there is a certain gain in pace, almost always in Harris, a former journalist (or for

Scully, also a writer for the popular press), a long practised skill. At other times, however – and again the effect of dictation is deleterious – Harris descends into mere chattiness about his subject to spin out his materials. Instead of facts, opinions, sometimes off the cuff, at other times long meditated, are offered. Some settle scores as Harris plays the curmudgeon and whip. For example, of the social agitator and Member of Parliament T. P. O'Connor, a journalistic giant in his day, Harris says that he 'survived until 1931 without ever having an idea later than 1865'; he characterises Shaw's vegetarianism as 'silly'; and although admitting that it is utterly fundamental to Shaw's dramatic impulse, also sarcastically lashes out at the playwright's Socialism: 'I know of no man living or dead who has made a capitalist fortune out of being a Socialist.' At times the judgements veer towards condescension: Shaw is 'our Bernard', 'our modern Don Quixote', a writer whose novels – granted, an early and unpromising vein – are 'duller than neglected pewter'.

Harris, a member of the 'lion-taming' school of biography, opened by Lytton Strachey in his genre-altering *Eminent Victorians* (1918), in no-holds-barred fashion treats the reader to a demonstration of some of its main arts: cutting down to size, putting on show the subject's warts, parading him round as a cowed captive whilst tweaking his nose – and energetically mocking the mote in his subject's eye while neglecting the beam in his own. Oddly, Harris proves an idealist despite himself, demanding a coherence and consistency of Shaw that he full well knows rarely occurs in life, let alone in that of a creative artist and a man in the public eye. Mockery is only part of his art, however; and he fully recognises Shaw's achievements as a music and drama critic, areas in which he fully discovered his talent for the stage. Harris pays Shaw his due, remembering his thorough professionalism – keeping to deadlines, scrupulously attending to proofs and striking an original note in writing that appeared artless because it was 'very simple, direct, and lucid'. The fly in the ointment, of course, is that work of this kind is almost as ephemeral as its topics: fame lies not in criticism but in the doing. Harris the editor had provided Shaw an opportunity eagerly seized upon, and in the box, night after night, Shaw, a keen opera enthusiast from childhood, was deepening his knowledge of the theatre and, in the presence of an audience, learning a craft he would make his own.

Harris is thoroughly unromantic about Shaw the playwright, attributing his turn from theatre criticism to play-writing to a happy combination of circumstances: a half-sketched-out topic beckoned, and the blandishments of the influential and well established proved irresistible. Shaw was fortunate to interest Harley Granville-Barker and J. E. Vedrenne, with the Court Theatre in effect 'his' house; once launched, he never looked back as small successes grew into large ones and first nights turned into revivals.

Perhaps Harris's life of Shaw most disappoints in its failure to convey Shaw's transformation from a journalist of genius to the major dramatist of his day. It seems simply to have happened: characteristically, Harris neglects to pin down the why, how and when of that crucial story – after all, the main one to tell of Shaw and begging for vivid, dramatic handling. Harris clearly discerns the need to please an audience and drama critics with topicality and how talented actors and actresses form the main ingredients for success, and full well knows that Shaw ably exploited these, but he misfires in declining to give the reader details, the very thing that would enliven and create atmosphere. This account of Shaw's life is, then, thinnest where it should be the most densely textured, Harris retreating with a wave of the hand from a great theme that he ought to have made his own.

Whatever the lack of resources, which undoubtedly discouraged greater precision and authority, Harris succeeds somewhat better, if briefly, in recounting Shaw's tussle with that quintessentially English *grande dame* Mrs Grundy in her form of institutionalised dramatic censorship. Those nightmarish and despotic figures the Lord Chamberlain and the Examiner of Plays (popularly, 'The Censor') much exercised the Edwardian theatre world – John Galsworthy and Conrad, among others, vigorously protested their arrogant reign – and provided Harris with a tale to tell. Proposing that nothing in Shaw is obscene, Harris notes Shaw's career-long fight against the hoary institution (established in 1737), which, while banning certain plays from the boards, provided free publicity to any play so banned.

The discussion of Shaw as man of the theatre closes with a chapter on 'Theatre Vicissitudes' and another on his women characters, the first an assessment followed by disproportionately long discussions of *Mrs Warren's Profession* and *Candida*, the second mainly descriptive and dissenting on a subject that Harris, a great womaniser, had declared himself a specialist. Both are strained, sitting oddly in a book nominally a 'biography', even one that wears its title loosely. The chapter on theatre airs Harris's opinion of Shaw's work – 'Others found so much of what we thought sparkling a generation ago dull today, and in all honesty I do myself' – the second, Harris's opinion of Shaw's women: they 'lack mystery, grace, divinity, allure, and charm'.

Once on the subject of sex, Harris is loath to let it go, and thus turns with a dutiful sigh, and with some amazement as to the psychological complexion of someone he characterises as 'a male flirt', to the subject of Shaw's 1898 marriage (a date not mentioned, although that of his meeting his future wife in 1896 is given). Harris shies from saying overmuch about the causes of the event; bride and bridegroom were both about forty; Shaw had led a remarkably chaste life, wholly out of sympathy with Harris's skirt-chasing predilections; and Harris, although he hints that Shaw possibly needed a mother substitute, depicts a marriage made up of parallel lives: 'Shaw spent his days in the reading room of the British Museum, and his evenings at public meetings or on his critical duties at the opera, the concerts, or the theatres. He had his midday meal at a vegetarian restaurant' (Chapter 15, The Male Flirt Marries). In Harris's view, Shaw married neither for love nor money nor even, it seems, for companionship, although the conventional arrangement – Shaw speaks of marriage as 'inevitable' in his 1908 Preface to *Getting Married* – brought him at least money. In the end, Shaw's fiancée and wife, the former Charlotte Payne-Townshend (1859–1943), wealthy, well born and Irish, remains so indistinct a figure in Harris's recollections that he throws in the towel, inviting the reader to make of her what he will: 'Readers are now in a position to imagine her according to their own taste.' (One wonders, in fact, if these chapters were mostly the work of Frank Scully, generally hostile to Shaw and not especially informed about the topic.)

After the account of Shaw's excessively genteel marriage, the biography turns to the playwright's relationships with his main actresses, in particular Ellen Terry and Mrs Patrick Campbell, and from them to 'Shaw's Sex Credo', an odd chapter title in an increasingly unconventional portrait. The first topic offers promise, but Harris proves as chary about it as he is about Shaw's marital situation, and picks it up teasingly only to drop it, its centrepiece a long, slightly waspish letter from Shaw in reply to a query from Harris, as is likewise the core of the chapter on Shaw and sex.

From this point on, the word 'biography' becomes increasingly irrelevant to Harris's aims and methods, with the narrative structure growing ever looser and the aim, obviously, to concentrate upon facets of Shaw's activities rather than to present a comprehensive account of his evolution and development as a man or artist. Thus, too, 'Shaw' becomes more and more a springboard for a display of Harris's attitudes towards the First World War and his preoccupation with religion and America, with side excursions made to treat of Shaw's dramatic technique, friendships and what Harris calls the *Saint Joan* 'controversy'. As the impressionistic method takes over, Harris inches ever more towards centre stage as the book borrows the generic features of memoir, becoming, in effect, 'What Frank Harris remembers and thinks of Bernard Shaw and his Beliefs'. As the obituary in *Time Magazine* quipped of a man who was an uninhibited self-promoter, fascinated by himself to a degree that went well beyond the confines of normal self-preoccupation: 'He wrote always of Frank Harris, even when his subject was another man' (7 September 1931).

With his focus blurred, Harris even more openly draws the reader's attention to himself, the chapters contentious in tone and, at times, self-justifying. His contemporary readers would, moreover, have been aware of his controversial stance towards the War and religion (by which he mainly means Christianity). In the popular mind, Harris was pro-German from the safe haven of the United States, a not wholly accurate impression, although it earned him the title 'traitor' as well as the undying enmity of the novelist Arnold Bennett among others. His youthful studies in Germany and tangles with British officialdom predisposed him to look at the motives and beginnings of the War with considerably more scepticism than was common during the heyday of jingoism and patriotic sentiment; his unpopular view, expressed in his book *England or Germany?* (1915) was that the United Kingdom was as responsible for the conflict as was Germany – 'a quarrel of two scoundrels whose aims are identical' – and that the United States should avoid becoming involved. Shaw, in failing to adopt Harris's views, is portrayed as 'pro-Ally' and a government 'decoy' neglecting to use his influence with the public (which he undoubtedly had won by 1914) to create a platform for the outright condemnation of the war as a 'crime' – Harris's word – and to make the case for peace and internationalism. Unshaken in his unpopular views, Harris cites Shaw's letters in order to denounce him as wavering and confused, making a rhetorically forceful if not an impeccably fair case. He likewise throws in Shaw's face his provocative *New Statesman* essay of 1914, for which Shaw was much vilified, for arguing that, once Britain had become involved, the winning of the War was a practical necessity although the conflict could have been avoided:

> What, it may be asked, of his *Common Sense about the War*? Nothing but a one-sided militarist appeal in the best Shavian manner. No wonder it failed of all effect, except to induce some old-women-men's clubs to pass condemnatory resolutions. When Dr Henderson [Shaw's official biographer] asked him what were the results of the appeal, Shaw truthfully replied: 'None beyond selling 75,000 copies.'
>
> [Chapter 21, In War and Peace]

The chapter is quintessential Harris: gloves-off, eager for a fight and pulling no punches, Harris energetically chews on a bone that no longer has much meat, revelling in the chance to settle old scores and to justify himself, however much the effort takes him off the immediate track.

Harris relies upon the same methods, and commits the same error of writerly judgement, in his discussion of Shaw's religious allegiances, again a subject dwelt upon at greater length than it merits because of his strong views, expressed in his biography of Oscar Wilde and in his unrealised plan to write a life of Christ. Harris's main line is that Shaw, the 'zealous apostle' of Socialism and 'the eternal compromiser', the author of *Androcles and the Lion* and of *Saint Joan*, lacks a firm ethical basis for his social vision and ultimately falls short as a reformer, because his views are insufficiently informed by conventional belief. No Christian, Shaw none the less saw in Christ a visionary 'reformer and thinker', but differed from Harris on Christ's historical existence and contended that 'Gentle Jesus, meek and mild, is a snivelling modern invention' unwarranted by the Gospels. The latter assertion, which moves Harris to take up the cudgel, occasions a long dissenting view, with Harris casting himself in the role of the Christian apologist. Harris the dyed-in-the-wool journalist, eager for a battle, insists on having it out with Shaw once more and on closing the debate with a sarcastic salvo: 'Evidently you know a great deal about Jesus, and Jesus does not elude you nearly as much as you would have us believe. Yours ever, Frank Harris.'

Writing about a living writer, Harris concludes, perhaps more predictably, with an assessment that hits home: 'Not an original thinker, not a great dramatist, Shaw will live for ages as a personality.' Time has largely proved Harris right at least on this point: a handful of Shaw's plays offering meaty roles for actors and actresses are occasionally revived in the English-speaking world, while interest outside it, once large, has faded badly. What Harris refers to as the 'talky-talky' ones are mainly forgotten, and the topicality and awkward construction of others have consigned them to the library, the long prefaces at times more compelling than the creaky dramas that follow. Harris also sees the fatal flaw in cleverness: 'The cleverness of his dialogue is stage journalism. There is not a single character in all his plays, nor a solitary line that haunts one's memory.' He is wrong about Shaw's characters, however; at least a few seem destined for immortality: Henry Higgins and Eliza Doolittle, perhaps Major Barbara and Captain Shotover. It may seem somewhat ungenerous to say that even less of Frank Harris's work has outlasted his time. He survives in an appropriately Harrisian way: by clinging to the coat-tails of greater talents – Shaw and Wilde not least among them, a 'first-hand' witness, if only sometimes reliable, to the literary developments and temper of his age. But he also remains an original and vivid personality, one of those 'larger than life' creations that manages – sometimes just manages – to escape oblivion.

Shaw, of course, survives his treatment at Harris's hands, and, ironically, a work mostly thrown together from shards of letters and laboured over by three writers – to leave Shaw out of the equation for a moment – proved to be Harris's best-seller. Shaw's own response to this portrait, the appended 'postscript', is remarkably judicious and even-tempered, perhaps as a matter of tactics; in a long and controversial career he had weathered fiercer storms. It would arguably have been even more gracious to remain silent, lurking behind the curtains, watching from the sidelines. On the other hand, Harris's recent death seemed to call for a response, and this 'Postscript' does double duty, at once an obituary appreciation of the man he calls 'the most impossible of biographers' and a not-to-be-missed opportunity to set the record straight about Harris's views. Shaw's tribute, that of a friend and compatriot, is deft and generous. Honest enough to admit Harris's faults and failures, it largely respects the spirit of the Latin dictum that nothing but good be said of the dead. Shaw shows himself well aware of Harris's self-destructive bent and of his many un-successful attempts to kiss the Blarney Stone. He winks at his friend's failure at that notoriously difficult task, for Harris, after all, was known not for his eloquence but his plain-speaking, all the more 'plain' in a society that he openly attacked for being hypocritical and mealy-mouthed. Many of his contemporaries could not abide him for this, or for pointing out their flaws, but Shaw proves himself the quintessential gentleman, letting the flaw-picking pass, and he even sees beyond Harris's loud buzzing (one of the pleasures of this biography) and his self-indulgent stings.

Few biographies end with a word from their subject. Bernard Shaw, an indefatigable public speaker on causes of moment, draws on his art and his experience here, his measured touch, his very temperateness, much more than raillery or shouting, alone pleading that the reader sift Harris's views on him. In its rhetorical strategies of restraint and gentle reprimand, the Postscript draws attention to aspects of Shaw unguessed at by his biographer, and thus urges the reader to reconsider and evaluate what has gone before – and season it with generous helpings of salt:

> In truth this book is valuable, not in the least as an explanation of my works . . . but as a demonstration of my reactions on Harris, who was interesting enough to make his reactions very readable. Now to produce a sufficiently strong reaction there must be some incompatibility; and I find this book amusing (in the best French sense of the word) in proportion to the clash made by our two temperaments as they collide.

Characteristically, Harris has amused, pirouetted, flailed about, but, most importantly, succeeded in arousing interest in his subject. The show is eminently worth the watching, but to swallow it whole or to take it too seriously, Shaw's lofty equanimity argues, would be unfair to him as well as to Harris. Not the traditional *plaudite* at the end of a comedy (the invitation to the audience to applaud the players and the play), the Postscript's valedictory note begs, with some coyness, for the reader's approval. Shaw's ploy works precisely because of its delicate manoeuvring and tendency to understatement, and one begins to reconsider, to weigh, to query. In so prompting the reader, doesn't Shaw, indeed, get the last and most authentic word?

J. H. STAPE
Research Fellow in St Mary's University College
Strawberry Hill, London

Biography

Born in Galway in about 1856, 'Frank' (in fact, James Thomas) Harris was the son of a seaman father of stern temperament. After his education in Armagh and Denbighshire, Harris in 1871 joined in the vast Irish exodus to the United States, where he studied law at the recently opened University of Kansas. Arriving in England in 1875, he tutored French at Brighton, and then turned to journalism, being appointed editor of the *Evening News* in 1883, a post in which he developed a keen nose for gossip and a tendency for audacious self-promotion. Named head of the *Fortnightly Review* in 1886, Harris embarked on an editorial career that involved sensationalism, contentious political views and canny choices (Bernard Shaw and Max Beerbohm served as his drama critics). On the *Saturday Review* in 1894, which he purchased and then ran for four years, he mingled brilliant editorial skills with an over-pronounced search for controversy. In 1898, Harris established himself in France and from then on led a bohemian life there and in London, until 1915, when he left for New York, editing *Pearson's Magazine* there from 1916 to 1922. Under his editorship, it took a hostile attitude towards Britain's war effort, and earned Harris the title of 'traitor', while his increasingly extravagant views saw him in trouble with American censorship. His personal conduct was of an unconventional and *outré* character and is described lavishly and at length in his autobiography, *My Life and Loves* (1922–27). Harris, who became a naturalised American in 1921, left the country for France in 1923, settling permanently in Nice where, impoverished, he died of heart failure in 1931. Among his works are plays, short fiction and biographies of Oscar Wilde, Shakespeare and Bernard Shaw. Married three times, he also had a long-term mistress. Colourful and reckless, Harris, who though he made many enemies also made loyal friends, served as the model for several fictional characters. The *Oxford Dictionary of National of Biography* remembers him as 'journalist and rogue'.

GEORGE BERNARD SHAW

I dedicate this book to
FRANK SCULLY
who goaded me into undertaking it
and then wouldn't let me have a minute's
peace till it was completed

Credentials by Bernard Shaw

London, January 18th 1930

MY DEAR FRANK – You really are a daisy. You put six questions to me, the replies to which would be the book: about a year's work, which you would then decorate with nonsense about impulses and resolutions and high purposes and all the rest of the literary junk which is *de rigueur* in biographies. Also you propose to endow me with a soul. Have you not yet found out that people like me and Shakespeare *et hoc genus omne* have no souls? We understand all the souls and all the faiths and can dramatise them because they are to us wholly objective: we hold none of them.

The odd thing about you is that though you can write, you have all the credulities and illusions and innocences of the amateur and the collector. I won't have you write my life on any terms: Nellie would do it far better. You made Shakespeare a cross between a sailor in a melodrama and a French criminal invoking the memory of his sainted mother. What you would make of me not even God knows. You haven't the very faintest notion of the sort of animal I am. If I had time I would tell you the facts just to see how utterly they would disconcert you: but I haven't, so you must drop it.

This is not my humour (you idiot!), but the solid prosaic truth.

Ever,

G. B. S.

London, March 3rd 1930

DEAR FRANK HARRIS – What a chap you are! You can, of course, compile a life of me as half a dozen other people have done – the sort of life that can be published whilst all the parties are still alive. Something, at best, like Morley's *Life of Gladstone*.

Also you can write an autobiography, as St Augustine did, as Rousseau did, as Casanova did, as you yourself have done, which is something more than a heavily padded *Times* obituary notice. A man cannot take a libel action against himself; and if he is prepared to face obloquy, and compromises no one except himself and the dead, he may even get a sort of Riviera circulation in highly priced top-shelf volumes. But you cannot write that way about other people. You have a right to make your own confessions, but not to make mine. If, disregarding this obvious limitation, you pick up what you can from gossip and from guesses at the extent to which my plays are founded on fact (in your Shakespearean manner), what will happen? Your publisher, believing me to be fabulously rich and an ill man to cross, will send me the manuscript and ask me whether I have any objection to it. Unless it is a Morley-Gladstone *Who's Who* job I will say that I have every possible objection and will assuredly not hold him guilt-less that taketh my name in vain; and I will point out that, even if I consented, I could not prevent the other persons concerned from seeking their legal remedy. And then where would you be?

You must not conclude that my private life has been a very scandalous one. But I once gave some autobiographical material to an Irish-American professor. He was the son of an Irish inspector of police; and he proceeded to investigate the case precisely as his father would have done. At last he produced a book about me which began by describing my mother as an adulteress and my father as a despicable fortune-hunter. Of course, Harpers would not publish this without my consent; and equally, of course, I could not consent; so the unfortunate author died of disappointment, aided by pernicious anaemia, cursing me for ruining him. Now the worst of it was that I could not deny that the information I had given him bore his construction; for as a matter of fact I was brought up in a *ménage à trois* (we kept joint household with a musician who was a bit of a genius as a teacher of singing and conductor, with my mother as his prima donna and lieutenant); and my father had married, at the age of forty, with nothing but a Civil Service pension of about sixty pounds a year, the daughter of a country gentleman with expectations from a rich aunt who disinherited her for not marrying an earl at least. The view taken by the police inspector's son of this domestic picture was wildly off the mark; but it opened my eyes to the impossibility of conveying a truthful impression, except by such a sketch of that house-hold and those persons as I alone could attempt. In my play called *Misalliance* the leading young man is 'the man with three fathers'. I should not have thought of that if I had not had three fathers myself: my official father, the musician, and my maternal uncle. So you see, long before my own adventures began, my story took a complexion that cannot be painted at second-hand. Nearly all the guessing is bound to be wrong. That is why I am afraid of your making either a ghastly mess of a biography, or a conventional affair that will add nothing to your reputation.

The prefaces to my early novels contain as much autobiography as is worth writing.

I must stop, or this letter will go on for ever.

G. B. S.

London, June 7th 1930

DEAR F. H. – I have been unable to write for many weeks, as my wife has had a serious illness. She now seems the better for it.

I have written the information you want with my own hand on the enclosed proof. When it is no longer private – say next year – sell it and have a spree with Nellie.

Ever,

G. B. S.

Malvern, September 18th 1930

DEAR FRANK HARRIS – An American firm is advertising your biography as being authorised and as containing fifteen thousand words by me. I have written to them to say that no biography of me except Henderson's is authorised, and that yours is especially deprecated. And if you publish a word of mine I'll have the law on you. I am not going to write your book for you: its sole interest for me, and value for your reputation, will depend on how you write your own book yourself. I have given you a look at certain things I have written about myself, and which I intend some day to publish myself; for if you insist on writing a life of me you may as well know what you are writing about; but you must tell the story in your own way and not in my way. Any fool can get a book published if he can persuade the publishers that I have written it; and the publisher can sell it on that understanding; but in that case all the reviews will quote me and be about me, and the nominal biographer will get nothing but his share of the plunder. Your publishers must withdraw their announcements of fifteen thousand words by me, and of an authorised biography. You are personally capable of writing a worthy successor to the Wilde biography without quoting a single word from my accounts of myself;

and I shall do everything in my power to force you to do so. There is no evidence in the Wilde book that you ever read a word he wrote; and as you have certainly not read more than three per cent of my stuff you will have to stick to your strong hand and paint the man and not the author. I can imagine nothing more ghastly than a literary shepherd's pie of Shaw and Harris horribly messed up together. Besides, the book should be an essay on our times and have sketches of all sorts of people in it. That is the sort of thing you can do; and if you do it in your best manner your abominable *Life and Loves* will be forgiven and forgotten.

You must die in the odour of sanctity, even if you persist in calling it the stink of respectability.

Faithfully,

G. BERNARD SHAW

London, November 3rd 1930

I sent the letters back to you yesterday in a hurry. One of them contains, I regret to say, the improper expression 'permanent whore'. Change the second word to 'mistress'. Our forecastle style will not do on the quarterdeck.

I give you a free hand as to these letters; but they are so condensed and so dependent on the context of our personal relations that expatiation may be better than quotation. I again urge that it must be *your* book. You must not let me play you off the stage.

Your publishers protest that all the announcements to which I took exception came from Nice, and that they are entirely guiltless. I have told them not to be alarmed; that I will see you through with plenty to quote.

G.B.S.

Introduction by Frank Harris

These prefatory letters show Bernard Shaw going all the way from absolute disapproval to conditional co-operation in less than a year, and they are strung together with the mischievous intent of showing how great minds don't always know their own. He will go to his grave believing he never approved of my biography, but the disapproval has all the coy refusal of a Victorian lady of easy virtue. Anyway, the result is the same: conception and the birth of an idea into a book in nine months; which seems to make everything quite all right.

To Shaw all biographies are lies. Not merely that, but deliberate lies. No man is bad enough or good enough, he insists, to tell the truth about himself during his lifetime. Why not? *I* did. Archibald Henderson, Ph.D., D.C.L., LL.D., Shaw's official biographer, tells us that 'Shaw once tried, within certain limits, the experiment of being candidly autobiographical.' How can anybody be candid within certain limits? Anybody, that is, who isn't a prude at heart. But then Shaw can do anything: within certain limits.

On the positive side he believes, and in this most of us, I think, will agree with him, that any man's childhood years are the most important. Even where some may not concur in this, they certainly will agree that these younger years usually make the most interesting reading. The later years of any great man are known to everybody who reads newspapers. More than that, once established and on his way, no great man differs much from another. You can find that out by bringing a group of them to dinner. But their childhood years are not so identical. And it's because Shaw's childhood was even more strange than that of most of us that I intend to please him, as well as myself, by dwelling freely on it in this work.

Astute critics, on reading the original draft of this work, remarked that the praise was most begrudgingly doled out at the beginning and only arrived at something approaching praiseworthy hysteria toward the end. I did not point out to them what will be obvious to less precious readers that this is a conscious design of the book and faithfully follows the public attitude toward Shaw. Viewed in historical perspective, was not the world cold to him when he had original things to say, and did it not acclaim him everywhere, even in England eventually, years after he ceased saying them? What, then, is wrong with my portrait? I don't expect to please them by it, but I do expect it to be accepted as a true picture. By everybody, that is, but Shaw. I long ago ceased trying to please him.

I don't know the relations of other writers with Shaw, but my own experience has been amusing. Whenever I've tried to do his portrait in the last twenty years, he has always begun by strenuously objecting to my doing the thing at all and ended by taking the brushes out of my hand and trying to do the things himself. I must have done a hundred bust-length portraits in several volumes of *Contemporary Portraits*, sketches of great men I've met in my lifetime, but Shaw is the only one who has always acted as if he could do his own portrait better himself.

Or perhaps it's only an over-zealous desire to help. Anyhow, twice on learning I was making an attempt he has deluged me with material – all of it so interesting and so well-written as to make it almost impossible not to use it. Always he objected at first; didn't want me to write about him; refused me the details I felt I must have to make a really full-length portrait. This was on learning I had begun his biography. I told him I was going ahead, anyway. Whereupon a month or so later he over-whelmed me with confessions, most of them new.

It could, of course, be maintained that, fearing a brutally honest picture, he decided the better course would be to give me all possible help and so soften my brush-strokes here and there, but I prefer to believe it was because his better side reasserted itself and he decided to help with all his might, not only to ease my difficulties, but to make this biography the best I have ever done of anybody.

He doesn't want it merely to be 'literature' any more than I do. He wants it to endure, to be in print what he believes Rodin's bust of him is going to be in sculpture. He wants it to have a scientific soundness about it. In this respect literature learns unwillingly from science, and it really could learn a great deal.

For example, a zoologist, let us say, finds a new sort of bird and sits down to describe it. He is far more than impartial; he knows that his description must be so perfectly accurate that another zoologist ten thousand miles away should be able to classify the bird from it as well as if he had the bird before him.

How many literary critics are there who reach such high detachment and show such scrupulous care?

The zoologist knows, too, that length of feather or peculiarity of colouring is not so important as structural differences in the skeleton, or such organic modifications as will affect the creature's chance of surviving and propagating his kind. Accordingly, he is on the look-out for peculiarities in proportion to their vital importance to the race or species.

But what literary critic uses such an enduring standard of values?

And when the man of science approaches the chief part of his task, he is even more careful: he must classify the specimen, decide what species it belongs to, and whether it is more nearly akin to this family or to that. A mistake here would expose him to the derision of every zoologist in the world, whereas if he performs his work beyond the possibility of fault-finding, he will only have done what is expected of every competent craftsman.

When will literary criticism even seek to attain such excellence?

You have a Sainte-Beuve comparing Flaubert with Madame Sand, and Eugène Sue regretting that the author of *Salammbo* does not write so well as the author of *Mauprat*, and that the creator of *Madame Bovary* has not such fertility of imagination as the author of *The Wandering Jew*. Or your Sainte-Beuve will tell you that Balzac's fame will be drowned in the sea of his impurities. That is to say, the most extraordinary specimen of man it was ever the good fortune of a Frenchman to meet, was so little out of the common that he was fated soon to be forgotten.

In much the same way your Matthew Arnold will call Byron a great poet and put him far above Heine, and will condemn Keats for writing sensual letters to his love, and for consequent 'ill breeding', apparently without even a suspicion that Keats is a greater poet than Milton, and Heine incomparably the first of all the moderns. Yet Arnold, as a poet, should have known that the *Hyperion* is dowered with a richness of rhythm and a magnificence of music to which *Paradise Lost* can lay no claim: while Heine's position is beyond dispute.

Yet, despite such brainless prejudice and shameful blundering as would ruin the reputation of any first year's student in biology, these so-called masters of literary criticism are not even blamed. And accordingly we find a Meredith at seventy declaring that his works have never been criticised, that no one in England has even tried to describe his productions fairly, much less classified him correctly.

While attempting to rival scientific exactitude and detached impartiality, the literary critic has still a further height to climb. His description may be exact, his classification fairly correct, yet we shall not be satisfied unless he reveals to us the ever-changing soul of his subject and its possibilities of further growth. In this way, art asserts its superiority to science.

When this ultimate domain is reached, a new question imposes itself. The portrait-painter is always drawn by two divergent forces; he must catch the likeness of his sitter and yet make his portrait a work of art.

This world-old dispute in portraiture, between realism and art, was settled for the artist by Michelangelo. Someone who watched him working on his great statue of Lorenzo dei Medici kept on objecting that it was not like Lorenzo, that he had known that great man for years, and that he would not have recognised him from the sculptor's presentment.

At length, Michelangelo turned on his buzzing critic: 'Who will care whether it's like him or not a thousand years hence?' In other words, the obligation on the artist is to produce a great work of art, and there is no other.

At the same time, the great portraits of the world, such as the picture of Charles V on horseback by Titian, and the Meniñas of Velazquez, and the Syndics of Rembrandt, manage to reconcile to some extent both requirements.

Likeness is caught most easily by exaggeration of characteristic features, but such exaggeration is apt to offend the modesty of truth and fall into caricature; whereas the work of art is always founded on truth, as a beautiful figure demands a perfect skeleton, and any heightening, even of the truth, must have beauty or some strange and profound significance as justification. How far, then, is exaggeration or modification of the fact allowed? I solved the riddle rather loosely in my own way. When my subject is really a great man, a choice and master spirit, I try to depict him in his habit as he lived, with absolute fidelity to fact. In the case of men like Emerson, Whitman, Wagner, Carlyle, and Meredith, I have taken no liberties wittingly with the fact; the real is good enough for me when it is halo-crowned, but when I am dealing with smaller men, whose growth has been dwarfed or warped or thwarted, I permit myself a certain latitude of interpretation, or even of artistic presentment.

Shaw, by his own estimate, and that of countless other critics, falls into the first category. He is big enough to be depicted as he is. One does not need to borrow colour from one's own personality in order to brighten his. On the contrary, Shaw is more colourful than all his portrayers put together. I have an idea he has always been aware of this.

Busy man as he is, he has contrived to be painted and caricatured and modelled by every artist of any worth. Among them he hopes a bust will endure a thousand years because it is a great work of art: greater, perhaps, than the subject, as Michelangelo's statue of Lorenzo was greater, as I have said, than the Medici himself. In fact, Shaw candidly says this was the reason he got Rodin, by hook or crook, to do that bust of him. It is possible that, for the same reason and with equal humour, he now puts at my disposal some material for a biography. If so, this frees me from all obligations. Anyway, I intend to tell the truth about Shaw and his work, and nothing but the truth as I see it. I don't see why I should pat him on the back now. I did that before most of his present sycophants were born, and at a time when he really needed it. He doesn't need it at all now.

In this Life I hope to show, as well as the shadows, the more unselfish, more generous sides of Shaw. He was more disposed to stand in life against any foolish, common prejudices than any of the great men of his time. I shall concede him that, but I don't intend to give him an inch of credit more than he deserves.

The portrait shall have, as I say, its shadows, deep shadows. It needs them to be a real likeness, but there shall be no slapstick, no caricature. I leave that to himself and the army of agile illustrators who have made his sardonic profile world-famous.

F. H.
Nice, February 14th 1930

I

Shaw, Then and Now

I remember Oscar Wilde bringing me one day, in the early eighteen-eighties, I think, a cutting from *The Westminster Gazette*, in which we were both mentioned, and rather contemptuously.

'Have you seen it, Frank?'

'Yes, I have seen it.'

'What have you written about it?'

'Nothing. I am not going to write about such nonsense.'

'Oh, Frank, you are quite wrong. They give you a column to write about yourself, and, what's more, they pay you too. You ought never to neglect such opportunities. That is the way to make yourself known.'

'I do not agree with you,' I said, 'and I am not going to bother about it.'

But I soon found that Oscar's determination to write about himself whenever he got the opportunity was the successful line to adopt, at any rate in a democracy. In a few years, Oscar Wilde was known to everyone: he had become, to this extent, famous.

Some years later, Bernard Shaw used the same method, and in his thirty years of longer life has achieved an unparalleled success. The majority of men believe that his name would not be mentioned so often in the papers if he were not a man of first importance, but is Coolidge, Chevalier, Baldwin, or Capone of first importance? Yet their names are in the papers every day. This is notoriety, not fame, and later we shall examine how Shaw used the circus-tents of publicity to clown his way to this notoriety.

There are Fleet Street journalists to this day who believe Shaw is a hard man to interview. Hence they grow elated every time they succeed, even if it's six times a week. Of course he differs from most notables in that he has something to say, but they don't care about that now. Anything he says is 'copy'. If he says, 'Nice day,' reporters laugh and look at the sky in doubt. There's a story in it somewhere. Of that they are certain. But I knew him when he had things to say and, sad reflection, when I had things to say myself. We have been friends for forty years and have disagreed no end of times. I am, I think, a good deal more serious than he is, more literal-minded, but his gayer touch, I concede, has allowed him to say just as many annoying things as I have without getting into half the hot water.

My first acquaintance with him was listening to him forty years ago at a Socialist gathering in the East End of London. He spoke under the auspices of the Social Democratic Federation of Hyndman and he spoke as a Communist, as a confirmed Marxian. He made a certain impression on me: he was very tall, over six feet in his boots and thin to angularity: a long bony face, corresponding, I thought, to a tendency to get to bedrock everywhere; rufous fair hair and long, untrimmed reddish beard; grey-blue English eyes, with straight eyebrows tending a little upwards at the outside and thus adding a touch of the familiar Mephistophelean sarcasm to the alert, keen expression. He was dressed carelessly in tweeds, with a Jaeger collar over a conventional tie; contempt of frills written all over him; his hands clean and well-kept, but not manicured. His complexion, singularly fair even for a man with reddish hair, seemed too bloodless to me, reminded me of his vegetarianism, which had puzzled me more than a little for some time. His abrupt movements – as jerky as the ever-changing mind – his perfect unconstraint – all showed an able man, very conscious of his ability, very direct, very sincere, sharply decisive – and, above all, a charming talker with enough brogue to make women appraise him with an eye to capture.

Our last meeting was in the summer of 1928. He had come to the Riviera for a six weeks' holiday from his labours on *The Apple Cart*, and after he had been adequately photographed in various stripped poses on the beach at Cap d'Antibes with cinema celebrities of sorts we finally fixed up a date to lunch together at my place, Villa Edouard VII on the Cimiez hill of Nice, ten miles from where Shaw was staying. But I had not figured on accidents. One happened to Shaw's bowels. He wrote explaining, or perhaps I should say complaining:

Hotel Beau-Site, Nino's Restaurant, Cap d'Antibes,
August 10th 1928

MY DEAR F. H. – I can't come tomorrow. Yesterday I was smitten with the most undignified form of *maladie du pays*. My interior became

a mere cave of the winds and waters; and I lay about unable to keep on
my legs longer than ten minutes at a time.

Today, after a good night, I am able to sit up and write and take my
meals (such as they are) out of doors. The winds have subsided, but
not the waters; and I dare not venture out of reach of the appropriate
seat until I am normally decent in that respect. I therefore propose
Wednesday instead of tomorrow. By that time I shall be either quite
well or dead.

Ever,

G. B. S.

Fearing he was seriously ill, I called the next day, but he had gone out
for an automobile ride. On returning, he wrote again:

It was most kind of you to come all that way to relieve my anxiety as
to the effect of my letter by tipping me a Sans Rancune. Thanks.

For the moment I cannot fix a day because I have given an open
invitation to Troubetskoy to rush over from Lago Maggiore, and until
I hear from him I am tied up. However, my telegram, despatched last
night, can hardly take more than a fortnight to reach him and elicit a
reply; and when he is disposed of I will fix a day for Cimiez.

G. B. S.

At long last we got into the same room at the same time. It was a
hearty enough greeting, but we were not really at ease together. A few
years before, his wife had carefully burnt some work of mine which she
thought her servants had better not read. He had written and told me
so. This was characteristic. Shaw handles his friends' feelings with the
callousness of a surgeon and discusses their affairs with the bluntness of
a family solicitor. His indelicacy sometimes takes away their breath. It
hurt me, and I didn't mind telling him that, if my wife had destroyed a
book of his, I should never have let him know.

Well, if one's wife dislikes one's friends, it makes visiting a little
difficult, but Shaw shouldered the burden like a man and came over to
Nice alone. We hadn't met in fourteen years, as I say, and we had a very
enjoyable afternoon. My foible, if foible it be, is to challenge every
opinion that I suspect of being contrary to my own. Small men take
offence at this and call me quarrelsome; and I am well content that they
should. But Shaw never contradicts. He is the most adroit plagiarist, the
deftest literary pickpocket in the world. However provocative or even

hostile your point of view, he instantly appropriates it, illuminates it, adjusts it neatly, humours it, and restores it to you so engagingly that you forget that he has just stolen it from you, and are enchanted with his imaginary fecundity. We got on together famously.

Besides, he can talk Shakespeare; and my interest and delight in Shakespeare are inexhaustible. Shaw's conviction that *Back to Methuselah* and *Heartbreak House* are works far beyond Shakespeare's utmost capacity is not to be shaken; but all the handsomer are his condescending admissions that Macbeth and Lear are unsurpassable in their manner. He would, he said, rewrite *Hamlet* some day when he had time, in such a way as to bring out its real meaning. All of which showed that he was as interested in Shakespeare as I am myself; and I asked no more. We argued for five hours about everything and anything, some of it the silliest stuff imaginable. Even compliments were conditioned. Shaw wondered what kept me looking so young. (I am six months his senior.)

'Good meat, good whisky, good wine, and plenty of them,' I said. 'And look at you – white, nearly bald, and thin as a rail.'

'My complexion is the admiration of Europe,' he said. 'I have not a bald spot on my dome; and my thinness is a quality, not a fault. And yet you enviously go around telling people I'm undersexed.'

'I never said it,' I cried.

'Yes you did – in a lecture in Berlin, last winter.'

'Well, if I did, it's true. You are.'

'It's not true. If anything, I'm *oversexed*.'

I looked at him in astonishment. Was he really serious?

'You oversexed?' I repeated. 'Why, you told me you came to London at nineteen and that your first overt act took place when you were twenty-nine. That's ten years! If that had been Shakespeare, it would have been eleven months, and if it had been Frank Harris or any other young blade, it would have been eleven days, or hours!'

'Ah!' he said. 'But then you and he had not been brought up on Handel and Mozart and Michelangelo and Raphael and Greek sculpture as I was. If your sense of beauty had been properly nursed you couldn't have touched anything so prosaic as a real woman at that age.'

At the time of this argument I was seventy-two and a half years of age, and Shaw seventy-two. Two old men dealing with such a young theme, in which at best their interest could not have been more than academic, seems funny to me on reflection.

Later in this work we will examine this side of Shaw more closely. His letter on the subject, which he wrote to me in the summer of 1930, will probably be the most quoted part of this biography. It certainly is his unabashed sex credo.

At this last meeting I speak of, Emma Goldman was present. Shaw and I talk a lot, but she has lived her convictions more than most of us and has been punished for them. Of course, I too have been in gaol – even as Shakespeare, Cervantes, Wilde, and nearly all the courageous writers (all seemingly but Shaw); but we went to gaol for our trumpery sins, and she for her deepest convictions.

Between Emma the Anarchist and Shaw the Fabian Marxist there could be no genuine *rapprochement*. In 1921, when Lenin was as busy shooting Anarchists as Trotsky shooting White Tsarists, Shaw sent Lenin a book with a laudatory inscription which is now lithographed and circulated through Soviet Russia. Emma Goldman looked to the revolution for the establishment of liberty. Shaw, who agrees with Mussolini that liberty is a putrescent corpse, looks to the revolution for the scientific organisation of slavery, which he declares to be the sole business of governments and an inexorable law of Nature.

I wondered what would happen if they got on to politics. But Shaw thought discretion the better part of valour, and talked at great length of how he had shown *The Movietone News* how they should have produced Mussolini's first talking picture. Everybody says this demonstration makes a great talking picture, that ten thousand pounds would have been a moderate sum to pay for it.

I never saw it. It wouldn't surprise me. Shaw was always a great actor, not a 'bit of an actor', as he says himself, and for some reason he insists on giving this talent away. He will not act, orate, or broadcast for money.

I recall in the war when Hearst had just paid him over a thousand pounds for an article. Even a genius can only write so much a day, and if Shaw wrote articles for nothing for me, that limited the time he had to devote to his bread-and-butter labours. 'I should be sorry to lose him as a contributor,' I said, 'but I can't pay him what he is worth.' I was at the time thousands in arrears, having lost heavily on my venture with *Pearson's Magazine* through interference and suppression by A. S. S. Burleson (as I always addressed him), Postmaster-General of the United States.

We discussed the matter in letters.

Finally, remembering the days when I made him repeat as a theatre critic the success he had made as a music critic, Shaw said, 'As long as you edit a magazine anywhere on earth, you can expect contributions from me.'

You couldn't ask more than that from a friend. It is this mixture that makes it easy to like Shaw. I have more of a liking for him personally than I ever had for Oscar Wilde, and I know him to be a far better man than Wilde. I came to the defence of Oscar Wilde when he was beaten, gaoled, thrown out of society. As the underdog he had entrée to my full sympathy and purse.

My *Life and Confessions of Oscar Wilde* could only have been written from a full heart. Now, Shaw has rarely, since I've known him at least, been the underdog, and so I suppose the impulse has been to bite at him rather than bark with him. But he hasn't always had the world as his pulpit, nor the pay-boxes of all its theatres as his purse. There was a time when he knew hardships, and long before that a kind of proud impecuniousness which can be more humiliating than poverty. I mean years before in Ireland.

2

Ireland in the Eighteen-Sixties

To tell Bernard Shaw's story one must go back several generations and sketch the Ireland that gave him birth.

The Ireland of seventy-five years ago was not by any means the Ireland of today. I don't need to reach for a textbook to confirm this, for I was born in one corner of it six months before Shaw was born in another.

Nor were we alone. It cannot be just an accident of history that a dozen or more persons who dominated the intellectual life of England for a generation, and, in Shaw's case, up to the present time, all sprang from the Ireland of the eighteen-fifties and -sixties. While General Grant was drinking his way to victory in America, Bernard Shaw, St Gaudens, George Moore, Oscar Wilde, John Redmond, Dion Boucicault, Sir Roger Casement, Lady Gregory, W. B. Yeats, George Russell ('A. E.'), Grant Allen, Conan Doyle, T. P. O'Connor, Lord Roberts, Sir Horace Plunkett, Lord Northcliffe, Sir Edward Carson, Lord Kitchener, and several others of the first minds of our times were playing childhood games in a conquered Ireland.

There were minor singers too – among them Francis Fahy, who wrote 'The Old Plaid Shawl', 'Husheen', and most of the Irish ballads which proved manna from heaven for later-day piracies by Jewish song-writers. Fanny Parnell, a sister of the political leader, was also a favourite. Her 'Post Mortem' was one of the most quoted things in Ireland fifty years ago. Lady Wilde, Oscar's mother, was a salon sort of poetess under the name of 'Speranza'.

Among novelists who were born about that time, there was Justin Huntly McCarthy, author of *If I were King*. His father, Justin McCarthy, wrote *The History of Our Own Times*. Conan Doyle came along a little later. His father designed the cover of *Punch*. Grant Allen was born about this time, and Shaw too. Their work, to fall into one of my old idioms, borrowed from Keats, is written on the forehead of time to come. Certainly the plays of Bernard Shaw and Oscar Wilde, the sculpture of August St Gaudens, the paintings of Sir William Orpen, the military skill of Kitchener of Khartoum and Roberts of Waterford, the acting of Dion Boucicault, the journalism of Lord Northcliffe, the poetry of William Butler Yeats, and the all-round genius of George Russell could not easily be excluded from any contemporary history of life and letters.

Almost anyone would say Ireland is no place to breed artists. Poets, perhaps, but surely not painters.

Yet Shaw in his youth there wanted to be a painter; Russell actually is to this day, and Moore, if he didn't succeed as one, certainly tried hard enough, as he relates in *The Confessions of a Young Man*.

Like Shaw, most of the great men of this renaissance I speak of had to leave Ireland to prove their greatness, but at least they were born there. They breathed from infancy its strange air of realism and mysticism, its dignity with poverty, its love of scholarship, its wit as distinguished from gaiety, and never got it quite out of their systems.

The fact that many of them were only recently transplanted Englishmen or Scotchmen, or, as in my own case, Welshmen, takes no more away from their being Irishmen than a New Yorker one generation removed from Warsaw is any the less an American.

What was this Ireland of the eighteen-sixties like? To Shaw, in all respects, it was horrible; but a good deal of that was due to the circumstances of his family. The members of it were not only at odds with each other, but with the community itself. In an intensely and poetically religious country, where a small aristocratic Protestant garrison ruled a poor but proud Catholic majority, and ostracised it vigorously, the Catholic was in Irish garrison society what the Dissenter was in English county society. An Irish country gentleman might be a Plymouth Brother or attend Methodist meetings without compromising his gentility in the least. He was a Protestant; and that sufficed. Shaw's father sent him to the Wesleyan Connexional School in Dublin because it was one of the genteel Protestant schools. But Shaw senior was not a Methodist, nor did the boy ever think of himself as one, or know what the words Wesleyan Connexional meant. Half his schoolfellows were in the same position. They were Protestants: that was all. They did not speak to Catholic boys, who were all destined to eternal damnation; but Quakers were quite in order.

You didn't have to be Irish, as I say, for seven hundred years, to share their innate love of freedom and culture, nor to share their pride of race. All you had to do was to be born there and, though your own parents may have been the most reactionary and domineering of English Tories, you would have grown up to love the land of your birth, for the Irish are a most lovable people.

You must remember that, in the eighteen-forties, Ireland had its black famine, and in the eighteen-sixties, when Shaw was a child, things were still oppressive. 'Talk is cheap,' they'd say, 'but it takes money to buy bread.' Life was an issue of just trying to live. Most families waited for the mail-boats from America, and the days these boats arrived you would see long queues at the post-offices. These people were waiting to receive letters from their illiterate sons in New York. Their postal money-orders always came in yellow envelopes. If the money arrived, it meant a cooked herring and potatoes dipped in the sauce. If it didn't, it meant a dinner of potatoes and 'point', for one had to be satisfied with just pointing a potato at an imaginary herring.

In times of famine even these potatoes were not at hand, as there was a blight that seemed to blacken them and ruin the crop.

Such a state of poverty was not helped any by an intolerable landlord system. If an Irish tenant improved the land, or any of the houses on it, all those improvements were the property of the absentee landlord – an English noble who left all the tyrannical details to an estate agent.

What the agent invariably did was to raise the rent on the strength of these improvements, and kick the tenant out if he did not pay the difference. With such injustices it was easy to see how Fenians and Home Rulers kept springing up regardless of the numbers imprisoned or deported for rebellion, or how much they were absorbed by America, Australia, and even London. Their only means of protest were *The Freeman's Journal* and *The Nation*, the latter edited by Sir Charles Gavin Duffy. Duffy was prosecuted by the Government and finally sent out as a felon. In time, of course, he became Prime Minister of Australia.

Isaac Butt, who started the Home Rule movement, was followed by Parnell, and even the destruction of Parnell could not kill the movement, because the causes were right in the soil. In fact, the agrarian movement was due to grievances economic, not political.

After famines, to be brutal about it, there was even no manure to nourish the soil – sweat, as has been well said, being the only manure Paddy could supply. They imported guano until such times as the land could support enough domestic animals to solve the problem.

Travel in those days of Shaw's childhood in Ireland was done generally in ass carts and jaunting cars. In the jaunting car, peculiar to Ireland as the hansom cab was to England, you rode back to back, facing right and left, on a two-wheeled frame with the driver on a perch in front. In the space between the passengers stood the luggage.

The principal cities were linked up with primitive trains. The minor connections were effected by the Bianconi cars. These were giant black jaunting cars with four horses. They connected the secondary towns somewhat as the trains did the big cities of Dublin, where Shaw was born, Cork, and Galway, where I was born. But, for the most part, jaunting cars or ass carts were the only means most Irishmen had for getting from one impoverished settlement to another.

A chief industry of those who could find any work at all during those dreadful times was poaching. This was simply hunting and fishing illegally on huge estates. To the nobility (who stole the land from the Irish), this poaching was stealing and as such was punished. To Americans, used to cattle-stealing (I rustled them out of Mexico myself when only eighteen), and to Chicago bandits, poaching may seem child's play, but in Europe it was considered disgraceful beyond words.

Jim Connell was one of the foremost of these poachers. He even wrote a book on the subject, the last blasphemy to English minds. It revealed the secrets of the craft and showed how one who had the right qualities and determination to succeed could become a better poacher, and perhaps in time graduate into more respectable forms of roguery – banking, possibly. Had not the noblest families of England started as robber barons, plunderers, pirates, and usurers? Well, then, poaching shouldn't be looked down on. It had a future. This, at least, was Jim's thesis.

One of the standard drolleries of the times is the story of a landlord overtaking a poacher on a morning's walk. The landlord explains that he is out getting an appetite for his breakfast, and asks the poacher what he is doing. 'Getting a breakfast for me appetite,' he replies.

This comic beggar prefaced all his remarks with 'Be-jabers', in a brogue you could cut with a knife. Playwrights had been chipping pieces of atmosphere off this Irish Blarney Stone for generations and carrying it to all corners of the earth. It was a language that theatre-goers liked. It helped them to forget that the real Ireland was a land of famine, starvation, absentee landlordism, pawnbrokers, and printers who made their living chiefly by setting up bankruptcy forms.

These 'Be-jabers' of the actors had only one good result; they created a goodwill so that the hard-hitting realistic Irishmen could get in their blows on an enemy who was in no position to fight back – an enemy relaxed, laughing.

There are actors known to this day who made fortunes and were known all their lives as great Irish tenors, but who were no more Irish than Calvin Coolidge. They simply knew the drawing power of the romantic Irish tradition as a modern cinema-producer knows sex appeal.

If Shaw had followed this laughing Irish tradition he might have succeeded quicker and died sooner; but, taking the line of most resistance, he reached the highest point, long afterwards, alone. He handled English with the Irish advantage of catching it in its Augustan phase, then a century out of date in England. He used it as an instrument, not as an art. 'Force of assertion is the alpha and omega of style,' he said later, and he certainly had an assertive style. You can judge how far removed he was from the stage Irishman by these facts: he did not drink, he was not devout one minute and hilarious the next, his smile was nearer a sneer than a laugh, he didn't love his 'ould mother', and, though Kilkenny and Dublin soil nourished his ancestors, he was anti-romantic, and patriotic only because the patriotic side was the side of revolt. If he ever paraded on St Patrick's Day, it is not on record, and if he ever wore a bit of shamrock in his tattered high hat or stuck a clay pipe in it, no photographer ever developed the plate for a ribald posterity to laugh at. He was even further away in feeling from the Twelfth of July Irishmen, the Orangemen of the north, who, however, counted for much less in lukewarm derisive Dublin than in Belfast.

The comic, jig-dancing Irishman, Shaw insists, is a stage fiction. 'Of all the tricks,' he wrote years later in *The Saturday Review*, 'which the Irish nation have played on the slow-witted Saxon, the most outrageous is the palming off on him of the imaginary Irishman of romance.

'The worst of it is that when a spurious type gets into literature, it strikes the imagination of boys and girls. They form themselves by playing up to it, and thus the unsubstantial fancies of the novelists and music-hall song-writers of one generation are apt to become the unpleasant and mischievous realities of the next.'

When Shaw says he is an Irishman he means that he was born in Ireland, that his native language is the English of Swift, spoken, as Beer says, like church music; not the unspeakable jargon of Oxford or the London newspapers.

'My extraction,' Shaw explains, 'is the extraction of most Englishmen: that is, I have no trace in me of the commercially imported North Spanish strain which passes for aboriginal Irish: I am a genuine typical Irishman of the Danish, Norman, Cromwellian, and (of course) Scottish invasion.'

By 1860, the shillelagh-swinging Celtic troubadours had disappeared, but goats and pigs still prowled through the sties that poetic peasants called home. This was the kind of shanty Ireland which surrounded the bourgeois Ireland of the cities, which was also the Ireland of the Dublin Shaws. These Shaws were highly pretentious socially: 'arrant snobs all of them' is Bernard's own description of them; though many of them were poor, judged by overseas standards of living. Shaw classifies them contemptuously as younger sons of younger sons, and calls his father a 'down-start', which is as good a description of their plight as any.

Without that Ireland he never could have written *John Bull's Other Island*, one of his better creations. Observe how well he catches its pain-giving mysticism which only drink can allay: 'Oh, the dreaming! the dreaming! the torturing heart-scalding, never satisfying dreaming, dreaming, dreaming, dreaming! No debauchery that ever coarsened and brutalised an Englishman can take the worth and usefulness out of him like that dreaming. An Irishman's imagination never lets him alone, never convinces him, never satisfies him; but it makes him that he can't face reality, nor deal with it, nor handle it, nor conquer it: he can only sneer at them that do, and be "agreeable to strangers" like a good-for-nothing woman on the streets. It's all dreaming, all imagination. He can't be religious. The inspired churchman that teaches him the sanctity of life and the importance of conduct is sent away empty, while the poor village priest that gives him a miracle or a sentimental story of a saint has cathedrals built for him out of the pennies of the poor. He can't be intelligently political: he dreams of what the Shan Van Vocht said in 1898. If you want to interest him in Ireland you've got to call the unfortunate island Kathleen ni Hoolihan and pretend she's a little old woman. It saves thinking. It saves working. It saves everything except imagination, imagination, imagination; and imagination's such a torture that you can't bear it without whisky.'

3

The Genteel Shaws

And whisky reminds us inevitably of Bernard Shaw's father. Of all the persons who contributed, however slightly, to Bernard Shaw's greatness, his father alone emerges dripping with human juices. His mother was a remarkable woman, but not the kind men die for. She lacked that kind of fire. But his father must have been easy to like – and even to live with when he was sober. As a provider, a father, he was of course rather a failure; but as a neighbour he must have been amusing.

What Bernard Shaw would have been without this waggish, irresponsible influence is appalling to contemplate – an Irish Anthony Comstock possibly; though probably not, for he had an irreligious Rabelaisian uncle, a ship's surgeon, who could even go so far in his blasphemous theories as to advance the hypothesis, in boy Bernard's presence, that the raising of Lazarus from the dead was all arranged between Lazarus and the Nazarene, a friendly publicity scheme to help Jesus – nothing more. Shaw's father never could go quite that far in disgracing the family. On the contrary, he was a mild conformer, only occasionally betrayed into blasphemy by an ungovernable taste for humorous anti-climax which was all he had to bequeath to his son. All he did was to disgrace his family socially.

These Shaws claim descent from Shaigh, third son of Macduff, Earl of Fife, who cuffed Macbeth. They came to Ireland toward the end of the seventeenth century by a roundabout route from Hampshire.

Cromwell's granddaughter married one of the Shaws, who were country gentlemen of sorts at Sandpits, Kilkenny. There always was an officer or a clergyman about. By 1802, even business men were tolerated in the family. One of them came to Dublin and founded the Royal Bank, long known as 'Shaw's Bank' in the city. He became Sir Robert Shaw, Baronet, of Bushy Park.

Bernard Shaw's Shavian grandfather, first cousin to the Sir Robert of his day, was a Dublin stockbroker who had married a curate's daughter.

He produced more children than profits, and on New Year's Eve, 1817, went on a spree over the birth of another son. This was George Carr Shaw. Except for playing the role of Prince Consort so that George Bernard Shaw might be legitimately born, George Carr Shaw's life couldn't in any sense be considered important. How he grew up nobody seems to have kept much track of. And yet he must have been a sweet old sinner, with a soft beard which he let grow at the suggestion of his infant son.

This George Carr Shaw managed to drink his way to the ripe age of forty before marrying. All we know is that, after quitting a job in an iron works, he got hold of a Government sinecure. It was such a sinecure that the office had to be abolished. The look of pain in his eyes at this bad news was too much even for politicians, so they gave him a pension of sixty pounds a year. He sold it; and it was on the proceeds of the sale that he went into business and, at forty, had the temerity to get married. A sober man would never have tried it, but then, as you gather, George Carr Shaw was not always sober. Outside of this, he had no apparent bad traits. Children liked him because of an amusing squint. Oscar Wilde's father, a famous oculist, had tried to repair the damage and had only made it worse.

If George Carr Shaw had had any social position it would have been fairly sound, for he came from the right people – baronets, parsons, officers, remember – but he had no money.

Curiously, his son Bernard arrived at forty in about the same position except, of course, that he did not drink and had no squint. They both followed the very practical course of marrying money, except that in George Carr Shaw's case most of the money disappeared as soon as he married it, for his wife was promptly disinherited for marrying a poor man, having been carefully brought up to marry a very rich one. This couldn't have bothered him much, for he was hopelessly unambitious, and could chuckle over his own misfortunes. They were anti-climaxes; and he always laughed at anti-climaxes. He was never known to weep. Shaw says that there was something of Charles Lamb in him. Yet he had black melancholies and remorses. One of the remorses was for having once set a greyhound to course a cat, which was slain. He declared that all his ill luck was a just punishment for this atrocity. No man who was any good, he held, would have done such a thing.

All these Shaws were a musical folk in a back-country way. They played by ear trombones, ophicleides (a monster keyed bugle, now supplanted by the tuba), violoncellos, harps, and most of them, the women particularly, fluttered over piano-keys. George Carr Shaw played the trombone.

Bernard Shaw's eldest uncle (he had fourteen uncles and aunts) was a university man. Some of his uncles made money. One even made a tidy fortune and lost it again developing the mineral resources of Ireland before railroads came in. Two of them emigrated, and did well in New Zealand and Australia. All these Shaw relations turned their eyes toward the baronet at Bushy Park – Sir Robert Shaw. George Carr Shaw and his young wife were invited there until George's tendency to arrive not quite sober and to leave scandalously drunk, made dropping him socially only a matter of time.

George Carr Shaw's mother – that is, 'Grandmamma' to Bernard – had a cottage outside Dublin known as 'Roundtown', in a suburb called Terenure. It remains to this day a Gothic cottage at the end of the trolley line. Her son George Carr was a mere item in her somewhat desperate budget; for she was left a widow with thirteen other children to feed and couldn't have spared much time on him.

At the baronet's, and among themselves, the clan got through their social evenings with the aid of their musical instruments. But they were more clannish than social, and seldom spoke well of the intruders who broke into the family by marriage.

One uncle, deciding to reform, gave up drinking and smoking at one blow and intemperately tooted the ophicleide instead. This not giving him sufficient solace, he married. Even that did not seem to give him the happiness he thought he deserved, so he bought a pair of opera-glasses and a Bible. When he tired of reading the Bible, he would turn the opera-glasses on the girls swimming at Dalkey Beach. This 'reformed' man finally committed suicide. The family thought of deeding his Bible and opera-glasses to G. Carr Shaw, but then they remembered that lightning never strikes twice in the same place. Besides, George Carr Shaw never read anything but newspapers. At least his son never saw him read anything else.

The realised capital value of the pension had been invested in a wholesale flour warehouse in Jervis Street. With it went a mill in the country behind Rutland House at Dolphin's Barn beyond the canal. Traces of it still exist.

Thither before breakfast once a week or so the father would walk with his little boy Bernard, and play at business while his son played about the millpond. It was a going concern when he bought it, and it survived all his efforts to ruin it, though the failure of one good customer once brought it to the verge of collapse. At such crises, George Carr Shaw, enchanted with the magnitude of the anti-climax, hid himself from his weeping partner and roared with laughter.

Even when his family deserted him for London he was able to send them a pound a week from the old mill, pretty generous of him considering everything.

Long before that, however, all doors were closed to him. George Carr Shaw's social isolation of course included his wife. She couldn't very well be invited without him.

'If you asked my father to dinner or to a party he was not always quite sober when he arrived, and he was invariably scandalously drunk when he left,' writes his son. 'Now, a convivial drunkard may be exhilarating in convivial company. Even a quarrelsome or boastful drunkard may be found entertaining by people who are not particular. But a miserable drunkard – and my father, in theory a teetotaller, was racked with shame and remorse even in his cups – is unbearable. My mother rescued herself from this predicament by her musical talent. My father reduced his teetotalism from theory to practice when a mild fit, which felled him on our doorstep one Sunday afternoon, convinced him that he must stop drinking or perish.'

So he stopped drinking, and in time, of course, perished. In spite of his abstinence he lasted until 1885. The old man kept the old mill till he died.

4

His Mother's People

About the time Europe was treating itself to its predicted 'Ouf!' of relief over the good riddance of a former Corsican corporal, and England was erecting statues to the Iron Duke from Ireland who had conquered him, a little town beyond Rathfarnham, to the south of Dublin, was gossiping about something important. Was the daughter of the Squire of Whitechurch, everybody wanted to know, going to be married to Walter Bagnal Gurley? Ordinarily the answer to this question might very well have been, so far as history is concerned, 'What of it?' But in this instance the squire's decision was important, because on it hinged the issue of whether he would be known one hundred years later as George Bernard Shaw's maternal great-grandfather.

The natives of Whitechurch could well believe the marriage would go through, for the squire's alliances were all limited to Protestant people of quality, county families, as they called them. Nobody knew how much of a noble he was himself. All they knew was that he had the cold manners of at least a marquis, and the wealth, even in times of famine, of a medieval moneylender.

This opulence would have been easier to understand if some of them, instead of poaching on his land when he left for a trip to Dublin, had hung on behind his carriage instead.

Once in the slums, they would have seen him enter Cullen's pawnshop in Bride Street and talk to the proprietor with the same lordly air that he talked with his hired hands. Being Irish, they would have made the astute deduction that the Squire of Whitechurch and the owner of Cullen's pawnshop were one and the same grand seigneur.

This moneylending landed aristocrat liked Gurley, who, like himself, was a country gentleman, but more of an aristocrat in the traditional manner of landed gentry. That is to say, Gurley knew nothing of money, how it was made beyond inheritance, or how it was replenished beyond mortgages.

The Squire of Whitechurch had enquired into Gurley's family tree and had heard a story about there being a Secretary for War in Oliver Cromwell's Cabinet somewhere among his ancestors. That seemed ample proof of the kind of hard-willed Protestant manhood he was looking for in a son-in-law.

Gurley had short, ginger whiskers, which embroidered his neck rather than covered his chin and cheeks. He could handle horses like a cowboy or a crusader. The Squire of Whitechurch thought him quite the man to marry his daughter.

So, in one of his spare moments away from counting the profits of the pawnshop and otherwise checking on poor Cullen's honesty, the Squire of Whitechurch married her off. It proved an unsound speculation. Walter Bagnal Gurley had no pawnshop to keep him in luxury, so whenever he needed more money he mortgaged his property.

His father-in-law used the pawnshop profits frequently to extricate Squire Gurley from his troubles. Gurley was not wholly incompetent. He could do many aristocratic things. He was a dead shot, a tireless fisherman, and could even make his own boats. He was usually well mounted, because he could master horses so wild that when others, thinking they could do the same, bought them for two hundred pounds, they were soon glad to sell them to him for twenty. Had he sold them dear instead of buying them cheap he might have kept out of debt. But he didn't. He played about, and loaned money to others as irresponsible as himself; and so his estate kept slipping through his fingers.

It all couldn't have worried him very much, for he lived to be eighty-five. His first wife died long before him. One of their children was named Lucinda Elizabeth and called Bessie for short. This Bessie is also important because she became in time the mother of George Bernard Shaw. After her mother's death, Bessie was taken in hand by a sweet-faced but tyrannical aunt for rearing. This aunt had a will like Bismarck's. She was hunchbacked to boot. She decided that the beautiful Bessie should inherit her money, and qualify therefore by becoming a paragon among ladylike young ladies, and making a distinguished marriage. That is to say, she must always sit straight, never talk in a loud voice, never learn anything useful, never know where the money that was keeping her in luxury was coming from, or otherwise rub her upright shoulders against the coarse realities of life.

To aid in these refining influences she was to learn the piano from the eminent Logier, and be grounded by him in the principles of his celebrated treatise on *Thoroughbass*.

This perfect young lady walked the streets of Dublin seeing nobody. She even (the supreme test) passed shop windows full of women's clothes without stopping. She loved flowers and dogs, flowers even more than people. She was exceedingly kind to people too, and showed great patience with her friends. But let a friendship be broken and she'd see that it never was renewed. She seemed devoid of jealousy and envy, and even of passion, so sexless in fact that it is difficult even for her son to believe that she bore two other children beside himself.

Her father she saw seldom. He managed to keep going somehow for twenty years as a widower by obtaining loans from rich, hunchbacked Aunt Ellen. Then, to everybody's consternation, he planned to marry again. His daughter unfortunately mentioned this in a letter to her Uncle John, son and heir of the original pawnbroking Squire of Whitechurch.

Uncle John acted promptly. Gurley incautiously left his house on his bridal morning to buy a pair of gloves; and, when he came out of the shop, Uncle John had him arrested for debt.

This left the horse-riding, bird-shooting, debt-contracting squire in such a state of fury that he forbade his daughter ever to enter his house. He was certain that she had engineered the whole thing. Such a humiliation demanded adequate revenge. He had a power of appointment over the money settled by the pawnbroker on his children; and he proposed to cut his daughter off from every penny of this. His solicitor, however, like most solicitors, would not let his client have his own way, and fixed it so that her children, if she ever had any, would get five thousand pounds when they came of age, though she herself would get no use of it in her lifetime. And very useful this money proved to Bernard in the lean years which preceded his long deferred acceptance as a writer. It made just all the difference.

This meant that Bessie would henceforth be wholly in the hands of her iron-heeled Aunt Ellen. She couldn't endure this much longer. Indeed, she was beginning to revolt against it long before her father made his new domestic establishment impossible for her.

Against this awful Aunt Ellen she finally revolted entirely, rejecting the religion and the prejudices to which she was brought up, and later, after marrying, leaving, her son insists, her children without any training at all. We shall see her becoming a teacher of singing late in life to support herself and her son too in his young manhood. She lived to be eighty, and kept her voice unbroken and unspoilt to the end in 1913.

'She amused herself with spiritualism in her old age,' Shaw writes me, 'to be able to play at communicating with her favourite daughter who had died; but she soon got tired of this; and the next thing that happened was that the lost daughter announced that they must separate, and left her to a certain entirely imaginary Father John, described by himself as "a Cistercian monk who lived six thousand years before Christ" '!

The last I see of her is in London, with a moving-van in front of her house, furniture standing on the pavement and men busy packing the van. The front door is open, the hall and downstairs rooms empty. Dan Rider, in search of old books, has popped his head into the large front room and drawn back in surprise, for there, in the midst of all this emptiness, sits Bernard Shaw's mother, an elderly lady in an armchair looking into a square, and meditating on the scene below.

When she died some years later, her son, who can show the same self-possession about all tragedies, or says he can, cheerfully accompanied her remains as one of two 'mourners'.

No one has accused him of being a bad son: his relations with his mother were apparently as perfect as anything of the kind could be; but, when she was cremated, Granville-Barker, whom he had chosen to accompany him as the sole other mourner, could say nothing to him but 'Shaw: you certainly are a merry soul.' Shaw was not only full of interest in the process and the ceremony, but full also of a fancy that his mother was looking on at it over his shoulder and sharing his delight at the points on which it appealed to his sense of humour. He is fond of saying that what bereaved people need is a little comic relief.

But long before death or séances cut an old lady off from this world's depressing realism, she had to meet a squint-eyed detrimental in Dublin and learn about romance from him.

5
The Innocent Triangle

Among the friends of Lucinda Elizabeth Gurley, daughter of an irate father who had turned her out of his house, and niece of an extremely severe aunt whose iron heel had proved intolerable, was George Carr Shaw. He was twice her years, with not only as little knowledge of making money as her father, but no knowledge of how to raise any. He was a Shaw, and therefore (so all the Shaws said) respectable. He kissed her on the cheek and proposed to her. Life being a terrible problem at the moment, she accepted. Had he kissed her on the lips, she might have learned something about his breath and rejected him; but, then, her ignorance of life was appalling. Still, if she were ignorant of life, her friends were not. They saw her practically obliterating herself at one stroke if she married George Carr Shaw. They told her as much.

'Why?' she wanted to know.

'The man drinks,' they told her.

'Why didn't you tell me this before?'

'You never asked us, Bessie.'

She got up and left them and went straight to him. She asked him if it were true.

'Is what true?'

'That you drink.'

'Drink? Why I'm a lifelong and bigoted teetotaller!' he exclaimed indignantly.

She believed him, as indeed he believed himself.

And so they were married.

The warehouse and the mill could not support her in the style to which she was accustomed. Before she discovered that out she discovered something worse.

The honeymoon found them in Liverpool. His behaviour there sent doubt panicking through her mind. Then one day the truth came out. Tumbled out, in fact. She opened a cupboard and found it crammed with empty bottles. Her one thought was to escape this disgusting scandal. She left the house and soon found herself wandering among the docks. The idea came to her that she might sign up as a ship's stewardess and so escape an intolerable situation. But the men about the docks were much rougher and more given to drink than the mild humorist she had just left. She could only go back to him and dree her weird.

Soon came children – two daughters and then a son. The son, not that it seemed to matter much then, was born in Dublin on July 26th, 1856, four years after her marriage, and named George after his father and Bernard after his uncle the ophicleidist.

He was taken once or twice to see Aunt Ellen, with the hope that a male heir might soften her heart. In this he failed, but the strange little woman, hunchbacked, with her clean little face and refined air, fascinated him. The fancy was not reciprocated. She took care that her fortune never got into the hands of his father, or himself and his sisters. When this aunt died, the boy went into the garden and wept bitterly. He thought his grief would last for ever. It lasted half an hour. From this he learnt, and never forgot, that floods of such tears are pure reflexes, worthless as manifestations of real and enduring regard for the dead.

His mother took the shock standing up. All woes were alike to her in those days of disillusion; her husband, their poverty, her husband's drinking, their children – all seemed part of the mess she had made of her life. So she left them all to Providence and took no interest in any of them, not even the children, after a few years.

'It would be ridiculous,' her son says, summing her up seventy years later, 'to call her a bad wife and a bad mother, because she was not a bad mother and was incapable of ill-treating anything or anybody, however deeply they might injure or bitterly disappoint her. She was simply not a wife or mother at all. Like my father, she was a hopelessly uncoercive person; and we as children had to find our way in a household where there was neither hate nor love, fear nor reverence, but always personality.'

From every point of view as much of a failure as her husband, Mrs Shaw, whose capacity for solitude made her exceptionally independent of society and circumstances, fell back on herself until she found a religious vocation in music. For the religious creed of her people she had no use; and the Life-Force credo of her son had not yet been thrust belligerently upon the world. So, until she took up spiritualism years later, music became her religion.

Her singing, which would have betrayed anything there was to betray, never expressed eroticism. 'I took her singing of Mendelssohn's "Hear my Prayer",' testifies her son, 'as a matter of course until I heard an ordinary English singer treating a concert audience to it. I was horrified: the woman produced the effect of indecent exposure on me.'

The discovery that she had a mezzo-soprano voice of peculiar purity of tone was made by a teacher of singing named George John Vandaleur Lee. Strangely he too, like her aunt and her husband, had an emphatic physical defect. He had fallen downstairs in his childhood and walked with a limp for the rest of his life, one of his legs being considerably shorter than the other. He was a celibate, though not wholly un-attractive to women, except that he insisted on putting music above them. Shaw knows little about his antecedents. He did have a tutor when a boy, but that ended when he attacked the tutor with a fishing-rod and drove him from the house. On growing up, he supported himself and a brother by teaching singing. The brother died, and after nearly going insane with grief, Lee got over it enough to nurse Mrs Shaw out of a serious illness, sweeping aside her husband and every-body else to accomplish the task. He actually cured her.

He was a physiologist of sorts too. He dissected throats till he knew exactly what a larynx was like. He watched an Italian operatic baritone, Badeali, whose voice was still perfect at eighty. From these sources he had perfected a technique of singing known in the Shaw household as The Method.

This came very shortly to be Mrs Shaw's religion. It would be easy to hint that she swallowed The Method to get at Lee. But the fact is, she was through with men as men. The bond between Lee and her was The Method. Any sex tie would not have lasted a year, Shaw says. The Method was eternal. 'While Lee remained faithful to The Method,' writes her son, 'she remained faithful to him as his prima donna, his chorus lady, his copyist of band parts, his harmoniser according to the rules of Logier's *Thoroughbass*, his lieutenant and champion. When, in the later days of his London vogue and decay, he dropped it and became a fashionable charlatan, she dropped him as unhesitatingly as her father used to shoot a sporting-dog at its first mistake.'

Lee lived with the Shaws after his brother died. He, needing a good address, had a house too big for him and too dear for the Shaws. So they combined forces and set up a joint household. In handsome Hatch Street this strange triangle – based, as Shaw says, not on adultery, but The Method – had its heyday.

The house was for ever rehearsing masterpieces of music. There was an amateur choral society and orchestra, with Lee conducting from a vocal score or a first-violin part. He could hypnotise an orchestra and was as good a conductor as Nikisch, though he probably had never seen a full orchestral score in his life.

In this atmosphere, Bernard Shaw was raised. To those who might doubt it was all as innocent as it seemed, I can only refer them to some authorities on sublimation. Shaw confesses that he had three fathers: Lee, his Uncle Walter, and George Carr Shaw. Only George Carr Shaw, however, had anything to do with his presence on this earth. The others contributed their parentage after the birth. And when you consider what a poor provider his father was, it is not surprising that others took it upon themselves to help fill his shoes.

Lee always walked about with a limp of studied elegance. Possibly this handicapped him completely in a matter of sex: at all events Shaw says that Lee was somehow unthinkable as a married man.

Lee's upper lip and chin were close-shaved. His face was framed with pirate-black whiskers. In his infancy babies wore enormous nightcaps, which occasionally caught fire. Lee's did; and for ever after his glossy black hair grew on his forehead like the 'join', as actors call it, of a wig. He was never carelessly or ill dressed; and he had personal style, physical adroitness, and the art of seeming to succeed in everything he attempted. Altogether a presentable enough singing-teacher. Anyhow, he was always accepted as a leader in his circle. In a group photograph taken by Richard Pigott, the forger of the famous spurious Parnell letters which deceived *The Times*, Lee is the centre of the picture, obviously by divine right.

For several years the Shaws and Lee lived together in Hatch Street. Then Lee, realising an ambition he had entertained for years, took a house in Park Lane and left Dublin for London. This left the Shaws without a paying guest in a house which they could not afford. Lucy Shaw, Bernard's sister, had been raised on The Method, and she and her mother decided the sensible thing to do now that Lee had left was to follow him. A possible London début under his auspices made the trip even more plausible.

George Carr Shaw could not keep the family together, as he was poorer than ever, and, indeed, he had lost all control long ago of this strange *ménage*. Uncle Walter, being an Atlantic liner's surgeon, was not in port often enough to make any difference. Left with no one to lean on, Mrs Shaw and Lucy followed Lee to London, taking a house in Victoria Grove down Fulham Road way. Mrs Shaw gave up her amateur status and began to teach singing professionally.

Lee's Method was doomed to failure in London from the start. It took three years to form and train a singer by it; and London wanted its Jenny Linds, Pattis, Melbas and Calvés turned out in twelve lessons.

'They did not want to sing like my mother,' said Shaw. 'They wanted to sing like harlots; and they did.'

Lee, seeing what way the wind was blowing, dropped the 'G. J.' initials and became 'Vandaleur Lee'. That only raised his fee to a guinea a lesson. He shaved off his black whiskers and grew a moustache. He waxed this, and his days of honest toil were over.

Mrs Shaw, observing that he was developing into a charlatan, would have none of him after that. This was particularly settled in her mind when he became susceptible to Lucy's adolescent sex appeal. No harm came of this because Lucy could not tolerate him.

Finally his fashion waned; and the flow of guineas ceased. He turned his Park Lane house into a nightclub, and dropped dead one night as he was getting into bed. The autopsy established a long diseased brain. He had come to London a doomed and decaying man. The Shaws were so far removed from Lee by then that who buried him, or what became of his effects, they never knew.

'With my mother he, of course,' writes Shaw, 'completely side-tracked my father; but there was no substitution whatever, and in the end she was more lenient to the husband than to the hero. Is it now necessary to add that my resemblance to my father is quite clearly discernible, and that I have not a single trait even remotely resembling any of Lee's? I do not want my mother to be the heroine of another Wagner-Geyer lie.'

Wanting further details on this strange household, I wrote Shaw in the summer of 1930. He replied:

London
June 20th 1930
MY DEAR FRANK HARRIS – As to your question whether Lee's move to London and my mother's were simultaneous, they could not have

been. Lee had to make his position in London before he could provide the musical setting for my mother and sister. But the break-up of the family was an economic necessity anyhow, because without Lee we could not afford to keep up the house. I was born in a small house in an unfashionable street (then half fields) at the edge of Dublin. No professional man of any standing could have received fashionable pupils or patients at such an address. The house had, in the basement, a kitchen, a servant's bedroom, and a pantry. On the *rez-de-chaussée*, a parlour (the *salle à manger*), a nursery, and a 'return room' which served as a dressing-room for my father, and subsequently as also a bedroom for me when I grew out of sleeping in the nursery with my two sisters. Upstairs was the drawing-room and the best bedroom; and that was all. It was 3 Upper Synge (pronounced Sing) Street at my birth; and one of my early recollections – coeval with the death of the Prince Consort, when the newspaper came out with a black border – was its change to 33 Synge Street when the three Synge Streets, upper, middle, and lower, were amalgamated.

The house we shared with Lee, No. 1 Hatch Street, was more fashionably placed. Being a corner house, it had no garden, but it had two areas and a leads. It had eight rooms, besides the spacious basement and pantry accommodation, as against five in Synge Street; and the rent, of course, was much higher. Without Lee's contribution it was beyond my father's dwindling means. Lee at last got his foot into England at a country house in Shropshire, where the lady fancied herself as an amateur prima donna; and he made smart acquaintances there. He had always said that he would take a house in Park Lane; and he did. No. 13 it was: a narrow house, but with one fine music-room.

When it was clear that he was going to stay there, and that Dublin had seen the last of him, the Hatch Street house had to be given up. So my mother took a London house in Victoria Grove, way down the Fulham Road, and settled there with her two daughters, whilst I and my father went into Dublin lodgings at 61 Harcourt Street. This must have been somewhere round about 1871.

Ever,

G. B. S.

Lee's presence in the Shavian household during the years when he was a really going concern made, Shaw admits, a revolutionary difference. If

Shaw has never slept with the window shut it is because Lee believed in fresh air. If Shaw has no reverence for doctors it is because Lee cleared the apothecary out of the house when he was an overdosed child and cured his mother by mesmeric induction of his own vitality. If Shaw was a nationalist it was because Lee's family had sheltered Fenians 'on the run'. And, by reaction, if Shaw has scourged artists for their way of forming poisonous little cliques to hate and slander all the other little cliques it is because the Dublin musical cliques loathed Lee, and the Lee clique would admit no virtue in the anti-Lees. And finally, Shaw did not fail to note the banal vanity of Lee's London 'success'.

It taught him more than all the universities in the world could have done. Even today at seventy-five you don't get him completely away from his work to play the vacuous rôle of a literary lion with manicured nails, sipping tea in Mayfair. Lee at least taught him to steer clear of that, except for what he could take out of it and put into a scene.

6

Boyhood in Dublin

In France you notice that, even in the wealthiest families, food is often served most sparingly. Nothing is wasted. I sometimes think this frugality may be in the blood, and that the cells themselves remember the frightful poverty of the Revolution.

In much the same way I can only account for Shaw's fierce hatred of poverty. He never knew the pinch of hunger; for his father was resolved that in his house no child should ever suffer from unsatisfied hunger, and a loaf and a lump of butter was always within Bernard's reach; but this did not save him from the wounds and limitations of chronic impecuniosity and the senseless falsehood of pretending to a superior social rank with less than half the income needed to make the pretence good. His dread of being credited with the least softness of heart is the result of his knowledge that such a reputation would bring all the beggars in the world down on him to strip him of all his goods. Detestation of poverty and riches alike goes to the roots with him.

He says he doesn't mind privations which only make success harder; he resents poverty which makes it impossible.

'Child poverty is the only sort of poverty that matters,' Shaw once wrote to Judge Henry Neill. 'The adult who has been poor as a child will never get the chill of poverty out of his bones; but he will make room for a better-nourished generation. There are no doubt property owners in America who tell Judge Henry Neill that it is confiscation to tax one man's property to pay for the education of another man's children. We have scoundrels of that sort in England, too.'

As the younger son of a younger son, a second cousin to a baronet, who knew all about Public Schools and universities, but could not go to them, Shaw might well look back on his boyhood bitterly; and yet those who remember him from those far-off days remember him chiefly for the dignity of his carriage and the condescending way he had with children, especially girls, older than himself. To boys he romanced about his courage and prowess with the reckless mendacity of a born storyteller whilst he was still an exceptionally timid child. 'I will strike you dead at my feet,' he declaimed at a daring older boy who called his bluff. But the caller faced this fearful death unflinchingly; and Sonny, panic stricken, fled disgracefully. Mostly, however, he was taken at his own valuation, and carried his arrant cowardice in his breast, a guilty secret that afflicted him horribly. He was excessively sensitive, and found his eyes filling with tears at the slightest rebuff. The struggle with this humiliating weakness was the beginning of the exasperating self-control he achieved as an adult.

Curious that he remembers so well the sadder side of those childhood years. Speaking of his mother, he says: 'She endured the children, their father, and the poverty and the drink and everything else, leaving them to the servants (and, my God! what servants! – except old Nurse Williams), and to Providence, and taking no interest in them after, say, six years old.'

It would be easy to connect this with his later belief that the State should compete with private individuals – especially with parents – 'in providing happy homes for children, so that every child may have a refuge from the tyranny or neglect of its natural custodians'.

But is this poverty and neglect? Nurses, servants – even bad ones? It is hard to believe this is Shaw. It sounds more like a born snob telling how hard times fell on him after the Russian Revolution and sent his titled parents packing. But, to people who never had servants to rail against, such 'poverty' is only skimming life's possible misfortunes.

Shaw's first literary composition was a prayer. He never used any of the ready-made liturgies. His prayer was in three paragraphs (or, as he calls them, movements) and ended with The Lord's Prayer.

He didn't beg from the Almighty, he performed for Him; an actor from infancy.

Even the Mephistopheles he grew up to resemble was a childhood hero. He remembers adorning the walls of his bedroom with likenesses of this tempter of Faust.

Only one thing could make him take a utilitarian view of his prayers. That was a thunderstorm. Two in especial nearly scared him out of his wits. On each occasion, he resorted to The Lord's Prayer as a lightning conductor. Mark Twain too had this feminine fright of thunder and lightning.

But storms didn't come often enough to keep Shaw's faith alive.

Before he was ten years old, family prayers and church-going were dropped in the Shaw household, and the boy Bernard certainly didn't show his independence by continuing on alone.

Seeing that it amused his father, he would often flout the Bible. At first this shocked his father, but as soon as the boy scored a point he would laugh, proud, no doubt, of such quips from the old block.

When a small boy he went swimming in Killiney Bay with his father. Swimming, incidentally, is still his favourite recreation. He recalls how at that time his father impressed him with the importance of learning to swim, telling him how when he was himself a boy of fourteen he had saved the life of one of his brothers. This left Sonny Shaw so in awe that the father, seeing a rare chance for an anti-climax, hastened to add, 'And to tell the truth, I never was so sorry for anything in my life afterwards!'

Then he laughed, plunged in the bay, and remained in a happy mood all the way home.

Here is Shaw's father when really himself, when not *blackjacked* into the code of the British garrison on his scanty income.

But Shaw recalls once playing in the street with a classmate. His father coming home questioned him about this boy. On learning the playmate was the son of a man who kept a hardware store, George Carr Shaw was appalled. He lectured Sonny Shaw never again to play with any children whose parents were engaged in retail trade. 'Probably,' writes Shaw, 'this was the worst crime my father ever committed.'

This could easily have crystallised a later opinion of Shaw's that 'we are, after all, social animals, and if we are let alone in the matter of our affections, and well brought up otherwise, we shall not get on any the worse with particular people because they happen to be our brothers and sisters and cousins. The danger lies in assuming that we shall get on any better.'

Shaw believes Ireland, at any rate as far as the Protestant gentry are concerned, to be the most irreligious country in the world. He was christened in his uncle's church. As his godfather was intoxicated and did not turn up, the sexton was ordered to play the rôle instead, 'precisely as my uncle might have ordered him to put more coals on the vestry fire'. Shaw was never confirmed, and doesn't believe his parents ever were either. They didn't need to be. They were Irish Protestants, and therefore eligible for heaven without confirming ritual.

He was sent to the Wesleyan Connexional School, now Wesley

College, Dublin. He had already been taught a good deal of Latin grammar by his uncle the Rev. William George Carroll, of St Bride's (now demolished). To the headmaster, the Rev. Robert Crook, D.D., there was only one subject of education: classics, meaning Latin and Greek. The first half-hour of the day was devoted to the Wesleyan catechism, with endless scriptural 'proofs' to all the answers; but Shaw escaped this, as the family had a cottage in Dalkey from which he had to come to school by rail, and was therefore privileged to be half an hour late. He was a dayboy; and if there was any religious atmosphere in the school for boarders it never touched him. Instead of learning anything he forgot what his uncle had taught him. He would not and could not read schoolbooks, though he read everything else he could lay hands on; and he could not attend to unskilled teachers qualifying for the Methodist ministry when his standards were set by the vital and mesmeric Lee. The school was to him only a hated prison where his parents got him out of the way for half the day.

It convinced him that the real object of our educational system is to relieve parents from the insufferable company and anxious care of their children. He thinks parents today ought to admit that children are nuisances except at playful moments, and that there should be some adequate defence of the comparative quiet and order of adult life 'against the comparative noise, racket, untidiness, inquisitiveness, restlessness, fitfulness, shiftlessness, dirt, destruction, and mischief which are healthy and natural for children'. He demands 'the organisation of child life as such' and the total abolition of schools as we know them.

On Sundays he most unwillingly patronised the Episcopal Church of Ireland, sitting with other infants on the knee cushions round the communion rails at the Molyneux church, after an hour of Sunday school. This experience left such a distaste in his mouth that when compulsion ceased he never entered a church again until, as an adult traveller and connoisseur, he began to visit Catholic churches in pursuit of works of art. His blood creeps every time, he says, he recalls that genteel Irish Protestant Church. He blames all the savagery and bad blood which has marred his literary work on that house of Satan, as he calls it.

No wonder he was hopeless, socially and scholastically. Here are some of his later conclusions.

'It is sometimes remarked that the school dunce often turns out well afterwards as if idleness were a sign of ability and character. A much more sensible explanation is that the so-called dunces are not exhausted before they begin the serious business of life.'

He gets in a good crack at schoolmasters: 'Mankind cannot be saved from without by schoolmasters or any other sort of masters; it can only be lamed and enslaved by them.' That is good individualism. Too good for Shaw.

Here's another: 'When a man teaches something he does not know to someone else who has no aptitude for it, and gives him a certificate of proficiency, the latter has completed the education of a gentleman.'

His three 'fathers' and his mother made school harder for him by treating him as an adult when he ceased to be a small child. They lived their lives and aired their views in his presence without troubling themselves as to the effect on him. When his uncle took him for long walks he entertained him with Rabelaisian stories and elegantly obscene limericks as if the boy were a liner's officer. Lee, a man of perfectly clean conversation, occasionally protested that nothing was coming of the schooling; but he was too busy teaching, and organising concerts and operas, to interfere seriously; and he also talked to young Shaw, when he talked to him at all, on equal terms. The case is common enough in Bohemian households where Art takes the place of business and religion, and discipline is unknown; but it makes school discipline and the attitudes of schoolmasters much more disagreeable than they are to children who are treated in the same way at home. The precocious Bernard disliked it very particularly. He was mentally older than his pastors and masters.

If Shaw could have seen more of his many relations, he thinks his dread of conventional society, founded on ignorance of drawing-room etiquette, might not have been so acute, and to this day he wishes his mother had drilled him socially as she had been drilled. This might have removed, he thinks, both his shyness and insolence. I think if he had been allowed to play with tradespeople's children, which he wasn't, some of this shyness would have been rubbed off twenty years sooner than it was. Anyhow, his first act on obtaining a reader's ticket at the British Museum when he came to London was to call for all the books on etiquette he could find in the subject catalogue; and he has ever since defended the author of *The Manners and Tone of Good Society* as gratefully and enthusiastically – and as unexpectedly – as Swinburne defended Bowdler.

The baronet at Bushy Park might have done much toward removing the boy's hidden humiliations, but Shaw remembers having been there only once – and then to a funeral. Their drinking father got them all dropped socially until Lee made the house a centre of musical society. And that, being largely Roman Catholic, was not tolerated by the snobbish Shaws.

'After my early childhood,' he writes in a preface, 'I can never remember paying a visit to a relative's house. If my mother and father had dined out or gone to a party, their children would have been more astonished than if the house had caught fire. My father's reform came too late to save the social situation; and I was cut off from the social drill which puts one at one's ease in private society. In consequence, all my life I have been a sojourner on this planet rather than a native of it.' He found comfort in a world of his own creation, and completely exhausted his taste for romanticism, he says, before he was ten years old.

'Your popular novelists are now gravely writing the stories I told to myself before I replaced my first set of teeth. Some day I will try to found a genuine psychology of fiction by writing down the history of my imagined life, duels, battles, love affairs with queens and all.'

He took to music as a duck takes to water. When a small boy, he was taken to the opera. He did not then know what an opera was, though he could whistle a good deal of opera music. He had seen, in his mother's album, photographs of all the great opera-singers, mostly in evening dress. In the theatre he found himself before a gilded balcony filled with persons in evening dress. He thought they were the opera-singers! He was puzzled when made to sit with his back to the singers. When the curtain went up, his astonishment and delight were unbounded. Before he was twelve he could whistle all the masterpieces, from their overtures to their last cadences.

Painting, too, interested him. At fifteen he could recognise the works in the Dublin Gallery of many Italian and Flemish painters without even a catalogue. He believes he was the only Irishman, except the officials, who had ever been inside the gallery. In the Municipal Gallery of Dublin today, any equally art-hungry boy can see a marble copy of Rodin's bust of Shaw which Shaw, not taking any chances, presented to the gallery himself.

Many who have no ear for literature or for music, he came to believe later, are accessible to architecture, to pictures, to statues, to dresses, and to the arts of the stage. 'Every device of art should be brought to bear on the young, so that they may discover some form of it that delights them naturally, for there will come to all of them that period between dawning adolescence and full maturity when the pleasures and emotions of art will have to satisfy cravings which, if starved or insulted, may become morbid and disgraceful satisfactions, and, if prematurely gratified otherwise than poetically, may destroy the stamina of the race.'

Nevertheless he received no technical instruction in music. When a small child he played the Guards' Waltz on the piano with one finger; but it never occurred to anyone that he, being a male, could have any interest in the young ladies' accomplishment of playing the piano. He never touched the piano again until the exodus to London of his mother and sisters left him with the instrument but without music. Then he taught himself to play from piano scores, and began to study the treasures of instrumental music that lay outside the oratorios and operas and overtures to which Lee's practice had been confined. By the time he followed his mother to London and again came into contact with Lee, he was able to act as accompanist at the Park Lane musical meetings. But the idea of his becoming a professional musician never occurred either to himself or any of his family, or to Lee. Once a friend who was an accomplished amateur oboe player offered to teach him that instrument. But Shaw senior, divided between his feeling that the profession of orchestral player was beneath the dignity of his illustrious family, and the difficulty of finding fifteen guineas to pay for an oboe, would not hear of it, although it was the only chance he ever had of giving his son a profession of any sort.

What is still odder, his mother never thought of teaching him to sing, perhaps because as a boy he was always singing. At all events, when he rejoined her in London as an adult, he had to insist on her imparting The Method and teaching him to use a voice which was at first, when properly produced, completely inaudible. She manufactured it at last into a presentable but in no way extraordinary baritone, with which, by transposing the notes that were beyond his range an octave up or down as the case might be, and whistling and imitating wind instruments as best he could, he was able to amuse himself by performing operas from end to end all to himself, to the distraction of his neighbours, and sometimes even of his mother, who could not bear the then novel harmonies of Wagner, and denounced his music dramas as 'all recitative', though she admitted that bits of *Lohengrin* were singable and even pretty.

What was the effect on Shaw of all this art and poetry? Many of his later opinions on child-training deal with work and play and were no doubt drawn wholly from his own boyhood in Dublin.

'Of the many wild absurdities of our existing social order, perhaps the most grotesque is the costly and strictly enforced reservation of large tracts of country as deer-forests and breeding-grounds for pheasants,' he once remonstrated, 'whilst there is so little provision of the kind made for children. I am sure that a child should not be imprisoned in a school. I am not so sure that it should not sometimes be driven out into the open – imprisoned in the woods and on the mountains, as it were. For there are frowsty children, just as there are frowsty adults, who don't want freedom. This morbid result of over-domestication would, let us hope, be cured by a compulsory minimum of fresh air.'

He must have been told too often in his childhood to keep quiet, for he returns to this theme often and with a good deal of fairness, as in this instance: 'The child at play is noisy and ought to be noisy. Sir Isaac Newton is quiet and ought to be quiet. And the child should spend most of its time at play, whilst the adult should spend most of his time at work. Therefore, Sir Isaac and the child are not fit company for one another.'

On discipline too he was, and is, sane: 'If you strike a child, take care that you strike it in anger, even at the risk of maiming it for life. A blow in cold blood neither can nor should be forgiven.'

And another instance: 'If you beat children for pleasure, avow your object frankly, playing the game according to the rules, as a foxhunter does, and you will do comparatively little harm. No foxhunter is such a cad as to pretend that he hunts the fox to teach it not to steal chickens, or that he suffers more acutely than the fox at the death.'

Shaw, I might say, though he has been a child, never has had any children. He recognises that he is not fit company for them. But he sympathises with them, remembering his own case.

As Shaw never did any school work out of school, nor indeed in it, and as he ran loose for long periods, he has no illusions about the imagined delights of having nothing to do. Discipline and duty there must be. If it can't be a spanking, what can be tried? Productive work, says Shaw. It is favoured by him because it's a discipline of impersonal necessity, not that of wanton personal coercion.

'Loathsome as we have made the idea of duty (like the idea of work) we must habituate children to a sense of repayable obligation to the community for what they consume and enjoy, and inculcate the repayment as a point of honour.'

Whoever consumes goods or services without producing by personal effort the equivalent of what he or she consumes, Shaw believes further, inflicts on the community precisely the same injury that a thief produces, and would, in any honest State, be treated as a thief, however full his or her pockets might be of money made by other people.

'There is every reason why a child should not be allowed to work for commercial profit or for the support of its parents at the expense of its own future,' he says somewhere else, 'but there is no reason whatever why a child should not do some work for its own sake and that of the community if it can be shown that both it and the community will be the better for it.'

That last is the stuff to give the Wesleyan troops. The Connexional School should be proud to hear its most distinguished failure on such sound doctrine, and the exploiters of child labour in the Methodist areas of America's southern States ought to be able to see community good in exploiting the young as it does. That's all they have to do to find solace in Shaw's statement.

For my part I prefer to throw the emphasis on child play rather than on child work. More parks for children and no idea of labour till they are old enough to vote for the jobs they will take – if there are any. But you cannot accuse Shaw in this instance of talking work and living ease. He began to work as early as Shakespeare did. Perhaps even a little younger.

7

And So to Work

At fifteen, shy Shaw was sent job-hunting. What were his qualifications? He could sing pages and pages of Handel, Haydn, Mozart, Beethoven and Mendelssohn, of Rossini, Donizetti, Bellini, Verdi, Gounod and Meyerbeer, and whistle what he couldn't sing. This seems no qualification at all for business, but suppose the office lacked a baritone for its quartet? Obviously such a learned lad could help out a lot.

He got an introduction to Scott, Spain & Rooney, cloth merchants. Scott saw no objection to taking him on. But Rooney had a fatherly conscience, and saw that the lad was not built for such common work. Shaw fled, grateful for the reprieve.

About the time I was quitting an English Public School because I didn't get a first prize for Cambridge which I had won, and was running away in a rage to America with the second money, Shaw got his first job – through avuncular political pull. At fourteen, I began (with no influence) as a sand hog, an under-river worker on the Brooklyn Bridge foundations. Shaw, a year older, got his in a Dublin land office, thanks to the wire-pulling of his influential Uncle Frederick. I got four dollars a day; he got four dollars and fifty cents a month. Today he passes for a millionaire and I am always skipping blithely two steps ahead of bankruptcy.

In 1871, Shaw entered Uniacke Townshend's land office in Dublin and stayed there five years. He began as a junior clerk. The place was overstaffed with gentlemen-apprentices who paid high premiums for receiving operatic instruction from Shaw when the boss was out. The Miserere scene from *Il Trovatore* was their favourite. Shaw very reluctantly accepted an obligation not to discuss religion with them, as his views on that subject were too subversive for so select an office. One of his duties as junior was to take the tram every Tuesday to Terenure and collect the weekly rents, ranging from a shilling to half a crown, from a dozen cabins called Dodd's Row on the Whitton estate, now replaced by more presentable dwellings. He had not forgotten this experience when he wrote *Widower's Houses*.

A year later the cashier, the most responsible functionary in the office, which was also in a limited way a private bank, had to leave suddenly. In this emergency the youthful Shaw was tried as a stopgap. He made good, was raised to forty-eight pounds a year and bought a tail coat. Things were going splendidly for him, and his father, now at last really a teetotaller, began to see blossoming the success he himself might have been. But Shaw himself loathed his servitude, and was only waiting to escape, not only from the office, but from Dublin 'that city of derision', as he called it, to London, where alone at that time an artistic career was possible.

Edward McNulty, afterwards an Irish novelist, was a schoolboy companion of Shaw's. While Shaw was balancing the cash in Townshend's land office, McNulty was working in the Newry branch of the Bank of Ireland. They carried on an almost daily letter-writing duel, an uncommon thing even for young men with a writing itch, though girls do it often. They had agreed to destroy the letters and so showed no reserve in expressing themselves. Whether the letters were ever worth this caution nobody knows. None seems to have survived, anyway.

The letter-writing became such fun that Shaw tried one on an editor. He had attended a Moody and Sankey revival meeting. Shaw wrote a letter to *Public Opinion*. It was inserted. It bore only one possible construction: to wit, that George Carr Shaw's son was an atheist. This did not shake the world perceptibly; but it shook the Dublin Shaws. The young reprobate's uncles conferred. But nothing happened. He was not even struck dead. And he had made his first appearance in print.

Daniel L. Moody, it might be explained to present-day readers, was credited in his evangelical zeal with saving one million souls from hell, the greatest of the breed since Wesley. He may have been shaken out of his terrifying Calvinism into a more humane theology by his failure to convert our young hero, though the about-face is generally credited to the persuasions of a Birmingham curate.

Anyway, later in life, Moody wrote, 'I used to preach that God was behind the sinner with a double-edged sword ready to hew him down. I have got done with that. I preach now that God is behind him with love.'

But in the eighteen-seventies he was still thundering about God's vengeance.

Considering that Shaw's mother had coldly rejected religion, that his uncle had vulgarly laughed at it, and that his father had never been able to resist the temptation to cap the solemnities of his efforts at religious teaching with a comic anti-climax, the boy's own announcement of atheism had all the originality of a young Rockefeller taking to the oil business. The editor, however, didn't know all this. Impressed by the renunciation of one of his readers, he printed the letter. It had been Shaw's second bid of the sort. *The Vaudeville Magazine* of September 1871 had received a letter of his with arguments so weighty they had to pay twopence extra postage for the privilege of opening and rejecting them. But this time his contribution landed.

Most scribblers have thrilled at seeing their work in print for the first time. Dickens has described how he felt when he opened the first of the *Sketches by Boz* in printed pages. Shaw missed this glorious sensation. Literature was so completely natural to him that he was unconscious of his own specialisation. 'It was no more exciting than the taste of water in my mouth' is his account of the matter. If a magazine had published a drawing by him; or if he had stood on the stage and sung 'Vieni, la mia vendetta' with full orchestra: that indeed would have been an event. But merely to write something! Anybody could write.

How much has he written since? Did he, the old accountant, ever tally those columns? Millions, perhaps trillions, of words – magazines, newspapers, books, political tracts, pamphlets, trade papers even. And how many letters to editors?

Sixty years have passed since that letter to *Public Opinion*, and he still gives his I's to the Press at the rate of a thousand a week. Did ever anybody write more? Not more volumes, I mean, but more words? I have turned out millions myself, though of late the grind is so wearying that I gladly dodge it for the sunlight of some sidewalk café. But Shaw keeps on at his old astonishing pace. Still he explains it well enough: he works, he says, as his father drank; neurotically.

He might have turned an envious eye toward the university. He was not too late even then. But he says he had no competitive instincts. To this day he craves no prizes, degrees, titles. He says he didn't compete for university prizes (to get a university education) because he had a too great sense of his own importance to feel he could be influenced by gold medals or prizes.

The great difficulty of dealing with his education lies in the fact that his culture, as he says, was so largely musical. No one without as much familiarity with the masterpieces of music as with those of literature could have written as Shaw did later about Wagner.

You cannot account for him by saying that he was steeped in Dickens, or even later in Molière. He was steeped in Mozart too; it was from him that he learned how art work could reach the highest degree of strength, refinement, beauty, and seriousness without being heavy and portentous. Shelley made a great impression on him. He read him from beginning to end, prose and verse; and held him quite sacred in his adolescence. But Beethoven and early Wagner were at work too. If he wasn't the Perfect Wagnerite he was at least an early one.

Socialism sent him to economics, which he worked at for four years until he mastered it completely, only to find, of course, he says, that none of the other Socialists had taken that trouble. He didn't then, nor does he now, read any foreign language easily without a dictionary, except French. His early operatic acquaintance with Italian expanded later into a tolerable facility in reading the Italian newspapers; and he doesn't believe you could put a German document into his hands without some risk of his being able to understand it. He learnt Spanish for a specific purpose, but did not keep it up. 'What you call knowing a language: that is, something more than being able to ask the way to the Bahnhof or the Duomo, puts me out of court as a linguist,' he admits. In fact, his command of foreign literature does not extend to any considerable conversational powers. Rodin's reply to a lady who asked him whether Shaw spoke French well has often been quoted. '*Monsieur Shaw ne parle pas bien; mais il s'exprime avec une telle violence qu'il s'impose.*'

'As to Latin,' he once wrote me, 'on which all my schooling was supposed to be spent, I cannot read an epitaph or a tag from Horace without stumbling. Naturally I make use of translations and musical settings. I know *Faust* and *The Nibelung's Ring* as well as the Germans know Shakespeare. I am very unteachable and could not pass the fourth standard examination in an elementary school – not that anybody else could; but still you know what I mean.'

In his youth there was no Gaelic League nor Irish National Theatre nor any organised belief that Ireland had a culture. Indeed, ambitious Irishmen all felt their first business was to get out of Ireland as quickly as possible, and Shaw did not differ from the others. He has been reproached for his lack of patriotism on this score. He replies that professionally he is not an Irishman but a classic. 'I belonged to European art, which included English literature, German music, Italian and Dutch painting. In 1876 Ireland had not come into the picture. If she has done so since, so much the better for her.'

In March 1876 he gave Townshend a month's notice. Shaw's father was not even consulted as to this move, though it threw away his son's only apparent opportunity. His wife and daughters were already in London. His son's going would leave him absolutely deserted. But he was by no means sorry to have his family taken off his failing hands and be left to his own ways. The only step he took was to prevail on Townshend to write for the deserter a glowing testimonial. It threw Shaw into a transport of scorn, in which he was unkind to his father. His business ability was nothing to him but a chain to bind him to an office desk. Was it any compliment to certify the future challenger of Shakespeare as a competent and trustworthy cashier?

Still, he has said that he can quite understand Dr Johnson standing bareheaded in the rain in Lichfield to expiate his inconsiderateness to his father. He has felt like that himself.

In April 1876, with no more hair on his face than a baby (that red beard did not grow till he was twenty-four), Shaw took his carpet bag to the north wall of Dublin, boarded a boat for England, and never went back to Ireland for thirty years, and then only to please his wife.

You will never convince him that Dublin is more to him than Stettin to Great Catherine or Ajaccio to Napoleon. 'No man,' he says, 'prefers the city that conquered him to the city he conquered.'

Whether this is anything more than swank, the fact remains he left a good job in Dublin for none at all in London.

And for the next nine years was a complete failure, and towards the end of them an unpresentably seedy one.

8

Lean Years in London

Shaw was now twenty. His boyhood had long been left behind. He had been earning money for four years in a responsible post in which he had replaced a man of forty, and had never been under any sort of tutelage at home. Before following him to London let us see what culture he took with him when he plunged off the deep end and crossed to Holyhead.

As a child he read everything he could lay his hands on, beginning with *The Arabian Nights*, *The Pilgrim's Progress*, and *Robinson Crusoe*, and going on to the snippets of Shakespeare attached to Selous' illustrations, to *The Faerie Queene* and *John Gilpin*, to Mayne Reid and Fenimore Cooper, to Scott and Dickens, to Byron, to Artemus Ward and Mark Twain, with *Household Words* and *All the Year Round*, and much miscellaneous romance.

Before he was ten, a move from commonplace Synge Street to a cottage on Dalkey Hill, where the whole sweep of Killiney Bay from Dalkey island to the Wicklow mountains could be seen from the front door and the whole sweep of Dublin Bay from Kingstown to Howth Head from the garden at the back. The place enchanted him. It gave him the vision of nature into which Shelley's poetry fitted when he discovered that poet later on and became an ardent Shelleyan.

When puberty came the analytical faculty which was the secret of his success as a critic, began to assert itself. He became interested in science, especially in physics, and read Tyndall's lucid accounts of the discoveries of Helmholz in his lectures on sound, light, heat, and the forms of water. He read Darwin, and studied the conflict between religion and science in the pages of Draper and in *The Westminster Review*, the organ of cultured agnosticism. But he just missed Clerk-Maxwell and the modern mathematical physicists.

He read the novels of George Eliot religiously. He read John Stuart Mill's autobiography, and experienced fits of depression like that which

Mill described so memorably. Mill on *Liberty* and *Representative Government* also left their mark on him; and he read some of Cobbett, and made his first attempt to teach himself French by Cobbett's quaint French grammar.

It will be seen that, compared with the average British journalist and author, Shaw knew too much rather than too little, even without counting the music. He has himself said that his difficulties arose less from what he did not know than from what he did not believe.

All through, from his very earliest childhood, he had lived a fictitious life through the exercise of his incessant imagination. In this dreamland he was as free from the need of money as Amadis de Gaul. He was eminent, fearless, powerful, victorious, a great fighter, a great lover, and everything else that, as a matter of cold fact, he was not. It was a secret life: its avowal would have made him ridiculous. It had one oddity. The fictitious Shaw was not a man of family. He had no relatives. He was not only a bastard, like Dunois or Falconbridge, who at least knew who their parents were: he was also a foundling.

It remains to be explained why Shaw, having no literary ambitions, went to London because it was the sole literary market in the islands. The answer is to be found in his one blank verse play, *The Admirable Bashville*, where the hero is admonished as follows:

> For know, rash youth, that in this star crost world
> Fate drives us all to find our chiefest good
> In what we *can*, and not in what we would.

Shaw had attended the Royal Dublin Society's School of Art only to be convinced that he was no draughtsman; and his private experiments in oil painting and watercolour had been wrecked by that scientific side of him, which insisted that though his pictures of Bray Head and his study in oils of a Delft teapot looked quite convincing at a little distance, their effect was an illusion, not a reality; and he had nobody to tell him that this was the utmost that could be said for Turner or Peter de Hooghe.

As to music, he had no marketable technical skill and no impulse to compose.

In short, as he could neither paint nor play, and could write, and as what else he could do – cashiering for instance – he was determined not to do, there was nothing for it but writing. On joining his mother and sister in London (the younger of his two sisters had just died in the Isle of Wight) he allowed himself to be pushed into one more commercial job. He was employed in the wayleave department of the short-lived Edison Telephone Company, and after a brief and irksome experience of persuading all sorts and conditions of London shopkeepers to allow telephone wires to be attached to their premises, was made manager of that department. When the company was bought up by the Bell Telephone Company, he seized that opportunity to break loose and settled down doggedly to write novels. Lee tried to help him by undertaking to act as musical critic to a paper called *The Hornet*, Shaw doing all the work and taking all the money; but the paper presently perished after the concert agents had refused to send it the usual tickets in consequence of the rawly contemptuous intolerance of Shaw for a musical London in which at that time there was not a single magnetic conductor. The crown was put on his impossibility when, on hearing Wagner conduct his own music at the Albert Hall, he wrote of him as a great composer instead of denouncing him as a cacophonous charlatan.

The paper soon failed. *The Hornet* lost its sting and the sting consequently lost its hornet. During the years of novel writing which followed from 1879 to 1883, during which he wrote five long novels and had them refused by all the London publishers and some American ones, Shaw earned by his pen precisely £5 15s. 6d. Fifteen shillings of it was for an article on Christian names, and the remainder for an article on patent medicines commissioned by a friendly solicitor, what for, Shaw never knew.

Meanwhile the pot had to be kept boiling somehow, no matter to what extremity of seediness Shaw might wear out his old clothes and boots. His father contributed a pound a week until his death in 1885. His mother was not successful as a professional teacher of singing with private pupils. It never occurred to her to relinquish her status as an Irish lady of county rank, or to defer in the smallest degree to English middle-class parents with daughters to be taught to sing the ballads of Virginia Gabriel and Arthur Sullivan. Not until she began to train choirs at the big public schools for girls, beginning with the North London College, did she fit into her place and enjoy a literally commanding success. But before this happened the family affairs were in chronic straits; and had it not been for the Whitechurch inheritance, which saved the situation by its gradual dissipation, and some Irish mortgage interest, Shaw might have been forced to throw down his pen and turn to like a man to save his mother from starvation. As it was, she was able to save him. He still chuckles over the fact that he gave more offence by insisting that his mother supported him when by all the rules of popular biography he ought to have supported her, than he could have caused by lying about it on conventional lines.

Shaw wrote his novels as a daily task without enjoyment, because he knew he must do something or perish, and has hated them ever since. The first lay unpublished for fifty years. The second discouraged the publishers who had been a little interested by the first, because in it Shaw unmasks his anti-bourgeois battery, and, through the mouth of a cultured proletarian, criticises conventional religion and conventional gentility implacably. In the fifth and last novel this attitude has taken shape as Marxism.

Although Emerson had said some years before that 'an Englishman's lot is still the best in the world', Shaw's jump from Dublin to London in 1876 belied it. The times were not the most prosperous for artists, because a depression had hit London in 1879 such as it was not to see again until the year 1931.

Unemployment was mowing men into idleness like harvested wheat. The previous spring had been disastrous – for farmers the worst of the century. Business was on the verge of collapse; and little shop-keepers, who in those days over-stocked their show-windows, looked out through empty panes.

All forms of entertainment were straitened; and the only places where people crowded were the public houses, and even there most could not pay for the beer they drank.

Things got so bad that even the rich began to worry lest the poor should revolt altogether. Those in better taste cancelled all their banquets, balls, routs, and other forms of elegant ostentation. The Prince of Wales (later, Edward VII) helped on relief work.

Food, coal, wood, and candles were at a premium. Factories closed down, and the London and North-Western Railway stood off five thousand workers. Sixty thousand Liverpool dock-workers went on strike. Then the Glasgow and Western Bank failed, nearly sinking the island altogether.

Fog came in November 1879, and lasted until February 1880. The fog was immediately preceded by Shaw's first novel. He was still un-conscious of all the political turmoil: the novel proves it. But in the autumn of that year he was induced by a friend to join a debating society called the Zetetical. Debating societies were then the fashion.

Of these the most noted, because the most heterodox, was the London Dialectical Society, formed to discuss the principles of John Stuart Mill's essay on Liberty. Being Millite, it admitted women on equal terms with men. In 1879 it was getting on in years; and the Zetetical Society was a junior Dialectical.

When his friend James Lecky lured Shaw to a meeting of the Zetetical, Shaw could not hold his tongue. He rose to his shaking legs in a pitiable state of nervousness, and addressed an audience for the first time. He sat down with a sensation of having made a complete fool of himself. Such a disgrace had to be redeemed. He swore that he would speak in public every week until he either mastered the art or died of the terrible heart thumpings that afflicted him at the very thought of facing an audience.

He kept that vow. He joined the Dialectical Society. He joined Stopford Brooke's debating society, the Bedford. He infested the meetings at South Place Chapel, then the headquarters of Agnosticism, graduating from little meeting rooms to big public halls. He became a plague and a pest wherever there was a public discussion; and London at that time was full of discussions. The Sunday papers announced whole columns of them.

Lecky introduced him to an old Alsatian opera-singer, a *basso profundo* named Richard Deck, a brother of the famous French ceramist but at irreconcilable odds with him. Deck was a disciple of Proudhon (author of *What is Property? Theft*), and was at this time living in Kentish Town in poverty, sustained by dreams of regenerating the world, and incidentally his own voice, by a Method. Shaw knew all about Methods; and he sat with the old man of evenings and listened to his outpourings in French; for Deck, after nine years' residence in London, hardly knew three words of English.

From Deck, Shaw learned three things. 1. To bank up his hair in the manner familiar to all his caricaturists instead of plastering it down on his forehead like a mid-Victorian female. 2. How to pronounce French vowels instead of British diphthongs. 3. How to articulate and emphasise his consonants for public delivery. Deck had been taught by Delsarte; and Shaw never thereafter had any difficulty in making himself heard and understood in the largest halls.

His haunting of public meetings for practice led him one evening into Farringdon Hall, where an American speaker was spellbinding a crowded audience. The spellbinder was Henry George, whose *Progress and Poverty* was just then a best seller.

This was Shaw's first real turning point. He was switched off from Victorian Agnosticism and on to economic Communism with a flash and a crash. He read *Progress and Poverty*, and broke out into advocating Land Nationalisation at the meetings of the Social-Democratic Federation. The Social-Democrats laughed at him and told him to read Karl Marx. He did so, in Deville's translation, and found that they hadn't. The arch-enchanter's exposure of bourgeois civilisation gave Shaw a scientific foundation for his revolt against it. He was by this time sufficiently practised as a debater to venture on extemporised harangues of an hour's duration as principal speaker. The Woolwich Radical Club was then under the influence of a Socialist Scot named Robert Banner. The Club invited Shaw to address it; and he accepted the invitation with some misgivings. The title of the address was 'Thieves'. The thieves were the landlord and the capitalist, with the proletariat crucified between them. The evening was a success.

For the next twelve years Shaw preached Socialism from platforms, pulpits, market squares, street corners, park pitches, dock gates, cellars hired by a few needy comrades or halls filled with assemblies of three or four thousand miscellaneous listeners. That soon rubbed off the last patches of his jejune shyness and nervousness. It put him at his ease with men of all classes, from bishops and cabinet ministers to coster-mongers and dock labourers. He harangued on every Sunday as a matter of course, sometimes morning and evening. He estimates that he averaged at least three orations (except that, like Lenin, he elaborated an art of talking to his hearers instead of orating at them) per fortnight: say roughly a thousand harangues in the twelve years, answering questions from all comers after each.

He did not join the Social-Democratic Federation. On the eve of doing so because there was nothing else to join, a leaflet entitled *Why are the Many Poor?*, unmistakably Socialist in its sympathy, fell into his hands. It was announced as the first publication of the Fabian Society. The name struck him as an inspiration. It meant literacy, culture, personal disinterestedness. He attended a meeting and found a handful of men of his own class in an Osnaburgh Street lodging. They were Civil Servants of the upper division, professional men, business men, suburban idealists with independent incomes, and one elderly and very quiet proletarian. The secretary was a stockbroker. They met in one another's lodgings or drawing-rooms; and the collective income of the Society was less than forty pounds a year. There was no fixed subscription.

Shaw had found his official *milieu*. He went away and returned with a Zetetical discovery of his: one Sidney Webb (later Lord Passfield), then resident clerk at the Colonial Office. Webb went away and returned with his fellow resident clerk Sydney Olivier (later Lord Olivier), who presently became the Society's secretary. Graham Wallas came later. Hubert Bland, a formidable amateur pugilist, then secretary to a hydraulic company but finally a noted journalist-feuilletonist and writer of *causeries*, was already there. No such team succeeded in holding together anywhere in the London movement; and it was by team work that they built up the Fabian Society and kept it going until it had brought about a Labour Party in the House of Commons and Revisionism in Germany. Shaw remained on its executive committee for twenty-seven years. It actually still exists.

Shaw was not the originator of the Fabian Society. We see him here as what he has always been, the Opportunist who has an eye for an opening, and, dashing into it, makes people believe that he has opened it. His perspicacity here seized on some vital points. His fierce Marxist reaction against his own bourgeois class and his championship of Labour could not mislead him into imagining that when it came to organising work he could go in double harness with illiterate manual workers. Their ignorance of history, their innocence as to the gulf between the shop window morality and democracy of the Radical shibboleths and the real machinery of government, and their inveterate and very justifiable mistrust of every black-coated bourgeois whom they could not idolise as a leader, made a segregation of the ordinary bourgeois Socialists an indispensable preliminary to getting any business done.

To the simple integrity of a miner's leader like Keir Hardie this seemed mere snobbery. In the name of fraternity and unity he called on the segregated societies to amalgamate. Shaw never said no. He said, 'Let us try.' Then he took care to be placed on the amalgamating committee and to set it by the ears. Keir Hardie divined that Shaw was determined that the amalgamation should not take place. He threw Shaw out; but matters went on worse than before. He threw all the Fabians out, which was what Shaw wanted. The rest quarrelled more than ever. When all the irreconcilables were thrown out there remained only one society: Keir Hardie's own. As it was in the beginning, so had it to be.

The Fabians were called drawing-room Socialists, armchair Socialists, gas-and-water Socialists, by the proletarian societies; but Shaw, though he would not pretend to do committee work with them, was one of their star speakers, rubbing shoulders with them in the friendliest way, and never shirking the rough and tumble of the streets and parks. At the same time he had no taste for martyrdom, and lent no countenance to the delusion that undrilled and unarmed men could cope with the police and the army. Only twice had he to volunteer for arrest and imprisonment; and he was lucky on both occasions, the police surrendering to the Nonconformist defenders of street corner meetings on the first, and another volunteer being elected on the second.

Events justified him in his choice of an organisation. The alternatives were to join the little proletarian retinue of the imposing Henry Mayers Hyndman which called itself the Social-Democratic Federation, or the even less sophisticated group of 'Anarchist-Communists' whom William Morris, the one unquestionably Great Man in the movement, called the Socialist League, and soon had to drop as impossible. The war against bourgeois religion was carried on by the National Secular Society, which could only organise meetings for the superhuman personality of Charles Bradlaugh, a hurricane fighter on the platform and in the law courts. His only peer was Annie Besant; and she left him and joined the Fabian Society on Shaw's nomination.

All these societies were no use to Shaw: he knew that the organisation of Socialism as a constitutional possibility was not a One Man or One Woman job, nor a fight with the police. He knew also that he had to fill up the gaps in his education by critical contact with differently educated men as clever as himself and better disciplined.

Also, the Federation and the League proposed nothing less than the enlistment in their membership of the entire proletariat subscribing a penny a week apiece. Shaw knew as well as Lenin that revolutions, peaceful or pugnacious, are the work of specialised minorities. The Fabian Society never got beyond two thousand members and did its best work with less than a hundred.

Meanwhile what had become of Shaw's Irish nationalism? It was completely sidetracked by Karl Marx. Though parliament in the eighteen-seventies and -eighties was raging with the Home Rule agitation, though the headlines were red with the Phoenix Park murders and green with the Parnell letters forged by Dick Pigott (whom Shaw had known in his boyhood), though the obstruction tactics of Biggar and Healy and Sexton, led by Parnell, were paralysing the Government, and moonlighting and the No Rent campaign exasperating Dublin Castle, Shaw, full of the larger issue of international Socialism, could not force himself to waste a moment on mere nationalism. At a Liberal meeting in the National Liberal Club he rose and asked the chairman whether there was anything except the Irish question on the agenda. The reply of the indignantly astonished chairman, Spence Watson, was in the negative. Shaw took his hat and solemnly stalked out. He had no patience with the fervent Irish patriotism of the English Gladstonians; and he declared that the British proletarians did not care a dump about Home Rule, having worse grievances of their own than the Irish. The Irish, he said, must help themselves. Only, he would not rise or un-cover for the English national anthem, nor drink the King's health at public dinners. This habit remained so strong with him that when the establishment of the Irish Free State removed his grievance he had some difficulty in dropping it.

I had some contacts with the Socialist movement in the early eighteen-eighties. But its societies could not hold me: I had none of the illusions as to their own importance with which they flattered themselves. Lord Randolph Churchill's Tory Democracy was really on the political chessboard; and to that I took my 'deep sounding voice' as Shaw called it, and such attention as I could spare from literature, journalism, and finance.

We had a mere glimpse of one another, and did not become properly acquainted until we met later on in the world of capitalist journalism as editor and contributor respectively. To tell the truth he attracted me as a literary artist and as a dramatist, not as a politician. I was not interested in his Fabian wire-pulling; and far be it from me to pretend that I ever tackled the endless volumes on bureaucratic history and political science poured out by his friends Sidney and Beatrice Webb. He attached importance to his political work, and has said that the years from 1884, when the Fabian Society was founded, to the slump in Socialism which preceded the South African war, were the most honourable and enjoyable of his life; but I did not and do not see it that way. I was always expecting more from him than he delivered; and I did not become really interested in his politics until the war of 1914–18, when, as usual, he disappointed me.

It really isn't worth spending much time on Shaw as a Fabian, except in so far as public speaking subsequently affected his style as a writer. To this day his work is full of harangue-writing.

If he ever tried to get on newspaper or magazine staffs, I find no record of it. Yet with a little bit of push he could have found a place for himself. If this seems like too debonair an indictment, I shall prove the case out of my own experiences in London at that time.

I did not know London at its worst, as I came there in 1882, by way of Galway, Liverpool, New York, Chicago, Kansas, Athens, Heidelberg, Plevna, and Paris, a journey that took me about fifteen years. Up to that time I had been an under-river worker, hotel manager, cowboy, college student, lawyer (I had retired from the Kansas Bar before I was twenty-five), and master at Brighton College. Afterwards I studied at two German universities and had stopped at Paris before going on to London.

I knew my Balzac well – one of the joys and master spirits of the world, but not intellectual enough, or perhaps not dreamer enough, to capture the imagination of all humanity. He knew women profoundly, as Shaw doesn't know them at all; but even his *Baronne Hulot* has not the significance of Goethe's *Gretchen*. In Paris, too, I had met Turgenev, far and away the greatest Russian writer. His Bazarof, the realist, was a masterpiece in character drawing. He came to life later as Bernard Shaw.

I knew, too, Catulle Mendès, a handsome journalist, a Jew, who could improvise and imitate every master of French prose. To me he was a perfect model of a man of talent, without a touch of the genius that might have ennobled or destroyed his unique gift of words. He was the most astonishing journalist I knew until I met Shaw years later in London.

When I reached London, I studied the city and it taught me a great deal about Englishmen. The city, like the men, was immense, no limit to its energy; healthy too, in spite of its wretched climate; well-drained and clean, but never rising high.

The East End was mean and coarse and grovelling, with narrow streets and cluttering hovels. In the West End you found the opposite, now comfortable, now pretentious, with, in between, grassy parks and open spaces and adventitious bridges. But there was no plan, or general idea directing this indefatigable activity. It was built by beavers and not by men; industry everywhere, but no great intelligence in the making of it. This often depressed the spirit. The smoke and the grime and the fog, all seemed part of the central idea: to eat well and to sleep softly. But there was no unnecessary noise; London still is the quietest of cities; methods of transport were cheap and excellent. If only its city fathers had followed Wren's wonderful plan, instead of rebuilding a wretched city to follow one more wretched that had been destroyed by fire!

This London was not a hard town on persons of artistic leanings. I knew no one. I had only a letter to Froude in which Carlyle said that he expected more things from me than anyone he had met since parting from Emerson. I went into the country to see Froude. He said he would be returning to London in a fortnight and would invite Chinnery, the editor of *The Times*, and other people of importance in literature to meet me. He would arrange a luncheon and so do his best, he said, to carry out Carlyle's wishes.

I had hardly left him when I realised that I should be a fool if I trusted to his help. 'Help yourself, my friend,' I kept repeating to myself; 'if he helps, so much the better, and if he doesn't it won't matter.' A morning or two later I saw in one of the papers something about John Morley in *The Fortnightly Review*. I took down the address, and without losing time called about 9 o'clock in the morning. The office was a sort of shop, the publishing house of Chapman & Hall. At about 10.30 Mr Chapman came in, and as soon as I heard his name I went up to him. He had nothing for me to do when I spoke about work, but finally he said I should come and see Mr Escott, who was acting as editor in the place of John Morley. I returned that afternoon, but Escott turned me down flatly. Rather, he said he would bear me in mind, but that amounts to the same thing in business. I asked him not to do that, but to let me come each day, and if he had nothing to do it would not matter. I would be on hand if unexpectedly he needed a proof to be read or a fact to be verified, or anything.

'As you please,' he said rudely, shrugging his shoulders as he turned away.

But every morning I was sitting in the shop. When Chapman came in he used to acknowledge my bow with an embarrassed air. After a week he told me politely that I could see now there was nothing for me to do; would it not be better to try elsewhere? I felt sure that Escott had suggested this to him, but I did not give up; each day found me at my post.

Meanwhile, I was stretching another string to my bow. I had met a man in a railway carriage who said he knew the editor of *The Spectator*. He told me to ask Escott for a letter of introduction, but I would not ask Escott for anything, and went round to the *Spectator* office on my own.

When the clerk came I said, 'I want to see Mr Hutton.'

'Have you an appointment?'

'No,' I replied. 'Tell me where Mr Hutton is and' – laying a coin on the table – 'that is yours.'

'On the second floor,' whispered the clerk hastily.

Once I got to the second floor I knocked. No answer. A minute or two later I knocked again and heard a loud 'Come in!' There was a big man seated at a table with his back to me. He kept on writing, and when I coughed emphatically he said, 'Goodness gracious, who are you, how did you come in?'

'My name does not matter much, Mr Hutton,' I replied, 'and I don't want to bother you. I want work.'

'We have too many writers here,' he ejaculated; 'we cannot find enough work for those we know.'

'There is always room at the top,' I countered. 'Suppose I can do better than any you have got, it'll be to your interest to use me.'

'Goodness me,' he exclaimed, 'do you think you can write better than any of us?'

'No,' I corrected, 'but there are some subjects I know better than any Englishman. I leave you to judge. The first ten lines of an article will tell you whether I am merely diseased with conceit or whether I am worth using.'

'That is true,' he said, getting up and going to the bookcase. 'Do you know anything about Russia?'

'I was with General Skobelef at Plevna.'

'Goodness me. Have you any special knowledge of the United States?' he went on, still peering at the books.

'I have been in a Western university,' I replied, 'and am a member of the American Bar.'

'Really,' he cried, 'well, here's a book of Freeman on America.'

When I got downstairs I showed the clerk the book as a proof that he would not be blamed for having let me in.

I did not go straight home and begin the job at once. It struck me that I ought to know the mark I was aiming at. To win R. H. Hutton I must know him first. Accordingly, next morning, I went to the British Museum and asked for all his books. I spent the next two days reading them. At the end of that time I saw the soul of Hutton before me – a gentle, pious spirit, intensely religious. I wrote the best stuff I could on the Russian book, and then slated Freeman. I took them to the Rev. John Verschoyle, who had come from Trinity College, Dublin, and was only kept from a great career by an untimely death. He criticised them harshly, for I was more at home with German than with English, and after he had gone through the two articles I had the best lesson in English I ever got. From that day, Swift and the Bible were ever at my side and I never opened a German book for five years. It took me years to learn German and twice as long to cleanse my brain of that tongue. No writer should ever try to master many living languages.

The next day I was back at my post at Chapman's and told him that I was now on *The Spectator*. He laughed, and said he was delighted. He called me in, a day or two later, and gave me a couple of books he wanted an opinion on.

'Meredith is our reader,' he said, 'but it takes him weeks to give an opinion, and I would like to know about these books as soon as possible.'

My chance had come. I thanked him, went straight home and sat down at once to read and re-read the books. I brought them back the next afternoon with my opinions. Chapman was greatly impressed.

'I thought you would keep them a week,' he said. Then he gave me a slip for two guineas, which would be cashed by the cashier. This I refused, telling him that I was heavily in his debt for bothering him as I had done. This pleased him, and in a little while Escott was giving me work to do on *The Fortnightly*. The opportunity that, in the Bible, won God, had been successful too in London.

Now all this time I had never heard a word from Froude, but a letter had come from *The Spectator* in Hutton's tiny script.

You were right, [he began] your reviews justify you; the one on Freeman is a gem, and the Russian one provokes thought and may lead to discussion. I send you the proofs of both, and should be delighted if you would call with them when corrected. I want more of your work.

Yours truly,

R. H. Hutton

I read the articles; the Russian one was certainly the better of the two, but the Freeman one was aimed at Hutton's heart and head, and that had won the prize. Food for thought in that. I began then to say to myself what I have since said often – 'that no one can see above his own head'.

In time, Froude carried out that dinner for me, but by that time I was making five to six pounds a week as a writer on my own, from *The Spectator* and *The Fortnightly*.

I mention all this to show how kindly London was in the early eighteen-eighties to any young writer who merited help and who had the backbone to go after it. If Shaw starved for nine years at that time, a good deal of this must have been due to his own lack of push. And yet, he says, he was incredibly impudent in his youth. That school of biography which has developed since Freud has become a household word would find an easy explanation for this in the theory of a defence mechanism to overcome an inferiority complex, and though the trouble with the Shaws was a superiority complex, and Bernard was certainly a chip of the old block in this respect, yet it is a fact that he was unbelievably shy as a boy.

I found it hard to credit this. As a boy I was quite the opposite. I was so sure of myself that nothing pleased me so much as to be asked to recite something. I recall once in an English school a master telling us Lord Macaulay knew *Paradise Lost* by heart – all of it. I asked if that were hard. A withering remark was intended to tell me how hard.

'Lord Macaulay was a genius,' I was given to understand.

In a week I said, 'Please, sir, I know *Paradise Lost* by heart.'

He tested me. He grilled me. Finally he conceded, disappointed, 'So you do.'

But he didn't say *I* was a genius.

Instead, the older boys when we got outside kicked and cuffed me for my pains. 'You show off! Do you want him to make us all learn that by heart? You smart Irish Paddy.'

Now, right here, you have the difference between English and Irish schools. For having brains I was cuffed by the boys and rebuffed by the masters in English schools. In Ireland I'd have been patted on the back as a bright boy, stood on a table and told to do it all over again for the village sages. But even the cuffings never daunted me.

So shyness like Shaw's was, and still is, a little incomprehensible to me. I realise, of course, that insolence is often built on insecurity and a sense of inferiority, though, at the other extreme, people who are very sure of themselves are also inclined to be brazen. Mussolini is a case in point. But impudence of the other sort, based on doubt of one's position, is so pitifully transparent. Shaw at his shabbiest, being still a Shaw, never doubted his position; but he did doubt his ability. He was diffident, not being at home in the real world.

In an age of blusterers such as overwhelm the world today, shyness may have a charm about it that many people, the blusterers particularly, envy. But in Shaw's youth the personality school of success was just beginning to assert itself. In America they called them 'go-getters'. I suspect I was one myself.

In the Dublin office Shaw's shyness wasn't such a frightful handicap, because he was doing a man's work in a boy's clothes, and knew he was doing it competently. For do not imagine that the cashier in the office of a leading Irish land office was like the clerk in *Misalliance*, a slave in a wire cage, taking money from shoppers and giving change. Every day, on fifty estates, he had to pay head rents, quit rents, mortgage interests, jointures, annuities, insurance premiums and what not, besides cashing cheques and receiving lodgments, and banking the rent collections sent up from the country. He could not do all this and feel like a child. He had a social status and never met the poor on equal terms. But in London he had to go out and really face the world. In that telephone job, for instance, he had to meet people and sell them a new-fangled idea, an idea which was, moreover, an encroachment on their privacy, in which he was wholly in the wrong and they wholly in the right.

You can't convince people to allow telephone-poles to be sunk on their property, and be both shy and uppish. You have to be something between a pirate and a shopwalker to break down their resistance. And that resistance in England, a place where the idea of a man's home being his castle is bred in the bone, was unusually strong. Your high-pressure talk under such circumstances had to be persuasive to the point of exhaustion to win. Shaw's courtesy wasn't quite right. It did not go down at the East End, where they think that if you give yourself the airs of a gentleman you should be doing a gentleman's job.

Shaw would never have succeeded for a minute were it not for a play he had seen in his youth, called *Cool as a Cucumber*. It was the story of a young man who had been sent on a world tour to cure him of bashfulness. He came back so brazen he insulted everybody, and actually won their hearts with his insolence.

To the potentially vegetarian Shaw, this was the kind of raw meat he needed most to build his frail personality into something overpowering. Like the Maurois character who read a Balzac story and then tried to mould his life to it, Shaw consciously tried to follow the Cucumber's technique so that he might be at ease in a world that, so far, had never been captured by shyness.

That his conquest of this shyness was not easy for Shaw is best illustrated by his own confession. In his early days in London he would walk twenty minutes up and down in front of the house to which he had been invited before screwing up enough courage to enter. Such a barricaded kind of courage, this brazenness which was easily turned into bashfulness, made novel-writing inevitable. There he could say all the fresh things he liked.

And so, through success as a cashier, failure as a contact-man for telephone-poles, he now became a novelist.

In 1879 he wrote his first story – *Immaturity*. He says he filled five quarto pages of his fine script (twenty pages) daily, rain or shine. By this method he produced five novels in five years, and trimmed his cuffs with his mother's scissors. Every London publisher, and some in America, rejected those books. His own explanation is that his Augustan style was a hundred and fifty years behind the times and his ideas a hundred and fifty years ahead of them. But perhaps his mistake of personally interviewing the publishers had something to do with it.

Besides *Immaturity* he wrote *The Irrational Knot, Love Among the Artists, Cashel Byron's Profession* and *An Unsocial Socialist*.

Blackwood, Shaw says, accepted one novel and then backed out. On his first effort, Shaw got a reader's long report from John Morley, my predecessor as editor of *The Fortnightly Review*, who later became Lord Morley. On the others, he got no encouragement whatever. In time, after he had become a successful playwright, these novels were published, of course. That first novel, which never got into print till fifty years later, I do not know how to compare, not having seen it. All I can say is the others are duller than neglected pewter.

He says himself they were 'very green things, very carefully written', for, in those days, Shaw had a style, a schoolteacher's style; that is, everything he wrote down had to be wholly intelligible to a foreigner with a *dictionnaire*. He borrowed freely from characters around him and his immediate experiences, which is a bad way to write novels unless you lead an adventurous life, and his, as we have already seen, was more cloistered than a curate's. You will find these early novels are full of autobiographical details, the prefaces particularly. For instance, *The Irrational Knot*, his second novel, tells all about his telephonic experiences.

In his own words, however, '*The Irrational Knot* may be regarded as an early attempt on the part of the Life-Force to write *A Doll's House* in English by the instrumentality of a very immature writer aged twenty-four.'

By the time he was twenty-four he was growing a beard, and it pleased him beyond words to observe that it was going Mephistoph-elean from the start – thus fulfilling a childhood ambition. From that time on he began to disagree with people violently. At such times he learned much from them, though now he feels that his *gaucherie* was awful in those first London years.

His ill-luck with his novels caused him to remark: 'They say that man in embryo is successively a fish, a bird, a mammal, and so on, before he develops into a man. Well, popular novel-writing is the fish stage of your Jonathan Swift.'

Love Among the Artists ran to four hundred and eighty-four pages in Shaw's fine handwriting with all corrections made with a circular motion so as to prevent anybody's seeing what the original words were. It was completed in 1881 and corrected in 1882 and again in 1883. Its composition was interrupted by an attack of smallpox, which accelerated the growth of the beard, and left him an Anti-Vaccinationist for life, but otherwise unmarked.

Shaw later met the charge of cribbing freely from Ibsen by pointing to the period in which these novels were written, insisting that this was before he ever heard of Ibsen – or de Maupassant either, for that matter.

Shaw claims that he has never had a novel accepted by a publisher. Four of the five written by him in these lean years which he has described in his preface (written fifty years later) to the first of them crept into print as padding for Socialist magazines, and were 'pirated' in America. They still sell in spite of his own neglect and dislike. But in the beaten way of business he must be described as a hopeless failure until he took to criticism.

And that opens a fresh chapter.

9
The Critic

Shaw, though he could now work, could not get work. He had never been really faced with the alternative of securing prompt employment or finding himself very hungry within twenty-four hours. I was faced with that when I became a sandhog under Brooklyn Bridge. Every navvy has been repeatedly faced with it; and in consequence the art of getting a job is as much a part of a navvy's equipment as a spade or barrow. He must go looking for it, ask for it, push for it, struggle for it.

Shaw, when his 'early struggles' are mentioned, repudiates the imputation. 'I never struggled,' he declares. 'I rose by sheer gravitation.' You can always trust him to find a new sort of swank. But this one is quite true. He was pushed into every job he got. And he always waited helplessly for the push.

William Archer saw this plainly when he made Shaw's acquaintance. Accordingly, being then one of William Stead's reviewers on the old *Pall Mall Gazette*, he handed a book over to Shaw, and told the editor that he had been forced to do so by pressure of work. Shaw made good with an amusing review, and thenceforth had as much book reviewing as he chose to do on *The Pall Mall* at two guineas per thousand words. If he was a feeble grabber he was a bulldog holder.

Presently Archer gave him another push. Archer was theatre critic to *The World*, then a leading fashionable weekly edited by Edmund Yates. Yates's picture critic died; and Yates asked Archer to take on the work. Archer, knowing nothing about pictures, repeated his *Pall Mall* trick and shoved Shaw into the job. Shaw knew all about pictures, and again made good. He became picture critic to *The World* at fivepence a line.

T. P. O'Connor started an evening paper called *The Star*. His lieutenant was H. W. Massingham. Massingham shoved Shaw on to T. P. as a promising young journalist with advanced ideas. T. P., who survived until 1931 without ever having had an idea later than 1865, was appalled at the Fabian stuff served up by the recruit, but had not the nerve to offend Massingham by sacking him. Shaw suggested a weekly column on music for two guineas. T. P. jumped at the compromise; and Shaw again made good by columns of outrageous clowning put forward as the work of a musical foreign nobleman styled Corno di Bassetto (the name of an obsolete musical instrument which figures in the score of Mozart's Requiem). Bassetto was a vulgar success.

After a couple of years of this *The World*'s music critic got into trouble and left the country. Archer instantly rushed to Yates and shoved Shaw into the vacated post as the only possible successor. Bassetto perished; his creator became G. B. S.; and the weekly two guineas became five pounds. Also Shaw discovered that Conservative papers can afford to give their contributors a much freer hand than Radical ones. He made good again; and soon the adjective 'brilliant' became as inseparable from his name as the adjective 'judicious' from that of Hooker.

When Yates died, Shaw left *The World* and began to look round for another editor who was not, like T. P., afraid of ghosts. 'I do not ask any man to go under fire for me,' he said, 'nor do I intend to venture so far myself. But I do want an editor who likes to go within an inch of the range, and wave his flag and shout as if he were in the thick of the danger zone. Men who dare not come within the sound of the guns are no use to me. My man must know good stuff and not be frightened when he gets it.'

The bill was not wholly flattering; but Shaw thought I filled it. I had asked him to contribute a fighting article to *The Fortnightly Review*, and had not blenched when he laid out William Hurrell Mallock with a broadside of rank Socialism. He had no fear of my spoiling good stuff or funking it. I suppose I looked plucky; for already I was described as a Literary Corsair: I do not know why. Anyhow I was not afraid of Shaw.

In the early eighteen-nineties I bought *The Saturday Review* and changed it from a Conservative weekly, living on a reputation which it had survived, to something alive which still haunts London on the reputation I renewed for it. I knew that Shaw was exhausted as a music critic and could now only repeat himself – he admitted as much – and anyhow I did not want Yates's leavings. When he had done a review or two for me I proposed that he should do a weekly theatre feuilleton for *The Saturday*.

He made two conditions. First, the paper must break its tradition of anonymity and the old-fashioned 'we', and print his articles in the first person over the now familiar signature G. B. S. Agreed. Second, six pounds a week. Agreed.

Of course he made good. It was the peak of his achievement as a journalist, and his last regular job in that profession.

Shaw's financial straits lasted for nine years from his arrival in London, and then suddenly cleared up – let us hope for ever. The situation had become badly strained by 1881, the year of the smallpox epidemic. The house in Victoria Grove had at last to be given up. It should indeed never have been taken; but Mrs Shaw took ten years to realise that it was possible to live without a whole house to herself, and that anything more than a second floor in a house with a ticket inscribed 'Apartments' in the fanlight was beyond her means. At last, when all the Whitechurch money was gone, and the fewness of her singing pupils had convinced her that she lacked the art of attracting them, she condescended to a first floor in Fitzroy Street. That was soon exchanged for a second floor in 36 Osnaburgh Street. The reconstruction of the house obliged her to move hastily to another second floor at 29 Fitzroy Square as a temporary makeshift; but she and her son had to make shift there for nearly twenty years.

Her daughter Lucy, three years older than Bernard, never lived there. She had found employment on the stage, first in Gilbert-Sullivan opera, and afterwards in a light opera called *Dorothy*, which had an interminable run in the provinces, where its soprano part broke every voice except Lucy's, which was fortified by The Method. She did not rejoin her family, and kept herself going until a bad chill on a draughty stage led to lung trouble and compelled her to retire, but not until Shaw became prosperous enough to maintain her in an establishment of her own. After a brief experience of marriage she separated from her husband, and later on, in a moment of irritation provoked by the discovery that at the time of the marriage there had been another lady in the case, divorced him, and then tolerated a friendly acquaintance with him until his death, which soon followed. She had no children. She died in her brother's arms in 1920.

In Fitzroy Square, mother and son held out on the paternal pound a week, on the interest on an Irish mortgage which came to as much more, and on such singing lessons as were to be had. Shaw, now lodged close to the British Museum, spent his days for many years in the great Reading Room, where Archer found him reading Marx's *Capital* with a Wagner orchestral score and a folio of Delacroix's *Faust* lithographs ready to his hand.

The paternal pound ceased on the father's sudden and peaceful death in Dublin in 1885; but, thanks to Archer, Shaw earned £112 by his first year's work as a journalist-critic, and Mrs Shaw found her place as a trainer of choirs. Money troubles vanished.

Shaw's first use of their comparative affluence was the renewal of his deplorable wardrobe. And thereby hang so many untrue tales that I may as well place the truth on record.

One of the most eloquent of Shaw's fellow-agitators on the Socialist platform was the Austrian orator Andreas Scheu, then in exile in London for his opinions. Scheu was commercially engaged in founding the Jaeger Company in London, Jaeger being a German doctor with a craze for regenerating the world by all-wool clothing. Shaw loved a fad, and jumped at this one when Scheu explained its principles. The Jaeger Company opened a West End tailoring establishment, for which the doctor designed new combined coats and waistcoats, made of brilliant stockinet cloths. In these Shaw hastened to invest himself, to the amazement of his friends, as the emergence of the Jaegerised butterfly from the desperately seedy chrysalis to which they had become accustomed took place quite suddenly.

Jaeger allowed his craze to run away with him. He designed an ideally healthy single garment or combination in brown knitted wool, complete from sleeves to ankles in one piece, in which a human being resembled nothing but a forked radish in a worsted bifurcated stocking. As it seemed clear that no man could appear in it in a London street without being mobbed, even Scheu had not the hardihood to put it to the proof. Shaw promptly ordered a specimen to his measure, and made a trial trip in it from Tottenham Court Road to the Marble Arch and back without molestation. After all, a man six feet tall, in the strength of his youth, and in a gymnastic-looking costume, is not lightly interfered with. A photograph of Shaw in this rig-out, taken by Sir Emery Walker, still exists. Shaw was content with the Oxford Street test and made only one or two more public appearances in it; but at the first performance of his first play, *Widowers' Houses*, at the Royalty Theatre in 1892, when the fall of the curtain was followed by a hurricane of hisses countered by Fabian calls of 'Author! Author!' Shaw stepped out before the curtain in a suit of dazzling silver grey stockinet and told the booing multitude what he thought of it, retiring amid good-natured general applause.

Such freaks cannot be indulged in without consequences. The tailoring establishment retrieved the situation by dropping the name of Jaeger, suppressing the knitted garment, and confining itself to a practice which followed, as far as external appearances went, the most unimpeachable traditions of Conduit Street and Savile Row.

Shaw did not get off so easily. Though the smart looking stockinet soon had to be discarded because it stridulated so frightfully, as the wearer's arms swung against his sides as he walked, that Lord Olivier, hiking in the country with Shaw, objected to his companion drowning his conversation by making a noise like a cricket, it was easier to get rid of the clothes than of the crop of legends they started about the rash experimenter.

The most persistent of these represented him as refusing to wear evening dress, and being thrown out of the opera in flannels or refused admission to theatres in consequence, with circumstantial accounts of his retorts on such occasions, of his offering to take off the offending garments, and so forth.

Shaw's unusual annoyance at these inventions was provoked by two circumstances. The first was that as it happened he, with Hubert Bland, was an ardent advocate of evening dress for men as the most democratic of institutions and as the blessed shield and refuge of impecunious gentility. The second cost him money out of pocket.

The late Robert Burdon Haldane, later Lord Chancellor, stood out among the Liberals in the eighteen-eighties by the long-sighted seriousness with which he took the oncoming Fabians and their little knot of clever leaders. He addressed Fabian meetings, and did what he could to bring about social contacts between them and the front bench men of the Liberal and Conservative Cabinets. He was on cordial terms with both; and Shaw, recognising in him every man's friend, put him on the stage in the unsuspected disguise of the benevolent Waiter in *You Never Can Tell*, perhaps the most amiable male figure in Shaw's *dramatis personae*, though Androcles runs him hard.

Haldane gave a very special dinner to which he invited Asquith and his famous wife Margot (later Lord and Lady Oxford), Arthur Balfour, and the attendant group of choice spirits and beautiful women who had come earlier into a select notoriety as The Souls. As it happened, they were all going on to some grand function later in the evening; and the men came with all their orders and decorations and the women in all their diamonds. Haldane seized the opportunity to invite Shaw; and, misled by the legends, he asked him to come in morning dress.

The stipulation filled Shaw with dismay. He could not disregard it;

for he concluded that he was being asked to meet some of the Labour MPs who regarded evening dress as a livery and refused to wear it. But except his evening dress he had no black clothes. The silver grey stockinets were all right for a *coup de théâtre* at the Royalty; but for a dinner-party they were out of the question. There was nothing for it but to dissipate a fortnight's earnings on a new black suit of the cut then affected by the Labour appendages of the Liberals in parliament, in which Shaw felt, as to the tailless double-breasted jacket, like a ship's purser at a wedding, and, as to the trousers, like a City missionary.

Thus attired, the unfortunate Fabian walked into Haldane's flat in Whitehall Court and found himself confronting his host's generous expanse of immaculate white shirt-front and a social galaxy which I could depict only by quoting Byron's description of the Waterloo ball at Brussels in 1815.

Shaw declares that he did his best to make them feel that they had all committed a painful solecism in dressing for dinner, and that he was the only correctly dressed man in the room. He took Margot into dinner with unshattered *aplomb*, and, on the whole, carried it off as best he could. But for ever after the surest way to make Shaw swear was to revive the legend of his objection to wear evening dress.

However, he backed up George Alexander, then actor-manager of the most fashionable theatre in London, against compulsory evening dress in the stalls, by example as well as precept. Alexander was a good man of business, having come from the City to the stage, and knew that if a City man cannot go to the stalls without first going home to the suburbs to change, the dice are loaded against his returning.

All this fuss about Shaw's clothes seems, I admit, beneath the dignity of literary biography. I should not plague the reader with it were it not that I believe it had a good deal to do with what I maintain is a part of a man's history without knowing which you do not know the man: I mean his sex history.

When I, Frank Harris, wrote my own sex history, I was frank enough to call it not simply my life, but *My Life and Loves*. I was so frank, in fact, that the book was burnt in the Shaw household lest it should inflame the passions of curious housemaids.

Shaw differed from me about this. When he read my conscientious avowal of what he calls, in his best bowdlerising manner, my gallantries, he said they added no more to his knowledge of me than if I had described all the occasions on which I had turkey and sausages for dinner. If that was all they meant to him, he was right to burn them.

Shaw had told me that he preserved his virginity continently until he was twenty-nine. Those who have read *My Life and Loves* will understand that I found this incredible and inconceivable on any assumption that Shaw is a normal man. I speculated on the possibility of some constitutional infirmity in him, and on the insufficiency of his silly vegetarian diet. But Shaw, though no athlete, has lasted into his seventies and seems pretty hale still. He had exceptionally capacious lungs, and could digest anything, even a vegetarian dinner chilled by a tumbler of Contrexéville water. Vegetarianism, whatever else it may do, evidently no more impairs a man's virility than a bull's bovrility or a buck elephant's elephantility. All Shaw's senses are intact; and there is nothing abnormal about his appearance.

The clue is to be found in a remark of his to the effect that the pursuit of women is impossible without pocket money. This is not at all true: Winston Churchill's great ancestor made his mistresses finance him; and many a humbler adventurer has lived on women, as the police reports testify. But Jack Churchill was not only a man of genius (Shaw might pass for that with a woman) and a handsome one at that, but well dressed and in a first-rate social position into the bargain. He had access to very rich women on very favourable conditions. Not so our Bernard. He has avouched that when he was at his seediest no woman of any fastidiousness could have persuaded herself to touch him with a pair of tongs even if he could have afforded to frequent the *salons* of the fastidious. The fastidiousness may have been partly in himself; for in sex every pot finds its cover. But the Shaws would not live within their means. Just as his mother took a house when she could barely afford a lodging, so her son went to Lincoln & Bennett's and bought a tall hat for a guinea, the top price in those days at the most fashionable hatter's, when a cheap bowler or even a shilling cap would have been a wiser investment. He had to wear the tall hat so long before he could afford another that in its last days it had to be worn tail foremost, as the front rim had become too limp to lever the hat off successfully when he had to salute a lady.

The coat, too, was of the class that had better not be worn at all than worn in anything short of the pink of condition. The change from blue black to tea green is worse than the ruin of an empire. Such coats insist on linen cuffs; and Shaw had to trim his fraying cuffs to the quick with his mother's scissors. And the last stages of his boots were worse than the last stages of his hat. Not such are the plumes and tunic of Don Juan.

Shaw's talk about the houris of the paradise of Art and the disadvantages of real women in comparison with the women of Praxiteles and Raphael and Mozart, is all humbug. The grapes were sour. If he could not have what he liked he must like what he had: that was all. The proof is that no sooner had the silver grey dragonfly burst from the seedy pupa than the saint became an unashamed sinner and remained so until his marriage thirteen years later. There is no getting over the exact coincidence of the dates.

No doubt the priestly continence so long enforced on him by his poverty effected a conservation of energy which may have reinforced the considerable vitality he still exhibits. Also, the unashamed sinner never became an intemperate one; for if the pursuit of women is impossible without money it is even less possible without spare time; and Socialism, criticism, and later on the theatre left Shaw no spare time. They made him, too, a conspicuous figure; and as, being an inveterate actor, he soon learnt how to play that part well, he was more pursued than pursuing. Let us do justice to his frequent comparisons of himself to Shakespeare. There certainly is a remarkable resemblance of their dramatised views of women as the aggressors in the duel of sex.

In a censorious world where moral judgements rush and react crudely from whitewash to soot I suppose I must make it clear that there is no evidence that Shaw was unscrupulous in his love affairs. He was not a wife stealer; he got no girl into trouble; and he had no purchased relations with the oldest profession in the world. His friendships with remarkable women were quite innocent in spite of the old-fashioned Irish gallantry of his ways with them. His famous correspondence with Ellen Terry is a masterpiece of tender Platonics on both sides, the two parties getting married – not to one another – in the middle of it without disturbing their affectionate relations in the least. But he was no ascetic, and had unquestionably one or two real affairs before he was married, and one or two attachments which were in the Wellingtonian sense 'very near things'. I am sorry to disillusion those disciples of his who would fain make a plaster saint of him; but I have his own word for it, and some corroborative evidence, that when he began writing plays, and at once shocked Archer by the sex episodes in them, he knew what he was writing about.

As no man ever had a sex adventure that gossip did not multiply by ten, and ladies make no secret of their successes with remarkable men,

Shaw soon had a reputation strangely opposite to the notion of him as an impotent Puritan that sprang up later on. But he had another reputation which he richly deserved, as he deliberately made it for himself, and by it lost in authority what he gained in popularity.

To illustrate this let me say that Leopold Godowsky, James Gibbons Huneker, and men of similar musical talent have told me that Shaw's knowledge of music was superficial, though to me he seemed an accurate and lively critic of music.

This will not hold water. Elgar, then ostensibly a young student of music, though really, like Sebastian Bach, an untaught and unteachable born master of it, read Shaw's articles with relish; and the friendship which sprang up between them when they first met as elderly men was prepared by Elgar's memories of *The World* feuilletons. I learnt later that Shaw had been steeped in music from his childhood.

Yet when, some months after he left *The World*, he met the acting editor Drummond in the street, and said, 'I see you have got Hichens to succeed me,' Drummond replied with conviction, 'Oh yes; *and he really knows about music.*'

Drummond firmly believed that Shaw's musical knowledge was a huge joke – a comic fake by a humorist who did not know B flat from a bull's foot.

It served Shaw right. He was, and is to this day, an inveterate and incurable clown; and Mrs Patrick Campbell was never better inspired than when she christened him 'Joey'. He had an uncanny *flair* for a laugh; and he never could resist raising it. Dyson's tragic caricature of the old man with cap and bells, looking at himself in a glass and wondering whether he was right to have ever donned them is a master-piece of criticism.

Take a case to show what I mean. Music is not my subject; and the jargon of music critics and programme writers about masterly modulations to the abdominant and the like have no sense for me. But I know that the symphonies of Beethoven rank with the plays of Shake-speare and the frescoes of Michelangelo, and should be treated with the same respect.

Now in the Victoria Grove days Shaw and his sister drove the neigh-bours mad by playing arrangements of the symphonies as piano duets. He knew them from end to end before he ever heard them on the band. When he had to criticise public performances of them pro-fessionally, it was a first-rate opportunity for a critic of his calibre to show his quality. He found such an opportunity when he had to write a notice of a concert at which the principal item was a great symphony by Beethoven – I cannot tell the number or the key; but it is the one called 'Eroica', dedicated to Napoleon when he was a republican general. When Napoleon made himself Emperor, Beethoven threw down the score and stamped on it in a fury. It contains a famous funeral march.

And what, if you please, was Shaw's reaction to this great work? His notice was a ludicrous description of a typical Shaw-family funeral in Dublin. His aunt Cha, or Charlotte, it seems, married the projector and resident secretary of the great Protestant cemetery of Dublin, Mount Jerome. The Shaws were borne from their intramural dwellings within the city to their last resting places in this cemetery, which was then separated from the town by a belt of country. The point of Shaw's description was that these inordinately long *cortéges*, to which the whole clan rallied with gusto, crawled with grief-stricken slowness until it got clear of the houses. Then there was a sudden clicking of coachmen's tongues, a tightening of reins, a jingling of bits, and away went the black procession at full gallop until the houses of Harold's Cross, where the cemetery was, were reached, when the tide of grief rose again; the mourning-coaches resumed their heartbroken *adagio*; and the defunct Shaw's bones ceased to be rattled over the stones and were conveyed decorously to the gates of Mount Jerome.

What, you may ask, had all this to do with Beethoven? Well, the funeral march, which is of course in a minor key, has a middle section in the major. This, I am told, is quite usual. But Shaw contended that the Beethoven family funerals must have been exactly like the Shavian ones, and that the episode in the major key followed by the relapse into the minor was composed to depict in music the run across country at the heels of the deceased.

No doubt this made funny reading. A few thousand unmusical stock-brokers and deaf mutes had a good laugh at it. No doubt, too, it was good for the paper; no editor would have turned it down and told his critic to take his business seriously. But will anyone blame Godowsky and Huneker and Drummond for refusing to see in such a *boutade* anything but an evasion and a cloak for utter ignorance?

I am not myself a professional humorist. Literature is to me too serious for tomfoolery. I was never able to accept the extravagantly high valuation placed by Shaw on Dickens and Mark Twain. Shaw's notion that all the great things in literature begin as jokes, and that the comic shrews of Dickens are the embryos of the tragically terrible women who prey on Strindberg's heroes, is ingenious; but it does not excuse Dickens for guying tragic themes. It is this street-boy guying that makes English fiction seem so silly compared to that of the Continent. For my part I would give ten volumes of Micawber for ten words by De Maupassant. When my stories – *Montes the Matador* and the rest – made some sensation in London, Shaw pleased me by calling me the English De Maupassant. If he had called me a Welsh-Irish Dickens or Mark Twain I should have asked him what the devil he meant by it.

They tell me that Micawber is Dickens's father. I reply that he most certainly is not; for old Dickens was at least a human being, and Micawber is not a human being: he is only a cheeky child's attempt to draw papa. Sam Weller has not a credible feature: he is just a funny middle-class make-up, dialect and all. The trial of Bardell *v.* Pickwick is supposed to be funny. *Is* it?

I yield to nobody in my appreciation and admiration of Shaw's literary art. I proved it by publishing articles of his that no other editor would have ventured on even if he had agreed with them; but Shaw repeatedly disappointed me by facing a big literary opportunity with the apparent strength of a giant killer, and evading and belittling it with some jape that merely made it ridiculous.

It is a hereditary defect in him; and it came from the parent who was 'the weaker of the two'. His mother never made a joke in her life. She never sang a song that condescended to even the mildest drawing-room facetiousness. It is not surprising that she had no respect for her husband, who made puns, and, as we have seen, never could resist an anti-climax. Shaw gave up making puns at the same age at which he gave up showing off his literary powers to the Almighty in his home-made prayers; but the anti-climax complex persisted, and will, I fear, persist until Beethoven's march is played at his own funeral.

His clever preface to Dickens's *Hard Times* in the Waverley edition is really an attempt to make out that tomfoolery is part of a great English literary tradition. If so, I am a heretic, and am content to remain so.

Yet I knew how valuable a sense of humour is to a satirist; for I was lacking in it myself and could by no means suffer fools gladly. I admired it immensely in Oscar Wilde; and it was what attracted me in Shaw. I had heard him lecture several times, and thought him an able icono-clast, with no profound originality, but with just this saving grace of humour. On the platform, Shaw was serious always. His proletarian audiences had no suspicion of the levities with which he loved to *épater le bourgeois*. Besides, I had now and again read his weekly articles on music, and admired the keen insight of them and the satiric light he threw on pompous pretences and unrealities.

Shaw says that I was the editor of *The Fortnightly Review* when I first met him about an article, and confesses he had an engaging air of being much more interested in me than in his article. He has the art of getting on intimate and easy terms very quickly, and at the end of five minutes, he insists, I found myself explaining to him how I had upset my health by boyishly allowing myself to be spurred into a trial of speed on the river in an outrigger, and over-straining myself in a fierce burst of speed. He gave his mind to my misfortune as sympathetically as my doctor, and asked me some questions as to what sort of care I was taking of myself. One of the questions was, 'Do you drink?' He says I was equal to the occasion and did not turn a hair, as I assured him that a diagnosis of delirium tremens could not be sustained.

This may all be true, but I do not remember it that way. The first interview I recollect took place in the offices of *The Saturday Review*, which I bought in September 1894, after resigning the editorship of *The Fortnightly Review*.

Shaw at this time was thirty-nine and thin as a rail, with a long, bony, bearded face. His untrimmed beard was reddish, though his hair was fairer. He was dressed carelessly in tweeds with the inevitable Jaeger collar. His entrance into the room, his abrupt movements – as jerky as the ever-changing mind – his perfect unconstraint, his devilish look, all showed a man very conscious of his ability, very direct, very sharply decisive, though a good deal of this may have been put on for my benefit.

I said I wanted half a dozen able men writing regularly, so that I might hope for three articles a week with something original in each of them.

'Who are your six geniuses?' asked Shaw.

'Well, I've got H. G. Wells to do the novel-reviews; D. S. McColl, the best art critic in England, is coming in.' (He later became the head of the Tate Gallery.) 'And Chalmers Mitchell will do the science.' (Mitchell later became the head of the Royal Zoological Society.) 'I think you'll be in good company, for Cunninghame-Graham, Arthur Symons, Walter Pater, Oscar Wilde, and a lot more will write occasional papers.'

Shaw found the difference between the leisure of a Persian cat and the labour of a Cockney cab-horse no greater than the difference between the official weekly play-goings of the theatre critic and the restless daily rushing to and fro of the music critic. His old job had kept him busy from three in the afternoon, when the concerts began, to midnight, when the operas ended. Reviewing pictures he had found nearly as bad. An Alpinist once, noticing the massive soles of his boots, asked him whether he climbed mountains.

'No,' replied Shaw, 'these boots are for the hard floors of the London picture galleries.'

Yet he found theatre-going so hard that the few years he was a dramatic critic, he declares, nearly killed him.

Well or ill, he was a most admirable contributor, always punctual unless there was some good reason for being late; always scrupulous, correcting his proofs heavily, with rare conscientiousness, and always doing his very best.

I soon realised that the drama of the day had never been so pungently criticised; I began to compare Shaw's articles with the *Dramaturgie* of Lessing, and it was Shaw who gained by the comparison.

His critical writing was exactly like his speaking, and indeed like his later creative dramatic work; very simple, direct, and lucid; clarity and sincerity his characteristics. No pose, no trace of affectation; a man of one piece, out to convince, not to persuade; a bare logical argument lit up by gleams of sardonic humour, humour of the head, as a rule, and not of the heart. His writing seemed artless, but there is a good deal of art in his plays: art, too, can be discovered both in his speaking and in his critical work; but whether there is enough art to serve as a prophylactic against time remains to be seen. You can best judge that for yourself by reading his three volumes called *Our Theatres in the [Eighteen-] Nineties*, of which I am the godfather. I rather doubt whether many will. Such things are of the moment. But in the eighteen-nineties, Shaw's serious-ness, sincerity, and brains soon brought the actor-managers out in arms against him. His tiff with Irving is best recorded in the long and affectionate correspondence of Ellen Terry with Shaw, published thirty years later.

At rare intervals I had to beg Shaw to shorten an article. For months together I had nothing to do except congratulate myself on having got him as a contributor; though at first he was strenuously objected to by many of my readers, who wrote begging me to cancel their subscriptions or at least to cease from befouling their houses with 'Shaw's socialistic rant and theatric twaddle'. On the other hand, thousands eagerly awaited each issue and devoured his stuff as avidly as that of his comparatively orthodox colleagues.

'The great panjandrum at that period was Clement Scott, who spread himself out in long columns in *The Daily Telegraph*,' writes Dan Rider in one of the less apochryphal passages in his *Adventures with Bernard Shaw*. 'After Frank Harris took over *The Saturday Review* we all swore by it; soon we all had copies every week, begged, borrowed, or stolen – I don't believe we ever bought one. Life was not worth living without it; it gave us the latest news from the front. And we craned our necks nightly over the gallery rails to see Shaw our champion take his seat among the well-groomed critics in their "glad rags". Shaw played up well to us in the gallery. We were proud to be able to point him out in his morning suit.'

An incident or two in our four years' co-operation may be cited, for they show, I think, the real Shaw. William Morris, the poet and decorator-craftsman, died suddenly. Shaw called just to tell me he'd like to write a special article on Morris as a Socialist and prose-writer and speaker. I said I'd be delighted, for Arthur Symons was going to write on his poetry, and Cunninghame-Graham on his funeral. I hoped to have three good articles. When they arrived I found that Symons was very good indeed and so was Shaw; but Cunninghame-Graham had written a little masterpiece, a gem of restrained yet passionate feeling; absolute realistic description lifted to greatness by profound poetry. Shaw too was overwhelmed with admiration of Graham's story.

'An amateur of genius,' I praised; 'it's a pity he hasn't to earn his living by his pen.'

'A good thing for us,' cried Shaw; 'he'd wipe the floor with us all if he often wrote like that.'

I came to regard Shaw as a realist by nature who, living in the modern realistic current, was resolved to be taken for what he was and what he could do, and equally resolved to judge all other men and women by the same relentless, positive standard. This love of truth for its own sake, truth beyond vanity or self-praise, is a product of the modern scientific spirit and appears to me to embody one of the loftiest ideals yet recorded among men.

It marks, indeed, the coming of age of the race, and is a sign that we have done with childish make-believes. From this time on we shall turn our daily job into the great adventure and make of its perfecting our life's romance. It was Shaw's realism, his insistence on recognising only real values, that called forth Oscar Wilde's epigram, which I must requote here.

'Shaw,' he said, 'hasn't an enemy in the world, and none of his friends like him.'

Mrs Patrick Campbell's correspondence with Shaw shows that he thought himself the kindest of critics while under my wing. 'If people had only known the things I didn't say,' was his pet defence. He wrote her a long letter fifteen years later, proving his case pretty well. She had reminded him of the 'odious things he had written about her in the past'.

Somebody wanted a copy of his *Saturday Review* articles. 'Before I sent it away,' Shaw wrote, with his reckless Irish gallantry all awake, 'I screwed up my courage and read the articles about you. And what a revelation! What a relief! What a triumph! Never did a man paint his infatuation across the heavens as I painted mine for you, rapturously and shamelessly.'

He asked her was she not afraid of drawing lightning down on herself, and challenged her passionately to produce a word ever written of her by anyone else that was more abandoned in its confession, that showed more recklessly to all the world that he was her utter captive.

In *Macbeth*, he did point out that his goddess could commit a few blunders, and he did not think she should play the dagger scene in her best evening dress of Lady Macbeth, but in a black wrap. He objected when she repeated the exit business by which Macbeth conveyed that he was going to see a ghost on every step of the stairs up to Duncan. She should have gone straight off like a woman of iron.

He thought she should not have forgotten that there was blood on her hand and on Macbeth's, and that they dared not touch one another for fear of messing their clothes with gore.

In the sleep-walking scene, he objected that she rubbed her hands realistically (drat the blood, it won't come off) and should not have worn an idiotic confection that wound her feet up more and more at every step and finally pitched her – off the stage – on her head. That scene needed the whole cavernous depth of the stage and the draperies of a ghost.

'It was maddening,' he summed up, 'to hear you deliver the lines splendidly and be in a different class to all the others and then throw it all away by half a dozen stupidities that the call-boy could have corrected.'

This intimate criticism hobbles Archer's contention – based chiefly on Shaw's abuse of Sir Henry Irving, whose leading lady, Ellen Terry, was an earlier recipient of Shaw's lavish letters – that, as a dramatic critic, Shaw was a paralysing and sterilising force.

Shaw, on the contrary, believed the function of the critic was to stir people, to make them think, to make them suffer, and under all his criticism lay the belief that the contemporary theatre was to our times what the Church had been to the Middle Ages.

'The apostolic succession from Eschylus to myself,' he once said in speaking of his *Saturday Review* primacy, 'is as serious and as continuously inspired as that younger institution, the apostolic succession of the Christian Church.

'Unfortunately this Christian Church has become the Church where you must not laugh; and so it is giving way to that older and greater Church to which I belong: the Church where the oftener you laugh the better, because by laughter only can you destroy evil without malice.'

Let me say a word or two further about this formative portion of Shaw's growth before I go on to speak of his later achievement. I had first heard of him in 1885, I think, and first heard him speak on Socialism in 1886; I had thus known him for more than a dozen years, four of which were spent in close, friendly, frank relations, though I didn't see him often for social purposes. He had grown in the twelve years, though even in 1886 he was in embryo the Shaw of 1898 and 1900. He had all the ideas at thirty which he has put forward later, and he was very articulate from the beginning. It seemed to me that the main part of his originality, a belief he has long since confirmed, came from the fact that he looked at England and all things English from the Irish point of view. British hypocrisy, formalism, convention, and cruelty shocked him. He was not to be imposed on by their pretended love of freedom; for example, the despots of Ireland, India, and Egypt could not delude him; nor by the love of free speech which the British are always bragging about; had he not seen Cunninghame-Graham and John Burns arrested and himself twice narrowly escaped imprisonment for trying to exercise the right? He knew that their sense of social justice was rudimentary, that one in every four Englishmen is buried in a pauper's grave. The ordinary Celtic view of England is a great part of Shaw's originality.

Towards the end of my tenure of the *Saturday*, Shaw had begun to make money by his plays, both in Germany, where Siegfried Trebitsch, his translator, was sacrificing his own career by his persistence in shoving Shaw on the German and Austrian managers, and in America, where Richard Mansfield carried him to the top as a box-office success with his triumphant production of *The Devil's Disciple*. Mansfield was not, like Trebitsch, devoted to Shaw. An American magnate publicly reproached him for not being sufficiently grateful for such a great play, adding that he ought to go down on his knees every night and thank God for it.

'So I do,' said Mansfield. 'Every night I kneel down by my little bed and thank God for that play. And the last words of my little prayer are "But, O God, why did it have to be by Shaw?" '

Mansfield loved Shaw no better than Irving did. In spite of the success of *The Devil's Disciple*, which established him firmly on Broadway, he never produced another Shaw play, though *The Man of Destiny* was written with one eye on Ellen Terry in England and the other on Mansfield in America. Shaw's American vogue consequently lapsed until Arnold Daly revived it with *Candida*.

Casually he told me one day that every article he wrote cost him much more than he got for it.

'I mean,' he said, 'the same time spent on a comedy would pay me ten or twenty times as much. I'm losing money every hour I spend on journalism.'

'You must stop writing for me, then,' I said, ruefully. 'But I'm about to sell the paper, and if you could have kept on for a couple of months, say till September' (it was then July or August, if I remember rightly), 'I'd be greatly obliged.'

'Say no more,' he reassured me; 'I'll go on till your reign comes to an end.'

'It's very good of you,' I replied; 'but I hardly like to accept such a sacrifice from you.'

'It isn't a sacrifice. I look upon it as only fair,' he replied. 'Your bringing me on *The Saturday Review* to write on the theatre has done me a great deal of good in many ways. You not only made me known in the theatre, but forced me to think out its problems, and so helped me to success. It's only fair I should pay you back a part of what you helped me to earn.'

'If you look at it like that,' I replied, 'I have no objection. You are making a lot of money, then, by your plays?'

'Not in England,' he said, 'but in America more than I can spend. I have actually opened a bank account; and my banker smiles when he sees me, and is in a perpetual state of wonderment, for, miracle on miracle, a writer is not only making money, but saving it.'

It was all for the best. As a critic he was written out. As in the case of his criticisms of music, he began to repeat himself; to fall into a style which to his great peril was recognised as partly serious. 'I found the pump tiring me,' he says, 'and the water lower in the well.'

No critic of the theatre, so far as I have observed, has matched Shaw since his time, except possibly George Jean Nathan. They both wrote with an air of men who were crammed with facts and who threw them overboard in sackloads in order to increase their speed.

Nathan, of course, has been more specifically outspoken, but it must be remembered that he was writing in America, where libel laws are not so hard on critics as they are in England. They both had a gay touch, though Nathan had Elizabethan tastes, as I had myself, and liked to write of belly-laughter and pretty girls.

In his avoidance of sex as 'a dull subject on paper', Shaw was a bad critic, and Nathan far ahead of him. But in England no critic has shown Shaw's force since his time until the present.

10

Seeing Red

To understand Shaw's career as a dramatist is impossible unless you know a bit of his social philosophy. His Socialism has coloured all his work. He is sincere in his opinions. If he does not live his beliefs any better than most of us, it is not because he cannot carry things to their logical conclusions, but simply because, as he tersely puts it, 'the police won't let him'.

Nor must it be held against him that his talk of equality of income does not seem to be borne out by his stout bank-balance in the midst of poverty. While I know of no other man living or dead who has made a capitalist fortune out of being a Socialist, Shaw, you must remember, has made it all honestly, though he denies this, declaring that he exploits actors and managers as his landlord exploits him. In this he is unique, I think. I know a good many men who have lost both fortune and social position by turning Red. Prince Kropotkin, for instance, and many others. Some of them have even lost their lives by it. I know others who, by raiding their organisation's exchequers, have enriched themselves while preaching the millennium. But Shaw alone has gained an honest fortune and high social position by telling the world unpleasant truths – certainly an exceptional achievement.

While I do not attach great importance either to his Socialism or his fortune, others doubtless do. For this reason some of his early researches in this field of hard-shelled idealism must be included in any biography of him, since they are at the base of my conviction that without his Socialism there would have been no Shaw, nor Shavian plays.

Before examining his skill as a playwright, or touching on his career as world's record-holder among plodding committee men, I shall therefore expatiate a bit on our modern Don Quixote's early ideas, since they form the background of his public career as a critic and dramatist – and frequently the foreground.

Don Quixote lived in an imaginary past; he cherished his beliefs and tried to realise the ideal of an earlier age. His present-day followers all live in the future and hug a belief of their own making, an ideal corresponding to their own personality.

But the lovers of the past and the future invariably start by despising the present; they are profoundly dissatisfied with what is, and in love with what has been or may be. The main difference between the rueful knight of Spain and Bazarof the Russian realist is that the don turns his back on the actual, whereas the modern thinker seeks to end or mend existing conditions, and thus found a new civilisation, the Kingdom of Man upon Earth.

Shaw is the best specimen of Bazarof that our time has seen; he is at once a greater force and more effective than his Russian prototype, for he attacks the faults of the established order with humour, a weapon of divine temper.

Once, on being told he enjoyed a great reputation in America, Shaw asked, 'Which? I am a philosopher, novelist, sociologist, critic, statesman, dramatist, and theologian. I have therefore seven reputations.'

Gladly making him a present of six of them, I cannot see for the life of me where he gets in as a philosopher, or even a laughing philosopher; at best a Court jester whose drolleries often contain sapient observations, a wit of the first water if you will, but not a philosopher, if you please. I have gathered heaps of notes that remotely touch this side of him, but, sifted out, they weigh almost nothing.

What is the first thing you ask of a philosopher? That he formulate a system of thought, of course – a school of thinking. From Plato to William James, from Aristotle to Comte, this has always been true.

Next you ask about his followers, his disciples. These carry on the work of the master, and sometimes the system of thought is strong enough to pass, by means of these disciples, through generation after generation for several thousand years. Who is there to carry on Shaw's school of thought? Obviously nobody, since he has founded no school and therefore has no disciples. Everybody who ever was inoculated with Shaw-fever has got over it in a few years. Indeed, Shaw has got over it to a large degree himself. So, as a philosopher, he simply doesn't exist.

But his claims as a social reformer rest on more solid ground. Briefly stated, Shaw's Socialism aims at the socialisation of the means of production and exchange by municipal or State control. He contends that all useful work is equally indispensable, and that it costs no more to support the scientist or philosopher than the bricklayer. He maintains that without equality of income no civilisation can survive. He repudiates as ridiculous the notion that any equation can be established between personal ability or virtue and money. He attempts to demonstrate that inequality of income upsets the social balance in politics, law, economic production, and above all in eugenics, with finally subversive and catastrophic results. He treats the social problem as one of distribution of the national income, and proceeds to reduce every possible plan of distribution to absurdity until, by elimination, he arrives at equal distribution as the only tenable one. He challenges every advocate of inequality to come down to pounds, shillings, and pence and say exactly how much Dean Inge should have and how much Jack Dempsey. No answer being possible, he points out that it is quite possible to give the dean half a crown and Jack two and sixpence, and that on no other terms can they found a stable society.

Shaw was the first Socialist to take this line on the Fabian platform; and until he put it into black and white in *The Intelligent Woman's Guide to Socialism and Capitalism* some twenty years later it made little way in Socialist circles, where equality of income had ranked as a crudity of the unlearned. Shaw thoroughly enjoyed making the stone that the builders rejected the head of the corner.

He has written voluminously on his economic credo, and he has summarised the whole of it in *The Intelligent Woman's Guide to Socialism and Capitalism*. His social beliefs up to then were scattered through his writings.

I could not stomach his equality of income. I used to argue in this fashion. Shaw is a vegetarian. He needs no meat and can get along on one meal a day, while I need meat and three meals a day. In short, I may have greater wants and needs than Shaw. Would equal incomes be just, then? It would be the rankest injustice, and surely Socialism does not intend it. The fact is that human nature and needs are so diversified that 'equality of income' would work fearful injustice to the whole of society.

Nor does food alone exhaust the problem. Some of us want music and the theatre and the opera, and now and then we require even greater luxuries. Shaw can live in frigid London houses: I need Riviera warmth, and steam heat and fireplaces to boot. In fact, what to other people may be a luxury is to me, and those like me, a necessity, a need without which we can neither work nor live.

Evidently, then, it should be the maximum of wants on which 'equal incomes' should be based. But Shaw derided me. According to him I was a miserable ascetic, eating and drinking unwholesomely and uncomfortably because I thought it was for my good, whereas he was a refined voluptuary, a connoisseur in the flavour of haricot beans and waters from the well, spending more money on his comforts than I. And as he ended by certainly having more money to spend, there was nothing more to be said.

And now compare Shaw's State, loaded with a statistical bureaucracy of huge proportions, and trying to solve unsolvable problems – compare it with Kropotkin's simple and just solution: to everyone according to his needs. Such Communism one can understand, but it is the free and anti-State Communism as opposed to the Shavian cell-block equality.

I could forgive Shaw his pre-war Socialism, but it is no credit to his thinking power that he still remains one. The war, the events that followed it, and the Russian Revolution in particular, have taken the bottom out of his ideas. But Shaw is proof against revolutions. He has actually visited Soviet Russia and returned to proclaim that Lenin was a Fabian, and that Stalin is carrying out Sidney Webb's plans, 'inevitability of gradualness' and all. The Third International, he told the Russians, is a Catholic Church with which the Soviet will sooner or later have to fight out the old Church *v.* State battle.

Dogmatists ever refuse to face life, and sneer at facts. Shaw insists on shutting his eyes to the débâcle of Socialist theories. He knows they have been disproved and discredited by actual application, and yet he continues to give Socialist advice and serve as its guide. Fortunately to 'intelligent women' only.

I have known Socialists that were bigger than their dogmas. Unfortunately, Shaw is not one of them. Dostoyevsky has said that a great man must be able to make a stand even against common sense. Shaw is all common sense. He thinks more of a drainpipe than a cathedral – the plumber-philosopher, if you will, but no Plato.

What ideas Shaw has today he picked up second-hand in the eighteen-seventies and -eighties, when the importance of an economic basis of history began to dawn on him. He had read *Progress and Poverty*, and its impassioned rhetoric fevered him like strong drink. It was while he was still inspired by Henry George that I first saw our hero in action. He spoke in favour of George's theory, only to be told that he should read Marx's *Capital*. He went to work on it at once, and came out with an original observation, but the wrong answer: 'It was supposed to be written for the working classes,' he exclaimed, 'but the working man respects the *bourgeoisie*, and wants to be a *bourgeois*. Marx never got hold of the worker for a moment. It was the revolting sons of the *bourgeoisie* itself – Lassalle, Marx, Liebknecht, Morris, Hyndman, Bax, all, like myself, *bourgeois* crossed with squirearchy – that painted the flag red.'

The study of *Das Kapital* made him, he tells us, a man with some business in the world. The choice of a Society for him lay between the Social-Democratic Federation on one side, and the Fabian Society on the other. The first was proletarian in its rank and file, aiming at being a large working-class organisation, while the Fabians were middle-class through and through.

'When I myself, on the point of joining the Social Federation, changed my mind and joined the Fabian instead,' Shaw once wrote, 'I was guided by no discoverable difference in programme or principle, but solely by an instinctive feeling that the Fabian, and not the Federation, would attract the men of my own bias and intellectual habits, who were then ripening for the work that lay before us.'

He joined the Fabian Society in 1884, and in time became the most famous of the band. Their whole idea was constitutional action, definition, permeation, educational propaganda, evolution, not revolution – and the difference between the bombs and bloodshed of 1848 and the Labour Government of today is their life's work.

In the beginning he performed on the platform or the cart-tail whenever he got the opportunity, and soon his humour and boldness gave him a unique place.

I remember his remarking that he was about the only person in England who understood Socialism. He had his own singular modesty from the beginning, you see. He knew Karl Marx by heart, he said. I had met Marx and knew the limits of his thinking. I was not only a Socialist, but an individualist as well, and believed that the whole effort of our time went towards a reconciliation of these two views. Shaw, though carried away by Marx at first, soon gave up defending his abstract economics. Philip Wicksteed converted him to the Jevonian theory of value, and he was presently fighting Hyndman and the other Marxists tooth and nail on this point. When *Fabian Essays* appeared under his editorship Marx was not mentioned in them; and his value theory was tacitly discarded for that of Jevons. But this did not prevent him from continuing to rank Marx as a giant, and making merciless fun of Jevons for proving that a State parcel post was an impossible extension of Socialism.

It was the late A. J. Marriott who insisted on Shaw's reading Buckle's *History of Civilisation*. It took Shaw a long time to get down to the three bulky volumes of Buckle, but finally he did. That he did not regret the time lost in studying the great historian is evident from this letter: 'I do not know how many years it is,' he wrote, 'since you undertook to make me read Buckle's *History of Civilisation*, and lent me your copy with that object. You must have despaired more than once of ever getting your three volumes back, much less inducing me to apply myself to them. But you will be glad to hear that I finished the last volume yesterday, having read every word of the three, notes and all, with the attention they deserve. And I assure you I am extremely obliged to you for making me do it. Out of the millions of books in the world, there are very few that make any permanent mark on the minds of those who read them. If I were asked to name some nineteenth-century examples, I should certainly mention Marx and Buckle among the first.'

It seems natural enough that, in the boundless Individualism of England, Shaw should have exaggerated the alleged benefits of Socialism. At any rate, that is what he did and, as a Freethinker and Socialist, he made himself widely known.

'Henry George,' he contended, 'saw only the monstrous absurdity of the private appropriation of rent, overlooking the fact that as practically all industrial capital is saved out of rent no Government could nationalise rent without undertaking the investment and control of capital and the conduct of industry as well.'

But, to an Englishman, that meant total industrial reconstruction, and the breaking up of their huge estates, and they would have none of either.

I remember when Shaw contested a seat at the London County Council election as a Progressive, after six years of drudgery on a borough council to which he was elected in 1897. The Free Churches were in a fury of Passive Resistance over Balfour's Education Bill, which threw the Church of England schools on the rates. Shaw declared that as half the children in the country had no other schools to go to, they should have public money in exchange for public inspection and control. To the Nonconformists this was trafficking with the Scarlet Woman, whilst the clergy at the last moment repudiated him angrily because he, the Freethinker, had put their case so well. His demonstration that the theological position of the Free Church leaders was precisely that of Voltaire did not help him. The result fully justified his opinion that no constituency would ever elect him on any terms, adult suffrage being a guarantee of second-best quality. He boasted that he got on the vestry and borough council not by a contest, but by making a bargain with the Conservatives that he should not be opposed. In his feeling about electioneering he out-Coriolanused Coriolanus.

Not only was he defeated for the Council by the defection of all the Liberals and temperance reformers (Shaw was a teetotaller), but the leading Progressive papers also exulted in his defeat as a most blessed deliverance. The only people who voted for him, he told me, were those who had never voted before.

He has written, of course, on the 'Impossibilities of Anarchism', and he would not go very far into Socialism without a fair-sized army and navy. Nor does he believe that the marginal man, the man on the verge of born scoundrelism, can be kept in order without an executioner in the background. He is against punishment on the ground that two blacks do not make a white; but he would ruthlessly exterminate idlers, parasites, unproductives generally, and violent and rapacious people who waste reasonable men's lives in looking after them. He would have us all appear before a Judicial Committee every five years or so to justify our existence and obtain a licence to exist for another five years. When Mussolini calls Liberty a putrescent corpse, Shaw applauds him and declares that what keeps men enslaved is their aspiration to be free for twenty-four hours every day. Government, he says, is nothing but the organisation of necessary slavery; and its first business is to see that nobody escapes his proper share of it. Liberty begins only when the day's work is over. Liberty is leisure; and the less Government has to do with that, the better. He is very civil to efficient dictators, holding that all rulers are dictators, no matter what they are called, and that our parliamentary plan of setting up one party to do the nation's work, and another party to prevent them doing it, is only an excuse for doing nothing but talk, and that it is bound to go down before the positivism of Fascism or Communism. Adult suffrage destroys responsibility: what is everybody's business is nobody's business. The problem of democracy is how to give rulers every power except the power to hold on to their job if they stop doing it. He warns you that the Socialist State is to be powerful, highly centralised, and supreme. It could *make* us good. Until then Shaw's ethics are on the loose.

'It does not concern me,' he says, 'that, according to certain ethical systems, all human beings fall into classes labelled liar, coward, thief, and so on. I am myself, according to these systems, a liar, a coward, a thief, and a sensualist; and it is my deliberate, cheerful, and entirely self-respecting intention to continue to the end of my life deceiving people, avoiding danger, making up bargains with publishers and managers on principles of supply and demand instead of abstract justice, and indulging all my appetites, whenever circumstances commend such actions to my judgement.'

His Socialist ideas, in theory at least, have not changed much in all these years. The child is born in due time, he argued years ago (and still does), and is raised and fed on credit. Consequently, when the child grows up it is inevitably in debt, and a social State would present it with a bill accordingly. The child, when it grows into a worker, must produce a sinking fund, thereby paying off his debt of nonage and providing a retirement at whatever age the community may desire to release him. If the adult does no more than this, he is a common fellow: if he does more, and leaves the world richer than he found it, he is a gentleman. Dean Inge endorses this definition.

Today, where the law is made by parasites for parasites, he argues, parasitism is privileged. That happens under capitalist morality, which looks on labour as a disgraceful vulgar necessity, a failure in life, whereas success means a character freed from all obligations to work. This means that if nine men all work hard they can support a tenth in extravagance, and the more poorly the nine live without disabling themselves the richer the tenth man will be. All slave systems are founded, he holds, on this maintenance of each one in the upper ten at the expense of groups in the lower nine.

So runs the Shavian theory. Today, as forty years ago, he is an old-time Communist. I think his creed is even worse and more short-sighted than a capitalist's. As, in the law of gravitation, the centripetal force is balanced by the centrifugal, so, in economics, Socialism and Individualism should be balanced, with Individualism first. The solution is what Carlyle and Goethe had in mind, the leaving to the initiative of the individual all things except the few which were obviously public in character, and I would rather be supported by Goethe and Carlyle than by Marx and Shaw. Shaw even attacks the right to strike, and challenges the Labour Party to abrogate it by making labour compulsory on all able-bodied citizens, whatever their income. Reformers of that sort use razors for ploughshares and end up at the same banquet-table with the Mussolinis, Stalins, and Garys.

In the last analysis you can judge a man and his ideals best by his heroes. Shaw, the Fabian, is really a direct-actionist. The desk-philosopher in this instance is at heart a terrorist. From his youth he was interested in prizefighters, and still is. In fact, the Carpentier–Beckett fight in London will only be remembered because Bernard Shaw and Arnold Bennett wrote about it, and Shaw knocked Bennett all over the ring. Then, when seventy-three, Shaw and Gene Tunney took a holiday together in Italy, where another of Shaw's gods, a man of action, held the whip hand.

Seriously, you could write Shaw's inner convictions and hidden aspirations in terms of Lenin, Mussolini, and Tunney. Mussolini and Shaw were two successes who started out as Socialists, and what Shaw admired most in Mussolini was the fact that Il Duce had been seemingly able to remould a whole nation to his bizarre tastes, while Shaw had only been able to talk about it and get nothing done.

I have felt all my life, through all the years that I have known Shaw, and from familiar knowledge of his works and life, that he feels himself defeated. 'I shall never have any real influence,' he says, 'because I have never killed anybody, and don't want to. And yet when I die and go to heaven I shall feel bound in intellectual honour to say to God, "Scrap the lot, Old Man. Your human experiment is a failure. Men as political animals are quite incapable of solving the problems created by the multiplication of their own numbers. Blot them out and make something better." '

It is this combination of a fundamental scepticism as to human possibilities, with an unbounded faith as to the possibilities of fresh creations, that weakens the original strength of his view of life as of his plays; at least of most them, and gives the impression of failure of achievement.

In *Widowers' Houses*, for instance, observe his hero. Realising that the wealth of his bride is ill-gotten, you would naturally expect him not only to feel outraged, but to do something about it. When he learns that his own wealth comes from similar sources he compromises. The hero, like Shaw, fails at the crucial moment.

Despite the fact that he is not a philosopher, he was the first readable philosopher's digest for many young men thirty years ago. He gave life a meaning which the dried-out sermons of their pastors had destroyed.

But after you had read all Shaw has written and said, you realised that his mentality was comically befuddled. His thinking was a broth, stewed by an Irishman, of the most varied schools of thought, chiefly from Schopenhauer, Strindberg, Butler, Bergson, Morris and Nietzsche, Marx, Tolstoy, Ibsen and Wagner. But he would not admit this, and in his *First Aid to Critics*, prefaced to *Major Barbara*, claimed that all his antecedents could be found in English literature.

Far be it from me to set any bounds to Shaw's pretensions in philosophy and science, religion and art. At one time he was fond of describing himself as an artist-philosopher. I have no doubt that after his *Methuselah* preface he described himself as an artist-biologist, though I never heard him do so. When he presumed to undertake the task of proposing Einstein's health at the banquet given in London to the supplanter of Newton, he claimed that the poets and artists were always ahead of the laboratory workers in science, and hailed Einstein as an artist-mathematician – apparently because Einstein can play the fiddle. In *Man and Superman* and in *Back to Methuselah* he has illuminated the Creative Evolution of Butler and Bergson with such a display of literary and theatrical fireworks that he may well pass as its inventor with those who know no better. Little as Shaw knows, there are millions who know less. Is it any wonder that they mistake Figaro for Aristotle?

So I get back to the beginning: he is no more a philosopher than I am. Our chief difference is that Shaw wanted to be a man of action, while I actually was. That also explains the difference in our heroes. His heroes are all contemporary men of action, skull-crackers, while mine are Cervantes, Shakespeare, and Heine – all gentle artists, and all dead.

And now let's ring up the curtain.

11

The Playwright

Superficially the public cannot help but assume that the harsh dramatic critic, goaded by the 'Try and do better' school of repartee, dropped his critical writings and tried his hand at play-writing to show them how easily it could be done. But this was not the case at all. As usual, Shaw had to be shoved by Archer into writing a play. Archer supplied a plot, and set Shaw to work on the dialogue. When a couple of acts were completed Archer found plenty of dialogue in them, but not a shred of his plot. He withdrew from the collaboration and gave Shaw up as a hopeless playwright. Shaw seems to have accepted his verdict; for the unfinished play lay untouched for years. Then Jack Grein, the Dutch admirer of Antoine and founder of the English Independent Theatre, shoved Shaw into writing a third act. The two performances, which were all that Grein's resources could compass, convinced Shaw that Archer was wrong, and that he really had a vocation as a writer for the theatre. Nevertheless his plays continued to be *pièces d'occasion*, produced in response to some external shove. Only three – *Man and Superman*, *Heartbreak House*, and the *Methuselah* cycle – were written in the air, so to speak, and from within. Thus *The Philanderer* was written for Grein, who could not cast it. *Mrs Warren's Profession* was a response to a demand from Mrs Sidney Webb, who, disgusted by the sex-obsessed women in *The Philanderer*, told him to write something about a real modern unromantic hard-working woman. It was strangled by the Censorship. *Arms and the Man* was hastily manufactured to save Miss Horniman and Florence Fair from having to close the old Avenue Theatre after a failure. *Candida* was written for Janet Achurch. *The Man of Destiny* was written for Richard Mansfield and Ellen Terry, neither of whom ever played in it. *You Never Can Tell*, so named by Sidney Webb, was commissioned by Cyril Maude, and withdrawn in rehearsal through a failure in casting. *The Devil's Disciple* was written for Terriss and Mansfield, who made it a big success in America. *Caesar and*

Cleopatra was written for Forbes-Robertson, whose Caesar was his finest achievement after his Hamlet. *Captain Brassbound's Conversion* was written for Ellen Terry when, on the birth of her first grandchild, she told Shaw that nobody would ever write a play for a granny. The famous series that followed, from *John Bull's Other Island* to *Androcles and the Lion*, were written by Shaw as playwright in ordinary to the Vedrenne cum Granville-Barker management and its sequel in the management of Lillah McCarthy. *Great Catherine* was written for Gertrude Kingston. *Pygmalion* was written for Mrs Patrick Campbell, and *The Apple Cart* for Sir Barry Jackson. None of these plays were spontaneous: they were handyman's jobs to get actresses, actors, and managements out of difficulties: all more or less, like *Arms and the Man*, stopgaps. It may seriously be questioned whether Shaw would ever have written a play if there had been no theatres to be kept open and no actors to be obliged.

Most plays have immediate successes or failures and then drop out of existence like leaves in the fall. Shaw's have proved immortal so far: how long they will last is a question for posterity. But in the main it is the stage societies, repertory theatres, coterie theatres, 'little' theatres, and amateur clubs that have kept them alive. There have been some fashionable box-office successes and long runs with star actors. Mansfield in *The Devil's Disciple*, Robert Loraine in *Man and Superman*, Agnes Sorma and Katherine Cornell in *Candida*, Mrs Patrick Campbell and Beerbohm Tree in *Pygmalion*, Cedric Hardwicke and Edith Evans in *The Apple Cart*, Sybil Thorndike in *St Joan*, besides starring tours like those of Ellen Terry in *Captain Brassbound's Conversion* and Forbes-Robertson in *Caesar and Cleopatra*. There have been the long runs of *Fanny's First Play* with Lillah McCarthy, and of *Candida* with Arnold Daly in New York; but the latter was in a tiny theatre; and neither of them was specially lucrative.

The Court Theatre during the Vedrenne–Barker adventure was really a repertory theatre where the length of the run was announced beforehand – six weeks at the utmost – making great money successes and ruinous failures alike impossible. Personal artistic successes, however, were conspicuous. Lillah McCarthy, a beautiful Siddons from the West Country, of Irish extraction, was the leading lady. Granville-Barker, also from the West Country, but with a strong dash of Italian blood, was the fascinating *jeune premier*. The late Louis Calvert, who abandoned the Shakespearean stage to play Tom Broadbent in *John Bull's Other Island*, was the 'heavy lead'. Florence Haydon, an ultra-Victorian lady, was an incomparable comedy actress of old women's parts. Lewis Casson, with a fine voice and an ear for verse, turned his hand to everything. With these for a nucleus, and the pick of the profession to draw upon when it happened to be out of a more lucrative job, Shaw and Granville-Barker, who were both born producers, and playwrights to boot, rejuvenated the sterile and perishing British theatre by a campaign which lasted until the war: roughly, the ten years from 1904 to 1914. The first half of it is chronicled in the history of the Court Theatre by Desmond McCarthy, a fine critic, and the only one who drew level with the new departure and fairly outmoded Archer and Walkley and the rest of Shaw's exact contemporaries.

Shaw made a desperate effort to bring the novelists into the movement, sometimes making the production of one of his plays conditional on the production of another by a novice. He tried Kipling; but Kipling was no revolutionist, and held aloof from the Shavian atmosphere. Maurice Hewlett was induced to try; but he confessed to Shaw that he could not take the theatre seriously as he took his novels, and did not persevere. Chesterton, though his single experiment, *Magic*, later on proved him a natural master of the stage, could not extricate himself from journalism and general literature. Wells replied with the unanswerable truth, 'Nothing can happen on the stage,' and refused to accept its limitations. The poet, John Davidson, with a great drama of transcendental materialism in him, said he could not afford to write it, because his family would have to starve for six months. 'How much can you earn in six months?' asked Shaw. 'Two hundred and fifty pounds,' said the poet. Shaw put down the money, and exhorted him to do his damnedest with no regard to anything but the utter satisfaction of his soul. The upshot was tragic.

Davidson, in a transport of gratitude, resolved to make Shaw's fortune. He produced what he conceived to be an ultra-popular romantic quasi-historical melodrama, calculated to attract full houses for at least a year.

When he realised that he had wasted Shaw's money and his own supreme opportunity, he committed suicide.

After that, Shaw knew better than to try to mould other men's destinies. The only authors who came in were those who needed no pressing: chief among them, Galsworthy.

At the beginning of the Court Theatre campaign, Shaw was ranked in the theatrical world as an unprofitable outsider of the coterie theatres.

At the end he was venerated as the most important British dramatist. The Shavians claimed that he was the greatest since Shakespeare. His own estimate was as modest as usual. 'I cannot guarantee myself as the greatest living hokum merchant,' he said; 'but I am certainly one of the best ten.'

Shaw still had no practical initiative. In his poorest days he had refused to go into debt. Friends pressed loans on him; but he was as resolute as he was seedy. 'A friend is worth more than a fiver,' he argued. 'I won't sell.' All very praiseworthy, no doubt; but when at last he had money to venture it was still the same: the probity revealed itself as timidity. Not a penny has he ever risked in any form of public entertainment, theatrical or other. When it came to putting in work, he could cast his bread upon the waters recklessly, just as both in clerking and journalism he had burnt his boats again and again. But nowadays a man who will not go into debt will not go into anything big. Wherever Shaw has succeeded you will find that he has attached himself to some more enterprising spirit who has taken all the money risks. I owe it to myself to admit that he picked his men well.

For in his journalistic phase he picked me, and was clever enough to let me believe that I had picked him. In his Fabian phase he picked Sidney Webb; and the firm of Sidney and Beatrice Webb proved a very sound political investment. And in this theatre phase of his he picked Harley Granville-Barker, who presently added Lillah McCarthy to the combination by marrying her.

But, as Swinburne sang, marriage and death and division make barren our lives. The war found Harley in New York; and there he fell wildly in love with a lady in the most plutocratic stratum of American society, who had literary enthusiasm, and several novels and a few poems to her credit. He proved as irresistible as he had been to the duchesses in the stalls of the Court Theatre. The intervening marriages were soon dissolved; and by the time the war was over, the lady, who was very well off, was established in England as Mrs Granville-Barker, and Lillah McCarthy was a handsome chatelaine in Oxford as Lady Keeble.

Unfortunately Mrs Granville-Barker's culture was Victorian. It stopped very decidedly short in the world in which George Meredith and Henry James were the gods of literary ladies' idolatry. In that world, George Bernard Shaw was not only non-existent, but inconceivable, except as a Red Spectre. Harley had to choose between an adored wife and his career in double harness with Shaw. Love kicked the beam; and the two adventurers of the Court Theatre saw no more of one another. Granville-Barker subsided into domestic bliss and contented himself with commentating Shakespeare and translating plays from the Spanish, of which language his wife was a mistress.

Shaw was left without a partner. And now, precisely as in the *entr'acte* between his partnership with me and his partnership with Granville-Barker, he had written a big play, *Man and Superman*, to propagate his views of Creative Evolution, so, in the interval that followed the dissolution of the Court partnership, he wrote the still bigger play, or cycle of plays, called *Back to Methuselah*, again about Creative Evolution, and the curious *Heartbreak House*, which is unlike any of the Sloane Square potboilers.

Let me not be understood as disparaging potboilers. Shakespeare's and Molière's plays – ninety per cent of them – were potboilers. Playwrights must live on their plays. Shaw, it is true, was under no such necessity. His marriage, to which I shall come presently, boiled the pot for him merrily without any subsidy from the theatre. But the late John E. Vedrenne, the business partner at the Court Theatre, and Granville-Barker, had not a rap that did not come in through the payboxes. And there were the actors to be considered. For them Shaw's plays boiled the pot, mostly with revival after revival of *You Never Can Tell*, until the whole repertory was nursed up to paying point.

Pygmalion was a culminating potboiler; but it boiled the pot of Beerbohm Tree and Mrs Patrick Campbell, and effected Shaw's only moment of contact with the fashionable commercial West End London theatre. He knew it was not his business to follow that up; and – the Granville-Barker connection being broken – he was at a loose end when he wrote *Heartbreak House* and *Back to Methuselah*. Then he formed a new association.

Unknown to him, there was a man in the provinces who had taken up the artistic running when the firm of Vedrenne and Barker, after an attempt to enlarge its enterprise which involved it at one moment in the management of several West End theatres, found itself hopelessly insolvent on such a scale. Barker sold all he possessed, and Shaw disgorged most of his royalties, to save the financial situation. The creditors were paid in full; and Vedrenne and Barker closed down for ever. But the man in the provinces, who was providentially a man of means, forged ahead, from larking about with a little strolling company of enthusiasts, to the building of the Birmingham Repertory Theatre.

He produced *Heartbreak House* there and made a success of it. Having thus introduced himself to Shaw, he proposed to produce the *Methuselah* cycle, to the amazement of its author, who asked him sternly whether he meant to take his wife and family to the workhouse and die there on the straw.

Barry Jackson replied calmly that he had neither wife nor family, and was prepared to stand the racket because he liked doing things of that sort. Shaw had found his man again; and since then he has worked with Barry Jackson, who presently became Sir Barry Jackson, established himself in London, and founded the Malvern Festival in the West Country on the Bayreuth–Wagner model, with Shaw as his prize author.

In America, too, a band of enthusiasts founded the Theatre Guild; and they also made a success of *Heartbreak House* and ventured on the *Methuselah* cycle without absolutely ruining themselves. Shaw at once reserved his potboilers for them, and reaped a series of lucrative revivals.

Meanwhile a British touring company called the Macdona Players, organised by Charles Macdona to exploit the old Court Theatre Shaw repertory in the provinces, made the astonishing discovery that *Man and Superman* in its incredible and impossible entirety, lasting about five hours, of which two were pure preaching, was sure of a full house everywhere at least once in the week. It became a question whether the stuff that Shaw himself, as well as the commercial managers, had assumed that the public would never tolerate, was not in fact exactly what a very large section of the public wanted. But that section was not the richest section: it could not afford expensive West End stalls. Shaw raised a cry for large theatres and low prices: sixpence, a shilling, and half a crown, with one night a week for intelligent plutocrats: all seats one guinea, if not five.

To sum up, Shaw as a playwright presents three phases. First, as an unattached free lance of the coterie theatres, snatching a few performances here and there, learning his business as a producer, and always getting the performances excitedly discussed. 'My reputation grows with every failure,' he said. Ten plays were his output during this period; and the first of them, *Widowers' Houses*, is still hardly known in London, and had to wait thirty-five years for its first big success, under the crisp title *Rents* (*Zinsen*), in Berlin.

Second, the association with Granville-Barker, and the campaign at the Court Theatre, in which both of them made theatrical history and emerged into established positions as the most discussed theatre men in

London. Granville-Barker, at the end of this period, was not only a leading actor and a great Shakespearean producer who had shattered the Irving tradition of recklessly mutilated texts, and restored Shakespeare's plays to the stage in their entirety, but a playwright who promised to rival Shaw on his own ground. It was Granville-Barker's second marriage and retirement that ended this phase.

Third, the association with Barry Jackson which still subsists.

And, between these phases, two intervals or *entr'actes*, during which Shaw wrote, not for immediate business purposes, but in a vacuum, and without regard to existing theatrical possibilities, first, *Man and Superman*, and then, in the second interval, *Heartbreak House* and the *Methuselah* 'metabiological pentateuch'.

And now I can discourse on all this at large.

I was curiously disappointed in the early plays. I had expected something more vital from Shaw. He sent me his first volume, *Plays Unpleasant*, and I could not see how they could succeed. All talky-talky, it seemed to me, where action alone is effective, and having written *Mr and Mrs Daventry* myself, a play which ran one hundred and fifty nights in London and brought money in floods both to Mrs Patrick Campbell and to me, I thought I knew the trick; yet Shaw's talky-talky later held the public and I confessed humbly that I did not know the game.

Success in the theatre, I said to myself, depends greatly on personal relationships, knowledge of the good and bad points of well-known actors and actresses, and the public demands of the moment (as true in the little theatres, the independents, as in the commercial theatres).

Shaw could always write good acting parts; but he only bothered the expensive West End stars, who got their big salaries for making non-existing characters seem alive and interesting. He did not want to exploit stage personalities: he wanted to give the public a stiff jolt and perhaps thus move the world nearer his heart's desire.

So, in his first play, *Widowers' Houses*, Shaw tried to picture middle-class respectability and young gentility, 'fattening on the poverty of the slums as flies fatten on filth'. And what was true of his first play has remained true of all the others, even if to a lesser degree. But in his later plays he has started out with a less violent theme and finished on a milder note. That has spoilt my interest in them. In *Widowers' Houses* he started out to destroy poverty and the causes of it, got halfway through, and turned tail. This is his real failure, not the paybox receipts, meagre as they sometimes were.

In a nutshell, *Widowers' Houses* deals with a gay and irresponsible Englishman and a painfully correct companion, who are travelling together in Germany. The irresponsible youth meets the daughter of a self-made English millionaire. They become engaged. Back in London from their holiday, he learns that the girl's father is a slum landlord, and being a young man of ideals, he refuses to marry into such tainted money. Later he learns that his own income is derived from mortgages on this same slum property. That fetches him. He acquiesces to 'the inevitable'. The realistic circle brings him back to the girl and the end of Shaw's first play.

You can readily see there is no point in bringing this all up unless you are going to do something about it, even if the thing you do is of no more moment than having a puppet on the stage stick to his guns.

Yet his Marxian conscience wouldn't let him escape so easily. He really wanted to do something about slums. He does to this day, but he can't seem to swing the axe all the way.

Here is a letter which the heirs of Marriott have sent to me. It shows Shaw still on the same subject – fifteen years after, when his play was still waiting for its success.

August 1st 1906

DEAR MARRIOTT – Certainly London is pretty bad; but I think it has passed its worst. The fact that it has begun to scatter is shown by the way in which some of the schools have been emptying. Of course, this scattering means the obliteration of the Welsh Harp and the filling up of such rural places as the valley of the Mimram with rows of houses; but this is better than the old congestion at the centre.

It is no use depending on the millionaires: what we have to do is to sit down and try to settle how many people should be let live on an acre of ground, and then pass a Building Act to enforce our conclusions. What maddens me is not so much to see houses cropping up over the old Sunday-outing places, but to see that they are cropping up in such a way as to form the beginnings of slums. It is our infernal improvidence and intellectual laziness that prevent us from stopping the reproduction in the country under our eyes of the evils that we have had such bitter experience of in towns.

You may remember from your reading that one of the things that infuriated the people under the old *régime* before the French Revolution was the furious driving of the nobles in their carriages.

The motor-car has shown that the world is much the same now as it was one hundred and fifty years ago. But the motor-car is doing one good thing. It is reducing rents on the frontages of the main roads; and it is possible that this may help to popularise your idea of strips of public gardens between the road and the houses.

But the more one thinks of it the more one is driven back to what I said before. It is no use grumbling: we must make up our minds as to exactly what we want, and then agitate for a national Building Act. Also, by the way, for a 'Right to Roam' (as Harold Cox used to call it), putting a stop to the 'Trespassers will be Prosecuted' business, except in cases where mischief would be done. The worst of it is that our present city-populations are so savage that they drive even the most public-spirited country people to put up barbed wire all over the place. They mean no harm; but if you let them near a bank of violets they leave it a mere dust heap, and are no more to be trusted with trees and animals than a baby can be trusted with a butterfly . . .

Yours faithfully,

G. Bernard Shaw

You see how, even in this letter, as in the play, he starts off to help and ends up a defeated realist. It's one of the keys to his failure.

When Archer planned *Widowers' Houses* for him in the middle eighteen-eighties, Archer borrowed the plot from *La Ceinture Dorée* and the proposed name, 'Rhine Gold', from Wagner.

'I perversely distorted it,' explained Shaw, 'into a grotesquely realistic exposure of slum landlordism, municipal jobbery, and the pecuniary and matrimonial ties between them and the pleasant people of "independent" incomes who imagine that such sordid matters do not touch their own lives. The result was revoltingly incongruous; for though I took my theme seriously enough, I did not then take the theatre quite seriously, even in taking it more seriously than it took itself.'

Archer disowned him, saying that Shaw's technique was to that of Scribe as a jellyfish to a racehorse, and left him two unfinished and condemned acts. When it was finished under pressure from Grein, who produced it at the Royalty Theatre in 1892, it was a seven-days wonder. For two weeks the newspapers discussed the subject of the play, and finally the text was published and all but drowned under a long preface and a bushel of appendices. This volume is now extinct.

As Shaw admits, he had not achieved a success, but he had provoked an uproar. It is undoubtedly true, as Shaw argues, that all plays which deal sincerely with humanity 'wound the monstrous conceit which it is the business of romance to flatter'. But here we are confronted, not only with the comedy and tragedy of individual character and destiny, but with those social horrors which arise from the fact that 'the average home-bred Englishman, however honourable and good-natured he may be in his private capacity, is, as a citizen, a wretched creature who, whilst clamouring for a gratuitous millennium, will shut his eyes to the most villainous abuses if the remedy threatens to add another penny in the pound to the rates and taxes which he has to be half cheated, half coerced into paying'.

To which the critics replied that playgoers don't want to be taught; they want to be entertained. There is unpleasantness enough in life without looking in a 'play-'house for it. They say this when the play is neither amusing nor tragic, but halfway between, and that's precisely where Shaw's plays invariably landed.

About one year after *Widowers' Houses*, Shaw wrote *The Philanderer* (1893). It is a topical comedy in which Shaw tried to paint the 'new' woman and, incidentally, also the 'new' man, who imagine they have outgrown conventional sexual compacts. The ordinary sex-life, Shaw argues, is based on our superannuated marriage laws, which are considered a political necessity, particularly for the other fellow. In *The Philanderer*, Shaw portrays specimens of modern and progressive people who ignore the outlived laws and who follow their love needs in their own independent manner.

A splendid theme. But Shaw has made of it a weak and preachy thing of compromise. His vaunted sex-rebels end up in conventional marriages, with Shaw, the male flirt, remaining the philanderer.

Curiously, but in my estimation very significantly, Shaw has classed *The Philanderer*, together with *Widowers' Houses* and *Mrs Warren's Profession*, among the dramas he called 'unpleasant'. As a matter of fact, it is nothing of the kind. Only a skimmer of life's realities and passions could consider the play 'unpleasant'.

If you compare this play with Shaw's letter to me on his sex-experiences, a classic confession which he wrote in the summer of 1930, you see the real connection between this philanderer and the author. The most Shavian speeches are put in the mouth of Charteris.

This *Philanderer* starts out with as lively a love-scene as Shaw ever wrote, and if this seems like faint praise it is not intended as such. It opens in a drawing-room in Ashley Gardens after 10 o'clock at night, with a lady and gentleman in each other's arms, seated affectionately on a sofa near a piano. Time is the elegant eighteen-eighties, as are all of Shaw's early plays.

To make sure you won't mistake that Shaw is Charteris, Shaw has him introduced to you as 'Mr Leonard Charteris, the famous Ibsenist philosopher'. And this famous 'Ibsenist philosopher' immediately proceeds to make a tract of the play.

It is an even bet whether it was Shaw the Socialist who wanted to air his views on marriage in *The Philanderer*, or whether it was the devil in the purist Shaw who attempted to free himself from his sex-inhibitions. I am inclined to think that both guesses are correct.

Shaw might have been more courageous in *The Philanderer*; but this can be forgiven him since it led to *Mrs Warren's Profession*. The only person who can't be forgiven in this latter instance is England's hired regulator of public morals.

12

Censors

By his own testimony and that of many friends, Shaw is a paragon of virtue. Can any other reformer point from infancy to thirty years of unbroken chastity? Yet what peace of mind has his continence and prudery in language brought him? He has got into as much trouble with censors as I, an admitted bad boy, have myself.

You cannot understand why from a reading of his plays. The naughty scenes in them are so spiceless they could hardly get into a benefit performance for the Girl Scouts. Try to recall them. There is a scene in *Back to Methuselah* in which a man, using television, gets a wrong number and finds himself looking into the bedroom of a partly disrobed negress; there is a scene in *Arms and the Man*, where a lady appears on the stage in a flimsy nightdress; there is a scene in *The Apple Cart* disclosing the king and his favourite rolling about on the floor. But she is only trying to prevent him from going home to tea with the queen. For the life of me, I can't remember anything else in all his thirty odd plays that could possibly be considered obscene.

For all his inoffensiveness, his career as a dramatist was nearly ruined at the very outset when *Mrs Warren's Profession* was suppressed by the Lord Chamberlain. Of course, in this instance, Shaw was dealing seriously with a subject (prostitution) that is only acceptable – at least, on the English stage – as long as it is treated lightly. But, then, *The Shewing-up of Blanco Posnet* and *Press Cuttings* were also censored. What can there possibly be in *Blanco Posnet* (a play dealing with a religious conversion), to bring down the disapproval of the official guardian of stage morals in a country which plumes itself on being the freest in the world?

All his adult life, Shaw has battered away at the institution of stage censorship as it exists in England. It seems to him that, with the best of intentions, the censors safeguard the very evils they are supposed to prevent. They do not bar plays which are frankly obscene. They bar those which seek to get rid of obscenity. Shaw began his siege in 1894, in the days when Victoria ruled British morals as well as British politics: he is still at it today. And for all his hundreds of perfectly logical arguments, the only change that has been brought about is that the tyranny of the official censor has been increased by an unofficial censor who certifies the propriety of every sex appeal from Hollywood, but bans attempts to show unprotected girls where they can find safe lodgings.

The establishment of the censor in England was due to Henry VIII, who appointed an officer of his own household to look after the job. Parliament never took control of the office. As a consequence, to this day the censor remains the Lord Chamberlain, who is part of the King's retinue and whose salary is part of the King's civil list.

Once, when asked by the Playgoers' Club how he proposed to abolish censorship, Shaw scandalised the members by replying: 'You must begin by abolishing the monarchy.'

In the beginning, censorship was chiefly political. Walpole, finding the playwrights too much for him, clapped the lid on them. He thus drove the public-spirited dramatists, Henry Fielding among them, out of the theatre, since which time the English novel has grown while the English play declined.

Years ago, Shaw announced in a facetious moment that he intended to apply for the post of censor at the next vacancy. Of course, he never made such an application. In fact, he said that if he were appointed he 'could no more help being odious and mischievous than a ramrod could if it were stuck into the wheels of a steam engine'.

Yet I can't help thinking the idea a salutary one. Shaw's own remedy: the licensing of theatres by the local authorities, does not appeal to me. But then I have never been a vestryman.

Shaw revealed the absurdity of the censor's position when he was still a young man. At that time he described him as 'a gentleman who robs, insults, and suppresses me as irresistibly as if he were the Tsar of Russia and I the meanest of his subjects'. The robbery, he explained, took the form of making Shaw pay him two guineas for reading every play that exceeded one act in length. 'I do not want him to read it (at least officially: personally he is welcome): on the contrary, I strenuously resent that impertinence on his part. But I must submit, in order to obtain from him an insolent and insufferable document which I cannot read without boiling of the blood, certifying that in his opinion – *his* opinion! – my play "does not in its general tendency contain anything immoral or otherwise improper for the stage", and that the Lord Chamberlain therefore "allows" its performance (confound his impudence!). In spite of this certificate he still retains the right as an ordinary citizen to prosecute me for an outrage to public morals if he should change his mind later on.'

If he really protected the public against an author's immorality, Shaw rubbed it in, why should not the public pay him for his services? The policeman does not look to the thief for his wages, but to the honest man whom he protects against the thief. If, having been paid, the censor is afraid to license the play – that is, more afraid of the clamour of the opponents than of the play's supporters – then he can suppress it. 'Since he lives,' Shaw realistically pointed out, 'not at the expense of the taxpayer, but by blackmailing the author, no political party would gain ten votes by abolishing him.'

His conviction that the censor was an unjustifiable tyrant is just as strong in him today as it was thirty-five years ago. In *The Apple Cart*, which was produced in 1929, Shaw makes his King Magnus remark somewhat irrelevantly: 'But you tell me that I can reign only by signing pledges which would make me a mere Lord Chamberlain, without even the despotism which he exercises over the theatre.'

The censor's strangle-hold on the stage has become such a familiar fact that the great majority of English playwrights no longer struggle against it, but allow the Lord Chamberlain to tell them how they must write plays, just as the writers of Hollywood let Will Hays dictate to them how they should write cinema scenarios. But it is a well-known fact that any play of vitality or imagination written in America (where there is no official stage censorship) has very little chance of passing the English censor. Serious dramas like Eugene O'Neill's *Desire under the Elms* can expect nothing but a blackball, and a sincere and moving play like *Green Pastures*, which inspired hundreds of audiences in New York, is rejected by the Lord Chamberlain because the representation of God upon the stage is against office rules. In this instance, the entire Press of London protested against the censor's decision, but usually they uphold him, rather liking to be led around by the nose. Certainly no London critic has smashed at the Lord Chamberlain as Heywood Broun has smashed, year in and year out, at the reformers who would like a Redford for the New York stage.

But even the rejection of such a play as *Green Pastures* is less ridiculous than the censoring of Shaw. Most of Shaw's admirers still believe his subjects are daring and his dialogue plain-spoken, but even his worst enemies would have to agree that he is absolutely free from the slightest trace of sensuality and is never offensive. In fact, that is what I feel is the whole trouble with him.

The first of these suppressions, *Mrs Warren's Profession*, shared its fate with Ibsen's *Ghosts*. Today both plays are prescribed to High School students, but in Victorian times, of course, the public could not be reminded that sex existed. Shaw's play was banned and remained on the black list for thirty years. In America, when it was produced at the Garrick Theatre, New York, in 1902, a frantic hue and cry was raised against it; and Arnold Daly and his whole company were taken to the police station on the fall of the curtain; but the police failed to secure a conviction, and the play, judicially whitewashed, soon fell into the unchallenged class.

In England it was not until 1924 that the Lord Chamberlain lifted the ridiculous ban and allowed *Mrs Warren's Profession* a public presentation in London. I do not know what Shaw actually thought of this tardy authorisation. In one of his typical interviews, he told a reporter that he deeply regretted the Lord Chamberlain's change of mind.

'The news is unhappily all too true,' he is quoted as having said. 'Now that I have reached the venerable age of sixty-eight years and am in the odour of sanctity, if one may so put it, the Lord Chamberlain has let loose this awful piece of mine, written nearly thirty years ago when I was only a young tiger believing in neither man nor God: a play which this terrible censor now authorises to prevent me from ending my days in peace. I cannot forbid the production, because it is as true and necessary now as in 1894; but, if one wants my personal impression regarding the necessity of producing it, I would say: "No, frankly, better never than late." '

This statement reminds me of Shaw's letters to me which form the preface of this book. Here we have the typical G. B. S., ever the coy Victorian lady, contradicting himself in the same breath, saying 'no' when he means 'yes'. We see him trying to make us believe the younger Shaw was an *enfant terrible*: he expresses horror at the lifting of the ban and then says, contradictorily, that 'this awful piece' is 'as true and necessary now as in 1894', and he winds up his statement with another contradiction by claiming that he sees no 'necessity' of producing this 'true and necessary' play. Moreover, he says that he cannot forbid the production. I would like to know what in blazes would prevent him from forbidding it if he really wanted to!

Shaw, in another of his countless attacks on the censorship, upbraided it for 'its scandalous laxity towards, and positive encouragement of, the familiar and customary pornographic side of theatrical art simultaneously with its intolerance of the higher drama, which is always unconventional and *super-bourgeois* in its ethics'.

One of the many inconsistencies of the British censorship is that, while the production of plays is subject to the will of the Lord Chamberlain, the Press is entirely free, as are, to a large extent, the publishers of books. It is but rarely that a book is suppressed in England (James Joyce's *Ulysses* and my *Life and Loves* are the only books of any consequence that have been suppressed since Fielding quit the theatre to write *Tom Jones*). And so, while the stage representation of *Mrs Warren's Profession* was forbidden and the English and Irish censors were quibbling about *The Shewing-up of Blanco Posnet*, there was no obstacle whatever to the circulation of these plays in book form. Indeed, the book sales of an American play were puffed up recently by a brilliantly coloured announcement on the dust-cover that the Lord Chamberlain had forbidden the play to be produced.

13

Theatre Vicissitudes

I find inscribed in my copy of *Heartbreak House*: 'Rightly spotted by the infallible eye of Frank Harris as My Best Play. – G. Bernard Shaw.'

On re-reading all his plays recently, I do not seem able to affirm this opinion made several years ago. In fact I have the greatest difficulty today in holding in my hands much of what he has written. Most of his pearls of great price slip through my fingers, almost while examining them, and disappear like drops of water. Whether this is due to my advancing years or the impermanence of Shaw's work I haven't yet decided.

Making a private poll among other old friends, and even among the younger converts to Shaw, I find them remarking the same difficulty. A revival of *Fanny's First Play* in 1931, for instance, twenty years after the original production, had the London critics asking why it wasn't played in costume? Hannen Swaffer, a fellow Socialist, even remarked, 'Shaw does not live on beans now, but has-beens.' Others found so much of what we thought sparkling a generation ago dull today, and in all honesty I do myself.

Of his thirty odd plays only *Candida* and *Mrs Warren's Profession* remain warm within me, and they were written during his years as a critic. In fact, really all his first successes were written, published, or produced while he was under my wing on *The Saturday Review*. At least, *You Never Can Tell, Arms and the Man, The Devil's Disciple, Mrs Warren's Profession, Candida*, and *The Man of Destiny*, fall into this group.

Three of these plays are among his best – one, *Candida*, actually his best, in my mature opinion. Of the others, *You Never Can Tell* has a good chance of surviving, because it happens to be the favourite of actors; and *Arms and the Man*, because it deals with humorous realism about men in battle and is caricatured in Strauss's operetta, *The Chocolate Soldier*.

Arms and the Man was Shaw's first regular West End professional production. It ran eleven weeks at the Avenue Theatre in London in

1894, and according to Shaw's well-kept statistics (he made careful entries in notebooks of all sums he ever earned in those days), the play grossed £1,777 5s. 6d. Eleven weeks may be considered a success for a playwright, but £1,777 5s. 6d. spread over that time spelled failure for the producer. If all the people had come in two weeks, Shaw's backers would have made money, but the customers took so long to straggle in that all the profits went out in general expenses.

The play opened in New York under Richard Mansfield, at the Herald Square Theatre in September of the same year, and though it was not an overwhelming hit, Mansfield put it into his repertory, and from that moment on, Shaw was established in America.

The Scandinavians always liked Shaw, being among the first to acclaim him after the Americans. This no doubt was due partially to Shaw's championing of Ibsen, and his free borrowing in his early days, despite his vehement denials, of the Norwegian's ideas. He knew not a word of Norwegian; but Archer indoctrinated him sedulously.

Germany was next after America to take him up, and between these countries he waxed prosperous until finally, nearly fifteen years after his first play in London, England became aware that it was housing a modern Molière. France held out the longest, despite the ceaseless fight of the Hamons, and even with the support of Rémy de Gourmont, who declared Shaw to be 'a dramatic genius'. The boulevards have never accepted him; the Comédie Française will none of him; and the few productions which followed the success of *Saint Joan* have been effected with difficulty at coterie theatres by the Pitoeffs, who are neither of them French.

When, in 1921, Paris first saw *Arms and the Man*, the material seemed familiar to them, and they had every reason to think it was, for, in 1845, Charles Mathews, in *Used Up*, was using up similar situations from a French farce. Mathews was, you may recall, the author of *Cool as a Cucumber*, which was Shaw's first lesson in how to get rid of shyness.

Shaw invariably answers any such deadly parallels with a remark to the effect that the thing actually happened in his family, or was told to him by one of his friends to whom it had happened. This is the formula of all amateurs, and Shaw does not seem ever to have outgrown it. Shakespeare, who borrowed anywhere and everywhere and enriched everything he touched, never seemed troubled by matters of this sort. But, then, Shakespeare did not have a social conscience.

France's unconcern over Shaw's greatness did not shake his conviction that Paris was to be pitied and excused beyond words. After all, he said, the Parisians had the original Molière and were playing him in the Comédie Française steadily; so why bring in foreign goods? He explained that Paris is coeval with Vienna and therefore one hundred years behind the other capitals of Europe; which, of course, must have made the only civilised city in the world laugh its head off.

The few that examined Shaw saw a bit of Gilbert (some more than a bit), snatches of Ibsen, Nietzsche, Sudermann, Hauptmann, Strindberg, Maeterlinck, and even their own Molière. So naturally they were disposed to make Shaw prove his case in a more original way before letting him into any of their theatres. He finally fetched them completely by *Saint Joan*, which, amusingly, as I will show later, is the least original of his plays, but because of its patriotic and religious appeal goes down with every Frenchman, completely swamping his critical faculties in the deluge.

It is odd that the realistic Shaw found that the way to riches in a theatre was through the use of romantic material. His first three attempts kept close to London and to his age. But his first successes found him far a field. *Arms and the Man* took him to the Balkans, *Caesar and Cleopatra* took him two thousand years behind the times, *The Devil's Disciple* to the American Revolution, *Captain Brassbound's Conversion* to romantic Morocco, and so on down the line. Since then he has even gone *Back to Methuselah*, back to Adam and Eve, in fact; and as far forward as thought can reach, with stop-over privileges in the Middle Ages.

His success as a dramatist, then, can be traced from the time he stopped dealing half-heartedly with immediate sociological problems, and projected himself in mind to other climes and times; and this is notable because Shaw is not by nature a traveller, and was severely immobilised by his early impecuniousness. His Hegira from Dublin to London was the only journey he took on his own initiative. Sidney Webb took him by the scruff of the neck to Belgium and Holland for his first trip abroad. His duties as critic took him to Bayreuth and Paris. His friends of the Art Workers' Guild made him join the excursions of that body to Italy. And when he married a nomadic wife, and had to see that she had holidays from housekeeping, and to gratify his own taste for mountain motor-driving, he wandered all over the Continent and French northern Africa, though he has never been nearer to America than Jamaica, never further south than Madeira, never further east than Moscow and Stamboul, never further north than Stockholm. Yet, though in his plays the atmosphere is always authentic, I do not attribute this to his globe-trotting. I should never have guessed from his conversation that he had ever been anywhere further than a mile from his house. After all, his fictitious atmospheres are not more authentic than Lemuel Gulliver's or Defoe's. Authentic atmosphere is a good story-teller's gift, not a tourist's reminiscence. If Shaw had been bedridden all his life he would have known where to borrow details for the more persuasive telling of his stories.

Another secret of his success was his aptitude for fitting actresses with tempting parts even in plays which they thought impossible. 'I am a good ladies' tailor,' he wrote to Ellen Terry. It was perhaps more by his good tailoring than by flattery, persuasion, sarcasm, humour, or straight, convincing arguments, that he managed to get Alma Murray, Kate Rorke, Lillah McCarthy, Ellen Terry, Mrs Patrick Campbell, Sybil Thorndike, Fanny Brough, Grace George, Gertrude Elliott, Gertrude Kingston, Winifred Lenihan, Phyllis Neilson-Terry, Forbes-Robertson, Richard Mansfield, Arnold Daly, Louis Calvert, Herbert Beerbohm Tree, Robert Loraine, Cedric Hardwicke, everybody, in fact, but Henry Irving, into his casts. Anyhow, you can see how well he digested the old saw about hitching your wagon to a star.

Shaw's later successes, such as *John Bull's Other Island*, *The Doctor's Dilemma*, *Heartbreak House*, *Back to Methuselah*, *Saint Joan* and *The Apple Cart*, I shall deal with elsewhere, if I deal with them much at all. For the present I want to concern myself with *Candida* and *Mrs Warren's Profession*, since the two together give a sort of measure of Shaw's best work.

Mrs Warren's Profession is undoubtedly the most characteristic of Shaw's plays – characteristic mainly of Shaw, for the play is both strong and weak, as is Shaw himself.

Unquestionably he hits existing conventions, prejudices, and stupidities straight from the shoulder, but when it comes to finishing them off he pulls his punches and the result is almost a draw.

For the benefit of those who are a little hazy as to what *Mrs Warren's Profession* is all about, it might be well to explain here that it concerns the oldest profession in the world, and would probably be titled today: *Whoring Mothers*.

There is no play in all Shaw's works as full of magnificent misses as this one. It could be one of the greatest dramas of all time and it is unforgettable, but it fails to achieve timeless greatness, either because he didn't know how to handle such a theme or was afraid to drive right through to the end of it. The play as it stands leaves everything as it was.

Take, for instance, his full-blooded attack on capitalist conditions and the fate of the poor working-girl, who is expected to be respectable, and self-respecting too, on a mere pittance.

'How could you keep your self-respect,' Mrs Warren indignantly asks her daughter, 'in such starvation and slavery? . . . scrubbing floors for one and sixpence a day, and nothing to look forward to but the workhouse infirmary.' With the lips of Mrs Warren, Shaw here actually seems to justify her profession. Indeed, he emphasises that the very people and conditions that demand virtue and chastity compel the girls and women to sell themselves – either into marriage or brothels.

And Mrs Warren cannot be gainsaid when she advises her daughter: 'The only way for a woman to provide for herself decently is for her to be good to some man that can afford to be good to her. If she's in his own station of life, let her make him marry her; but if she's far beneath him, she can't expect it: why should she? It wouldn't be for her own happiness. Ask any lady in London society that has daughters; and she'll tell you the same, except that I tell you straight and she'll tell you crooked. That's all the difference.'

That's the truth, and it shows Shaw's courage to say it so frankly and bluntly. Nobody in the world can present a case better; it's in the winning of it he always falls short.

Nor does he fail to point out *where* the real crime and immorality originate. As in the scene of the capitalist Crofts and Vivie Warren: 'Why the devil shouldn't I invest my money that way? [In brothels masquerading as hotels.] I take the interest on my capital like other people: I hope you don't think I dirty my own hands with the work. You wouldn't cut the Archbishop of Canterbury, I suppose, because the Ecclesiastical Commissioners have a few publicans and sinners among their tenants. And do you expect me to turn my back on thirty-five per cent, when all the rest are pocketing what they can, like sensible men? No such fool! If you're going to pick and choose your acquaintances on moral principles, you'd better clear out of this country, unless you want to cut yourself out of all decent society.'

With admirable skill, Shaw shows in this play that society expects you to be respectable, whatever else you may be, and will not enquire too deeply into the sources of your well-being.

Obviously Shaw sees clearly, and makes the theatre-goer see that fashionable morality, in the words of Mrs Warren, is all a pretence. It's not Mrs Warren who is the sinner; it's society, which dooms to a sinner's life a mother who only wants to be good to her daughter, provide well for her, and secure her. Indeed, there is no tragedy greater than hers, the mother's, when the only being that she did good to turns against her!

Shaw is cruel when Mrs Warren, the ex-whore procuress, to hold her daughter's love, offers her every luxury and compares it to the drudgery refusal would entail. 'I know what young girls are,' she says, 'and I know you'll think better of it when you've turned it over in your mind.'

'So that's how it's done, is it? You must have said all that to many a woman, mother, to have it so pat.'

This isn't mother and daughter, but the realist Shaw unsexing both.

I consider Shaw's indictment of society in *Mrs Warren's Profession* powerfully dramatic and unconditionally sincere. Alas, neither his courage nor his dramatic quality enables him to cross from indictment to cure. Here is where he fails again, and leaves himself and a great play hanging in the air.

The weakness of *Mrs Warren's Profession* is not precisely the same weakness you find in his other plays. Here the heroine, Vivie Warren, on learning the polluted source of her income, at least does not bow to it as the hero in *Widowers' Houses* does. She quits the comforts of home and goes out on her own to confine herself henceforth to such a sex-free subject as actuarial mathematics.

I think it is a perversion of appreciation to consider, as almost all critics persist in doing, that *Mrs Warren's Profession* is an attack on female prostitution, on the Mrs Warrens and their aids. Shaw goes deeper than that, for he sees the world and life clearly. He knows that it is not only the women of Mrs Warren's profession who are prostitutes or live on the proceeds of that vice.

'We not only condemn women as a sex to attach themselves to bread-winners, licitly or illicitly, on pain of heavy privation and disadvantage,' he writes, 'but we have great prostitute classes of men; for instance, the dramatists and journalists, to whom I myself belong, not to mention the legions of lawyers, doctors, clergymen, and platform politicians who are daily using their highest faculties to belie their real sentiments: a sin compared to which that of a woman who sells the use of her person for a few hours is too venial to be worth mentioning; for rich men without conviction are more dangerous in modern society than poor women without chastity.'

But what is the cure and how to be achieved? Shaw, the hard-hitting social critic and indicter, falls short again as the direct-actionist. He wants to 'replace Sartorius's slums with decent dwellings, Charteris's intrigues with reasonable marriage contracts, and Mrs Warren's profession with honourable industries guarded by a humane industrial code and a "moral minimum" wage'.

I know of no proposal that could be more weak, inadequate and ineffectual. Certainly he knows that the social evil is not due to unreasonable or reasonable marriage laws. It has existed long before there were any marriage laws. He knows, only too well, that it is not laws which are responsible for prostitution, but poverty, misery, human degradation, and loneliness.

Fundamentally speaking, in *Mrs Warren's Profession*, Shaw attacks the conventional view of the social question, the view of fashionable morality – no doubt because his own career has been conventional: living one life and believing in another. I hold that the convention view is wrong here, as everywhere. Shaw ought never to have stirred the matter up at all if he had not been prepared to go to the full limit of our modern morality and to declare that the mother's profession had nothing whatever to do with the daughter's character. He failed in his promise.

Janet Achurch, who, I believe, created the rôle of Candida, had once mentioned to Shaw a French story, possibly *Yvette*, as having a dramatisable *Mrs Warren's Profession* in it. She dramatised it herself under the title *Mrs Daintry's Daughter*.

'Oh,' exclaimed Shaw, 'I will work out the real truth about that mother some day.'

But he didn't. Not the real truth, at any rate; not even the half of it. But, as he foresaw, even half of it was too much for the censor. As he wrote: 'Crime and lust and horseplay, deprived of all moral significance or psychological analysis, are the only permitted alternatives to conventional romance. We are allowed and encouraged to make the stage an attractive advertisement for prostitution and to drive the young to the brothel by the most potent of aphrodisiacs; but when I dramatised the truth about prostitution in *Mrs Warren's Profession*, the play was at once prohibited.'

I recall how excited London was by this suppression. Shaw had very little trouble in proving to his friends that the censor was at fault, and he,

Bernard Shaw, was well within his rights. The friends of the censor, on the other hand, hinted that Shaw had introduced a Gaiety girl; but that had been done before, and all the pleasures of vice flaunted for the benefit of the vicious. So about all the quarrel amounted to was that *Mrs Warren's Profession* was not up to a sufficient standard of immorality. It was true to life and not spicy enough to pass the censor.

However, it is from a man's best work that we learn most. His failures count no more than the spots on the sun. It is by the light he gives forth that he must be judged. And so I turn to *Candida*.

Nothing abler has been done in our day than *Candida*. It is worthy of Goldsmith at his best, and is a vital, powerful, humane, and perfectly charming play.

It deals with a woman who must choose between a husband who needs her and a poet who adores her. The poet has no sense of responsibility and no definite purpose in life except to be shocked because the hands of Candida, made for kissing and adoration, have been soiled by peeling potatoes in the kitchen.

Candida sees that he is in love with being in love, whereas her husband, Socialist clergyman, is in love with her and his work and needs them both to make life remotely supportable. When her husband gives her the choice between himself and the poet, she decides to remain with her husband. It is Candida who comes out of the struggle a great woman.

The Stage Society tried its hand at *Candida* in 1900, with Janet Achurch; but the play's popular success began in Germany with Agnes Sorma. In London it was Harley Granville-Barker's memorable impersonation of the poet at the Court Theatre in 1904 that laid the foundation of the epoch-making Vedrenne–Barker management. Perhaps the finest Candida, however, was Katharine Cornell's in New York in 1925. I didn't see this, but critical opinion was unanimous as rating it one of the season's sensations. Shaw himself, not having seen Miss Cornell, gives the palm to Phyllis Neilson-Terry at Malvern in 1930. He declared that Sybil Thorndike was under-parted in it, and that Janet Achurch, though incomparable in its most difficult passages, on the whole 'kicked the part round the stage instead of playing it'. He wrote the play for Janet and – very foolishly – reserved the part for her for ten years. Her comment on hearing him read the play was 'I can be that woman – *for two hours.*'

I think that, in *Candida*, Shaw has not only given us a great play, but – what is far more important – he has created a great and noble woman.

In the portrayal of her character – her growth and self-realisation – Shaw has transcended anything else he has done in character painting. Surely the spirit of genius hovered over him and inspired his vision while the soul of Candida was revealing itself to him.

True art consists in the author remaining superior to his characters, to the emotions and situations he depicts. In no other play has Shaw succeeded so perfectly in this as in *Candida*. To be sure, there is enough of the Socialist Shaw in the type and talk of Candida's husband, the Socialist preacher Morell, though Shaw has described him as a portrait of Stopford Brooke with touches of Fleming Williams. Anyhow, there is enough in him also of the inherent respectable Shaw. But his portrayal of Candida shows that he has succeeded in eliminating himself entirely, and has for once cut loose the wings of ideal hope and vision.

I am sure the average theatre-goer applauds *Candida* because of the virtuous ending of the play: after all, the unconventional and 'immoral' things said in the play notwithstanding, the story ends conventionally. But such an attitude is both false and stupid. It merely shows how fearfully a play can be misunderstood. I count it particularly to the credit of Shaw's courage that he did not pause with fear at having his meaning misconstrued. He had the courage to make the play end true to the character of Candida, true to life as to art, even at the risk of the conventional ending stamping the play as unoriginal.

This courage was a master stroke. The entire play hinges on it and is made strong and vital by it.

There are few Candidas in the world, yet there are some, and the world is the better for them. She sees through the vaunted strength of her legal provider and protector, the honest, good, virtuous preacher, and she realises how weak the alleged strong sex really is. Her husband, Morell, the celebrated orator and powerful influence for good, is, in fact, so sure of his strength that, when Candida decides to give herself 'to the weaker of the two' men, Morell mistakes her intention.

Psychically blind to everything about him, understanding nothing of the real nature and needs of Candida, the great teacher and preacher thinks that his wife means to go with the poet. To him, typical good Christian man that he is, the helpless and lonely poet, impecunious and impractical youth, is the weaker of the two. He offers Candida 'my strength for your defence, my honesty of purpose for your surety, my ability and industry for your livelihood, and my authority and position for your dignity'.

He hasn't the least inkling that Candida possesses a soul, that she yearns for understanding, for someone to share her idealist dreams and longings. So little conception, indeed, has her husband of his wife's mind and heart, that he closes his offer by saying, self-confident in his manly philistinism: 'That is all it becomes a man to offer a woman.'

Her husband's offer completely strips him in her eyes of the last vestige of nobility and understanding. Quietly she says to the poet Marchbanks: 'And you, Eugene? What do you offer?'

MARCHBANKS: My weakness! My desolation! My heart's need!

The naïve, impractical, and inexperienced young poet instinctively knows the need of the woman. A woman like Candida does not hunger for protection or support. 'It is she who wants somebody to protect, to help, to work for,' he tells her paternalistic husband, 'somebody to give her children to protect and to work for; some grown-up man who has become as a little child again. Oh, you fool, you fool, you triple fool!'

The poet's intuition has seen through Morell's shallow goodness, and with equally clear eye he has read Candida. He has nothing to offer her but his weakness, his desolation, and heart's need.

How well he understood Candida, and how powerfully has Shaw thereby brought out the real strength of the young poet! Candida is quick to realise which of the two men is the weaker. Marchbanks's answer decides her.

CANDIDA (*impressed*): That's a good bid, Eugene. Now I know how to make my choice.
She pauses and looks curiously from one to the other, as if weighing them. MORELL, *whose lofty confidence has changed into heartbreaking dread at* EUGENE's *bid, loses all power of concealing his anxiety.* EUGENE, *strung to the highest tension, does not move a muscle.*

MORELL (*in a suffocated voice – the appeal bursting from the depths of his anguish*): Candida!

MARCHBANKS (*aside, in a flash of contempt*): Coward!

CANDIDA (*significantly*): I give myself to the weaker of the two.
EUGENE *divines her meaning at once: his face whitens like steel in a furnace.*

MORELL (*bowing his head with the calm of collapse*): I accept your sentence, Candida.

CANDIDA Do you understand, Eugene?

MARCHBANKS Oh, I feel I'm lost. He cannot bear the burden.

MORELL (*incredulously, raising his head with prosaic abruptness*): Do you mean *me*, Candida?!!!

CANDIDA (*smiling a little*): Let us sit down and talk comfortably over it like three friends. (*And then she continues*) . . . Ask the tradesmen who want to worry James and spoil his beautiful sermons who it is that puts them off. When there is money to give, he gives it: when there is money to refuse, I refuse it. I build a castle of comfort and indulgence and love for him, and stand sentinel always to keep little vulgar cares out. I make him master here, though he does not know it and could not tell you a moment ago how it came to be so. (*With sweet irony*) And when he thought I might go away with you his only anxiety was – what should become of me! And to tempt me to stay he offered me (*leaning forward to stroke his hair caressingly at each phrase*) his strength for my defence, his industry for my livelihood, his position for my dignity, his – (*reflecting*) ah, I am mixing up your beautiful sentences and spoiling them, am I not, darling? (*She lays her cheek fondly against his.*)

MORELL (*quite overcome, kneeling beside her chair and embracing her with boyish ingenuousness*): It's all true, every word. What I am you have made me with the labour of your hands and the love of your heart. You are my wife, my mother, my sisters, you are the sum of all loving care to me.

CANDIDA (*in his arms, smiling, to Eugene*): Am I your mother and sisters to you, Eugene?

MARCHBANKS (*rising with a fierce gesture of disgust*): Ah, never. Out, then, into the night with me!

MORELL (*rising from his knee, alarmed*): Candida: don't let him do anything rash.

CANDIDA (*confident, smiling at* EUGENE): Oh, there is no fear. He has learnt to live without happiness.

MARCHBANKS I no longer desire happiness: life is nobler than that. Parson James: I give you my happiness with both hands: I love you because you have filled the heart of the woman I loved. Goodbye. (*He goes towards the door.*)

Many critics have claimed that Shaw was laughing behind his hand at the poet, but how can you reconcile that with his willingness to give the poet lines which so well reveal Shaw's own early longings? Recall the poet's cry that 'All the love in the world is longing to speak, only it dare not because it is shy, shy, shy,' and then recall Shaw's bashful youth and you will well understand that if he were laughing at the poet at all it was from the other side of his mouth. Who has caught better the day-dreaming of poets than Shaw in this: 'That is what all poets do: they talk to themselves out loud; and the world overhears them'?

As in the poet, so in the woman, Shaw presents a nobler conception than he ever did before. Candida is not merely a parson's female, but a warm woman, a one-time woman with whom the poet would not be long satisfied, as life for him is in the chase, not the fireside. Shaw has him leaving with 'a man's voice, no longer a boy's', since he has learned to do without personal happiness, and this I think is well expressed. In fact, the entire character of the poet is well done, but the great achievement of the play is Candida; and why Shaw couldn't have grown from Candida to hallow-crowned heights will for ever remain a mystery of his career. Half a dozen women like Candida, and he would have made himself the greatest of all Irish playwrights, greater than Sheridan or Wilde, certainly, to name two outstanding in the field of social comedy. Candida's straightforwardness, her ability to see through her husband's supposed strength to his very real weakness and hence need of her, is the work of a master, as vital in conception and as powerful and moving in execution as the best of English classics.

I have always thought Candida Shaw's finest creation, though Shaw once argued with me that she was as unscrupulous as Siegfried. He went on: 'She is a woman without "character" in the conventional sense. Without brains and strength of mind she would be a wretched slattern and voluptuary. She is straight for natural reasons, not for conventional ethical ones. Nothing can be more cold-bloodedly reasonable than her farewell to Eugene: "All very well, my lad; but I don't quite see myself at fifty with a husband of thirty-five." It's just this freedom from emotional slop, this unerring wisdom on the domestic plane, that makes her so completely mistress of the situation.'

Shaw's apprenticeship was now over and done with. He had reached the point where he began to produce as a master and show his true essence. There will be nothing novel in his growth, nothing that should surprise us; he developed normally, naturally, and his life's history is to be found in his works.

It is a peculiar dominance of mind over heart and over body, a rooted preference in Shaw for reflections and ideas, with a contempt of sensations and even emotions, that gives the Mephistophelean cast to his personality.

His excessive preoccupation with the play of mind often hurts his dramatic writing. It did in *The Devil's Disciple*, after *Arms and the Man* probably his most popular early play, though by no means near his best.

But in *Candida* and *Mrs Warren's Profession* I think I show that Shaw had found his outlet and had come into his own: he had at length done something not to be overlooked, something that belonged to English literature; and I am glad to tell him so frankly. *Candida* will live.

14

Shaw's Women

Barring Candida and Lady Cicely (in *Captain Brassbound's Conversion*), two characters with sweet Ellen Terry unquestionably as the original living model, Shaw's women, from Blanche, his heroine in *Widowers' Houses*, to Vivie Warren in *Mrs Warren's Profession*, are distinctly unpleasant, practically unsexed women. Their bodies are as dry and hard as their minds, and even where they run after their men, as in the case of Ann in *Man and Superman*, the pursuit has about as much sex appeal as a timetable. Whether such women ever existed, or whether in creating them Ibsen convinced Shaw they ought to exist as a counter-irritant to the romantic, swooning, novel-reading females of our boyhood, is an open question.

In my long experience with women, both modern and antique, I've known only one who could be as calculatingly cruel to a mother who had done everything for her as Vivie Warren is to Mrs Warren. And I've seen few girls who could even be mean and realistic to their mothers for more than a week at a time. The rest, thousands, get on after a fashion and try not to be more annoying in asserting their own personalities than necessary.

Of course, in much of this it's a matter of the personal equation. I've known avowed worshippers of the Shaw creed, women who have earned their economic independence and managed to keep free of emotional enslavement to any one man, who have never got rid of their mother's influence. One in London I knew at sixty, though directing a big organisation alone for twenty years, was still in mortal fear of her eighty-four-year-old mother, though they were separated by two hundred miles ten months in the year. Strong woman that she was, university graduate, club-leader, Socialist, reformer – everything, in fact, that her mother was not – she didn't dare argue such an obvious false doctrine as 'Prosperity by Tariff' with her octogenarian mother for fear of getting rapped on the knuckles with a ruler. In her forties, after twenty years of freedom, this 'independent' woman fell in love with a man much younger, an inevitable thing, I have observed, with 'strong' women who choose careers when they're twenty and have a Puritan aversion to normal love-making. After that her deadly fear was that her mother would find out the true state of affairs. It wasn't long before her young lover discovered it was a battle between him and the mother for the daughter. After ten years he gave up the fight and learned, in Shaw's phrase, to do without happiness. If Vivie Warren had been that mother's daughter, or, indeed, if any of Shaw's independent, desiccated young women had been her daughters, they'd have wept freely. She'd have broken Shaw himself under her iron-willed, rosy-cheeked and white-haired, but unsexed personality.

Between these extremes, however, is the vast army of normal women, mothers and daughters who love and quarrel, kiss and make up, are alternately secretive and confiding, and generally striving to be generous to one another without completely blotting out their own place in the sun.

Though derived in much from Ibsen, Shaw's women do not resemble the human heroines of the great Norwegian. Nora, in *A Doll's House*, 'new' woman that she is (or was at the time when Ibsen wrote), strong-minded and determined once she comes to know the truth, is at the same time very feminine, far from Shaw's sexless ones. She resents being considered a doll, for she feels herself a human being, a personality; she wants to be treated as a full-grown woman, with her woman's needs for understanding love and passion.

Where are the Noras and the Hedda Gablers in the plays of Shaw? In vain I search for them. His are the sexless dolls which Ibsen threw out of the doll's house.

I do not think that Shaw himself 'believes' in his women. At least there is no evidence of it in his own life. He married a woman who could disagree with him about his friends, a woman so old-fashioned that she never seems to have been even photographed with her prince of publicity.

We know only too well how the First Lady of the Land looks; the Queen of England's hats are all too familiar to us, and even the wife of our friend in retirement at Doorn has been shown often enough to us in newspapers. But how does Mrs Bernard Shaw look? Has the wife of the propagandist of the 'new' woman no personality of her own? Or has she too much of it? Has she no statements to make to the Press on every subject under the sun, or is she the old-fashioned, home-loving wife who 'leaves all that to her husband'?

Shaw's relations with women have always been gallant, coy even. The number he has surrendered to physically have been few – perhaps not half a dozen in all – the first man to have cut a path through the theatre and left it strewn with virgins. If the virgins were anything like most of the women Shaw has portrayed in his plays, I can well understand why they remained so. Everybody has noticed this vital defect in Shaw's women, their lack of mystery, grace, divinity, allure, and charm. All he can fill them with is pre-occupation with the Life-Force, which sounds like a laboratory experiment at the Rockefeller Institute.

'Every woman,' he says, 'is not Ann; but Ann is Everywoman.'

To which most of us instinctively shout, 'Every woman, but not mine.'

If he meant he discovered that, when a woman falls in love, she pursues her man till she gets him, that was no discovery at all. As Chesterton pointed out (the only writer on Shaw, incidentally, who has interested me), 'The trap may catch the mouse, but it's a little difficult to imagine the trap running after the mouse.' Still we could grant that to Shaw, if he didn't insist it had to be such an unattractive trap. If it were, the race would have ended long before he was born.

On a certain occasion, while discussing the subject of people dying because of unrequited love, Shaw found most of the group sceptical that this could lead certain people to premature death. He interrupted by saying that personally he could cite a case of a friend who was in love with a girl who refused to marry him on account of her poverty.

'And did he die?' asked a flapper.

'He did,' assured G. B. S., 'he died of it fifty years later.'

In *The Devil's Disciple* the heroine, pretty and young, reaches her own conclusion as to why the hero saved her husband vicariously. He could only have done it for love of her, she is certain, which is the correct answer, even if Shaw insists on the hero's saying he doesn't love her at all, and would have done the same for anybody in obedience to 'the law of his own nature' if she had never existed. We have the same hero remarking, 'Now, now, come, come! I don't mind being hanged, but I will not be cried over.'

What nonsense! Shaw's strong reaction against what he calls 'nine-teenth-century amorism' would have landed him in a monastery in the

Middle Ages. He argues that chastity is so powerful an instinct that its denial and starvation, on the scale on which the opposite impulse has been starved and denied, would wreck any civilisation. He insists that intellect is a passion, and that the modern notion that passion means only sex is as crude and barbarous as the ploughman's idea that art is simply bawdry. Well, he himself has tried to keep the race going, using intellect as a passion, but I haven't noticed any of his offspring about. He tries to show that art flourished splendidly when sex was absolutely barred, and cites as examples Victorian literature (which produced Dickens), painting in Italy, and sculpture in Greece, maintaining they were nursed to their highest point within the limits of a religion and a convention which absolutely barred pornography.

And that is exactly his whole trouble. The periods he speaks of were not less pornographic than our own, but more; and, even if this were untrue, what records has he of the copulations of any period in the history of art and literature? He can only guess, and having lived such a cloistered life himself, Shaw's guesses are more likely to be wrong than the ploughman's, since the latter probably never knew that Greece or Italy ever had a past.

Nobody is claiming that the current femininity in men and virulence in women is of Shaw's making. All that, too, has been going on since the Greeks and before. But it is certain that any attempt to destroy the womanly woman can only succeed in destroying equally the manly man.

It has been advanced by someone that Shaw's women are singularly English, and he certainly has declared himself that Blanche in *Widowers' Houses* was as specifically an Englishwoman as were Vivie Warren and Ann Whitefield. He even bragged that Ann, being his most gorgeous female creation, could no more be appreciated in America than Anthony Trollope's novels could be written there.

I don't think anyone could quarrel with that, or would care to.

The Male Flirt Marries

I must now tell the story of Shaw's marriage. It is perhaps the most neglected incident in his whole career, and this is a grievous oversight, for I do not think any passage in his plays is as humorous as his description of how he finally was brought from green pastures to the harness-room of life's stable.

There are many versions of this. I recently ran into a French one recounted by Maurice Verne. According to Verne, Shaw was in Florence in the middle eighteen-nineties, travelling with some friends. He fell ill, and his friends had to go on, but one of them refused to leave him to the mercies of an Italian *cameriera*.

This friend nursed him through the illness and, by the time Shaw could sit up and take notice, the situation had become so precarious that he grew alarmed.

'Heavens, what have you done?' he exclaimed to the amateur nurse.

She looked at him surprised.

'Do you realise what your friends will think?' Shaw continued. 'Nobody would believe that you did this simply out of disinterested devotion. In the eyes of the world you are lost!'

The lady wanted to know what they had better do about it; possibly the safest course to pursue, she thought, would be to remain the rest of her life in Italy; but Shaw, knowing how easily the canons of respectability can be satisfied, decided that the simplest way out would be to marry.

Thus Shaw, according to Verne, saved the honour of a lady.

As amusing and as romantic as this version is, it is not the story Shaw told me. According to my recollection, he knew his wife as a girl in Ireland. Her name was Charlotte F. Payne-Townshend and he had long been attracted by her. In the late eighteen-nineties, while cycling in the neighbourhood of her country house in England, he fell and hurt his ankle badly. He was carried into her house and she gave him first aid. That first aid grew into an overnight stay, and the overnight stay into weeks. Presently Shaw realised that the situation was getting too serious for him. But he found it very difficult to forgo his charming philanderer's speeches, especially to someone who had been so kind and sweet and such a good nurse, so helpful in every way.

'It suddenly became quite clear to me,' he later related to me, 'that if I kept on I had to make love to her and ask her to marry me, and I didn't intend to do anything of the sort. So one night I made up my mind to leave, and next morning got up very early. I started to sneak out at dawn, but the floors were of polished oak and I had a long flight of stairs before me. On almost the first step my lame leg buckled under me and I fell headlong to the bottom. Almost immediately she came out, hurried down the steps to where I lay, and helped me to my feet.'

I regret to have to add that my story is, if possible, further from the truth than the Frenchman's. The Terry correspondence has, I confess, exploded it. My excuse can be given in Shaw's own words. Paraphrasing Falstaff, he said, 'I am not only a liar myself, but the cause of lying in other men.' The two tales are built on two grains of fact. Miss Payne-Townshend did actually go to Rome before her marriage to study Italian municipal administration. But she left Shaw behind. Shaw did actually not only sprain his ankle but crash down from his crutches from a first floor to a tiled hall and break his arm; and the same lady had to put him in splints. But she had been Mrs Bernard Shaw for some time when this happened.

What really occurred was as respectable and prosaic as everything that happens to the would-be revolutionist Shaw. But to understand it, it is necessary to hark back to Shaw's domestication with his mother in their second floor in Fitzroy Square with one maid-of-all-work.

Domesticity is hardly the word for that *ménage*. You picture to yourself, doubtless, the orderly breakfast with George kissing his mother good morning, the neatly served daily meals at regular hours, and the day ending with George kissing his mother good-night. Nothing could be wider of the mark. This extraordinary pair, though in such complete accord that no unkind word ever passed between them, yet never touched one another, never had a meal together, never discussed anything with one another, in fact, though there were absolutely no reserves between them, may be said almost never to have talked to one another. They did not 'look after' one another, nor take care of one another, nor ask questions about one another's movements. Shaw spent his days in the reading-room of the British Museum, and his evenings at public meetings or on his critical duties at the opera, the concerts, or the theatres. He had his midday meal at a vegetarian restaurant. Morning and evening the slavey brought to Shaw, in the tiny room with wide open window which was his workroom, a tray with cocoa and brown bread and eggs or whatever needed little or no cooking, and dumped it on the heap of papers in which his table was smothered, and which he cleaned up two or three times a year at most, usually gaining a treasure trove of forgotten and overlaid cheques and post office orders in the process; for the ex-cashier was still as careless about his own money as he was meticulous about other people's. He rose according to circumstances, went to bed when the last post, which was then 3 a.m. in London, had gone, and in all his movements, his presence and his absence, was unnoticed and unquestioned. And his mother went her ways similarly. After his bout of smallpox in 1881 they were never seriously ill: Shaw paid for everything with a bad headache once a month or so. If they were indisposed they got over it as best they could, neither of them ever dreaming of such a resource as a doctor. Sometimes there was no maid-of-all-work; and then a charwoman came in for an hour a day for five shillings a week and also took in the washing, the net result being, as Shaw has described in *The Intelligent Woman's Guide*, that she stayed half the day and that he could not lay his handkerchief out of his hand for a moment without danger of its being snatched away to add to the wash. As such costly luxuries as painting and decorating were out of the question for at least fifteen years after the move to Fitzroy Square, Mrs Shaw had to hire a music-room when she had any pupils to accommodate.

Thus the mother and son lived their own lives and went their own ways and dreamt their own dreams without a moment's friction. Asked about his mother, Shaw said, 'Our relations were absolutely perfect; but what do I know about her? What does any man know about his mother?' He found it hard to realise that most people know too much about their mothers, especially daughters; though here he had had some enlightenment from the fact that the relations between his mother and sister were anything but perfect, and that whilst they had lived together he had had to act as peacemaker, mostly by provoking them to agree that it was all his fault.

Anyhow, the conditions at Fitzroy Square suited his temperament and his mother's precisely. They both found a happy home in having, according to the usual domestic standards and ideals, no home at all.

But this is not the whole story. Bachelors (or grass widowers) of the Shaw calibre easily find a cuckoo domestication in the houses of married friends to whom they become attached by common tastes, sympathies, and interests. Sometimes the cuckoo arrangement breaks down, as it did in the case of Wagner and the Wesendoncks when Wagner borrowed endlessly from Wesendonck and made love boundlessly to Wesendonck's wife. Sometimes it develops into an agreed and successful polygamy, as in the case of Nelson and the Hamiltons. But if the cuckoo is a reasonable sort of cuckoo, and his attachment to the nest is genuinely disinterested and the lines loyally drawn, such arrangements may be quite idyllic. The Thrales did very well with Dr Johnson. Coleridge was a real asset to the Gillmans in spite of his opium eating. Lee had not done so badly with the Shaws. And Herbert Spencer had done quite irreproachably with the Potters and their nine remarkable daughters.

Now quite the most remarkable and attractive of the remarkable Potter daughters was Beatrice. She, well launched in London Society, escaped all the seductions of the marriage market, became a self-made investigator of social problems, worked in disguise in sweaters' dens to see what they were really like, wrote a book on Co-operation, helped Booth in his enquiry into London poverty, arrived at Socialism entirely on her own observation and reasoning, and accordingly took a look at the Fabian Society just as she had taken a look at the sweaters' dens.

She sampled the Fabian leaders methodically, and picked her man without hesitation, the man being Sidney Webb. Precisely, you will observe, what Shaw had done when he sampled the Zetetical Society in 1879.

When she became Mrs Sidney Webb, she found herself loaded up with Sidney's friend Shaw. Her reported remark that 'You cannot love a sprite' indicates that the connection was not one which she herself would have chosen. And he perhaps came as near being an undesirable acquaintance at that time as anyone could be, short of the dock at the Old Bailey or the divorce court. But he was thoroughly sound on the subject of Sidney Webb; and that carried the day with Mrs Webb. She tried him during one of his holidays as the family cuckoo, and he answered almost as well as Herbert Spencer. Apart from his vegetarianism he was no trouble in the house; and he was a helpful animal to a hard-writing young couple who were still modest as to their literary skill. He had unexpected views and angles of vision to sharpen their wits, and was good fun for visitors into the bargain.

The experiment was a success; and thenceforth Shaw spent his autumn holidays with the Webbs. During his Easters he had another home with the Henry Salts. Salt, now well known as the biographer of Shelley and the author of an amusing autobiography entitled *Seventy Years Among Savages, by One of Them*, had thrown up a lucrative position as an Eton master to live the simple life according to Thoreau and Edward Carpenter, and to let himself loose as a ferocious humanitarian, vegetarian, and Shelleyan. Mrs Salt had two pet pianists to play duets with: Carpenter ('the Noble Savage') and Shaw. With the Salts, Shaw was placidly happy, with the Webbs terrifically active.

Such was the pre-marital domesticity into which Charlotte Payne-Townshend burst in 1896.

This lady had, like Beatrice Webb, been launched in Society by well-to-do parents, and had run the gauntlet of the fortune hunters of Dublin Castle and the London fashionable marriage market without compromising her spinsterhood. And she, too, was a *revoltée*, having social compunctions and religious scepticisms and general intellectual interests which finally led her to enquire into Socialism. She consulted an aunt; and the aunt introduced her to Mrs Sidney Webb. The Webbs were at that moment trying to establish the London School of Economics (as it afterwards became) with an inadequate sum bequeathed to Webb for subversive purposes at large by an eccentric town clerk of Derby. Miss Townshend reinforced the bequest to such purpose that the Webbs were able to take Number 10 Adelphi Terrace as a provisional home for the school, the lady easing the situation further by making the two top floors her residential flat.

Through the friendly relations thus established with the Webbs, Miss Townshend was invited to spend the autumn holiday with them at a rectory taken for the purpose at Stratford St Andrews, near Saxmundham in Suffolk. She accepted the invitation, and presently found herself living in the rectory with Shaw, who was at first only one of a company of disciples which included Charles Trevelyan, Graham Wallas, and another Charlotte: no other than the witty rhymester and feminist Charlotte Stetson, who, however, found the atmosphere of perpetual Fabianism and hardy bicycling only an aggravation of the dullness of a Suffolk village, and soon fled, leaving the hostess and Miss Townshend in sole feminine possession. The men also came and went; but Shaw went on for ever. The Webbs were preoccupied intellectually with their monumental work on – whichever it was just then – and sentimentally with one another, leaving their visitors plenty of time to entertain themselves.

The result was fairly inevitable. We find Shaw soon writing to Ellen Terry that he thought he would fall in love with Miss P. T. He was at this time a man of forty. Having worn out a few 'mere love affairs' and made some enduring friendships with women, he knew how to make himself agreeable to them. The lady was not unskilled in her part of the business, having seen something of the world and known some interesting men fairly intimately. This does not come to much, perhaps; but I think I know where Shaw's real charm came in, because, as I have already hinted pretty plainly, I was myself the victim of it. He had the power, or the trick, of raising great expectations as to his future possibilities. In my case he always disappointed them, and in all cases he disconcerted them; for when his opportunity came he invariably behaved with the most desolating conventionality, whilst on no provocation at all he would unexpectedly go off the rails and upset all preconceptions.

Anyhow, his trump card with Miss Townshend, I feel sure, was that he seemed a first-class investment for her money and herself, knowing that both could be useful to him. Whether she too was disappointed I have no means of knowing.

At all events when Shaw, having finished *You Never Can Tell* in Suffolk, returned to Fitzroy Square, he began spending his disengaged evenings at Miss Townshend's flat at the top of 10 Adelphi Terrace; and, as the Terry correspondence shows, she was taking part in his work as a volunteer secretary. If they were not engaged they were very clearly 'keeping company'.

But there were difficulties. Shaw was, to put it mildly, not a marrying man. It will be remembered how, in that imaginary life of his, he was never a husband and father, never even a son or a brother. He was a foundling and a free lance. His 'perfect relations' with his mother were relations which no wife could tolerate. It will be remembered too what he said of Lee: that nobody could think of him as married or marriageable, and that he never thought of himself as a married man. Shaw seems to have modelled himself unconsciously on Lee in this respect. There are many such natural bachelors in the world: Arthur Balfour for a conspicuous instance! Shaw was fond of quoting a saying of Nietzsche's to the effect that a married philosopher is ridiculous. In Shaw's *Man and Superman*, Tanner's intense repugnance to become a

married man in his last struggle against his capture by Ann is unmistakably an authentic document: no author who had not felt it could
have invented it. Shaw was more than ready to court the friendship of
any eligible woman; but if an anxious mother had asked him what his
intentions were, he would have taken to his heels at once.

On the other side Miss Townshend was a strong feminist, in revolt
against domestic ideals, jealous of her independence, very loth to change
her name, on her guard against fortune hunters, quite prepared to defy
convention, and attracted by Shaw's apparent readiness to do the same.
Between such a pair there was no reason why their association should
not continue indefinitely without any compromise of their freedom.

But the situation altered decisively. After a second autumn holiday
with the Webbs in Monmouth, the Webbs went off for a voyage round
the world. During their absence Shaw's health suddenly broke down.
He had overworked for a long time: his evenings in badly ventilated and
crowded concert-rooms, theatres, and political meetings, his Sunday
harangues, his unpaid contributions to Fabian literature and his bread-
and-butter critical articles, his play-writing and his heavy correspondence, with an occasional bout of electioneering for some Socialist
candidate or other, at last reduced him to a state in which a too tightly
laced shoe produced an abscess on his instep which, on being opened,
revealed necrosis of the bone. The mischief was not serious; for Shaw's
complete abstinence from stimulants of any kind did not permit of
his staving off a collapse beyond the possibilities of rest and rapid
recovery. Unfortunately for him, at that time the Listerian antiseptic
treatment of wounds was still in vogue; and the sinus left by the oper-
ation was stuffed with iodoform gauze at every dressing, with the
result, now well understood, that it would not heal; and Shaw was an
invalid on crutches for eighteen months until the Listerian antiseptic
was discarded for pipe water, when he immediately recovered, and
became a furious anti-Listerian just as, after his smallpox, he had become
a furious anti-Jennerian.

As an invalid, Shaw presented a new problem to Miss Townshend.
She had for the first time to visit him in Fitzroy Square. The mother-
and-son *ménage* horrified her. All the ceremony of illness to which she
was accustomed was missing. Mrs Shaw seemed to take almost no
account of her son's illness. The second floor, the appalling disorder of
Shaw's poky little study, the way in which the maid-of-all-work in any
sort of dress would appear with a meal of lukewarm eggs and put it

anywhere within Shaw's reach, usually on a heap of dusty papers, the revolting apparition of Shaw's insolvent maternal uncle the doctor, now terribly decayed as to his dress and dying of diabetes, but still addressing her with all the assurance of an Irish gentleman, and making fun of the case (of which, by the way, he was not professionally in charge), the remoteness of the last painting and papering of the premises – in short, the absence of everything demanded by a rich woman's notion of decency and order – seemed to her to ensure only one sequel: the patient's speedy death from neglect.

She took prompt measures in the shape of a house on Hindhead in Surrey, to which salubrious air she proposed immediately to carry off Shaw. His mother had not the smallest objection. Whether he went off to the Webbs or the Salts, or to an unmarried lady, was not her business: he was always going off to some house or other; and she was content provided it was one where he would be better taken care of than at the Square.

But Miss Townshend reckoned without the conventional side of Shaw. He had always scrupulously avoided doing anything that could compromise her. Whenever women had consulted him – as they often did, apparently – as to whether they should throw their bonnets over the windmills, he had always warned them to insist on the status of married women and to do nothing for a man without the guarantee of marriage. The appearances that shocked Miss Townshend had no terrors for him: he could pig through it at Fitzroy Square; and if not, he could die, not of the bad foot, but because Mozart and Raphael and Schiller died at his age, and he should either die as they did or survive like Goethe through a similar breakdown, and live to be an old nuisance. No woman's dignity was to be wounded on his account.

But Miss Townshend would have none of this nonsense. Come to Hindhead he must, and be properly nursed and fed and taken care of. The irresistible force had met an immovable obstacle; and as the immovable obstacle was a woman and the irresistible force only a man, he had to find a way out. 'Go out and buy a ring and a licence,' he said. And within a week Miss Townshend found herself a married woman; and Shaw was a married man. When the Webbs returned from their circumnavigation of the globe they found the pair on Hindhead completely settled. Shaw, no longer a free lance, took on the appearance by which this generation knows him; that of a country gentleman up in town. And he became an armchair Socialist. The dock gates, the parks, the suburban commons, the street corner pitches, the market squares, and the town halls had seen the last of him; and the Sunday At Home became a Shavian institution.

I, in my innocence, believed that people married either for love or money. Shaw would not allow that he had married for either. 'We married,' he said, 'because we had become indispensable to one another.' And that appears to be the plain truth.

He was still very ill when they were married by the West Strand registrar, still on crutches and wearing a jacket which, he swears, his crutches had worn to rags in the armpits.

Graham Wallas and Henry Salt acted as witnesses.

'In honour of the occasion they were dressed in their best clothes,' Shaw continued, as I remember his relating the incident. 'The registrar never imagined I could possibly be the bridegroom; he took me for the inevitable beggar who completes all wedding processions. Wallas, who was over six feet tall, seemed to the registrar to be the hero of the occasion, and he was calmly proceeding to marry him to my betrothed when Wallas, thinking the formula rather strong for a witness, hesitated at the last minute and left the prize to me.'

Shaw, with his Fitzroy habits of life strong on him, must have been a fearfully trying husband, especially when he was respecting his wife's independence as scrupulously as he had respected his mother's. And no doubt, having never known a disciplined house, he must have occasionally wished he could run away from domesticity without hurting her feelings. However, they stuck it; and the marriage held fast whilst divorces were flying in all directions.

Mrs Shaw saw that he was the most independent of artists and should be kept free. Provided with a comfortable home and an assured income, there were no limits to what he might do, and it is a fact that all the fruits of his successes date from the year after his marriage, though a good deal of the seeds had been planted long before. And this was Mrs Shaw's grievance, because she had bargained for an unconventional husband whose greatness would not be recognised for at least three hundred years, and presently found herself attached to a very conventional one whose popularity became more vulgar and fashionable from year to year, and on whose rapidly filling pockets her income was wasted. All marriages have a tragic spot somewhere.

I used to think of Shaw on the verge of marriage as portrayed, not by Tanner, but by Captain Brassbound. 'Look you,' says Brassbound to

Lady Cicely, 'when you and I first met I was a man with a purpose, I stood alone: I saddled no friend, man or woman, with that purpose because I was against law, against religion, against my own credit and safety. But I believed in it; and I stood alone for it, as a man should stand for his belief, against law and religion as much as wickedness and selfishness. Whatever I may be, I am none of your fair-weather sailors that'll do nothing for their creed but go to heaven for it. I was ready to go to hell for mine. Perhaps you don't understand that.'

I think Mrs Shaw did, but she didn't think anything would be gained by letting him do it. So she took him two flights up towards paradise. There isn't a chance now of his ever going to hell. Like Oscar Wilde, he's too good company.

When I came across her, however, she puffed him up beyond all bearing. I recall our meeting at the first performance of Shaw's *The Dark Lady of the Sonnets*. Some years before, I had written a play, *Shakespeare and his Love*, and when Shaw's playlet was announced publicly I wondered what borrowing he had been up to. For not only did he, like Molière, take his goods where he could find them, but what was more terrifying was that in his reaction against the nineteenth-century vanity of originality he would accuse himself of plagiarisms that did not exist, and make fulsome acknowledgements of indebtedness to authors to whom he really owed nothing, often to their great embarrassment. This time, however, he had protested that he had not plagiarised me, and had declared that I had made Shakespeare like the sentimental sailor in *Black Eyed Susan*, though God be my witness my only fault was that I had not made Shakespeare like George Bernard Shaw.

The afternoon of his play I went to the theatre and met Shaw in the entrance. He came forward in exuberant good humour. 'The very man,' he cried, as soon as he caught sight of me; 'I've been telephoning for you everywhere; but first let me introduce you to my wife and then take your place in the author's box and witness "your play".'

I was glad to meet Mrs Shaw, I replied; but I wouldn't take any responsibility for his bantling. He insisted we share his box. Finally we yielded to him, and my wife and myself went up to his box. Mrs Shaw gave us seats and tried in every way to make us comfortable.

'But Shaw,' I finally protested, 'where's he to sit?' for I saw there were only three seats.

'Oh,' Mrs Shaw replied naïvely, 'the Genius will stand there.'

When we protested, she informed us that 'the Genius preferred it'.

Later on, Robert Loraine, the actor, came in to see Shaw about a play, and poured butter over him in a stream till the stomach of one's sense turned at the apparent flattery. Ten years earlier, no actor in Loraine's position would have taken Shaw seriously as a dramatic author. Loraine, however, had staked his last penny on *Man and Superman* in America, and won. He was quite sincere.

The next day I proved (or so Arnold Bennett assured me) that Shaw's *The Dark Lady of the Sonnets* was misnamed. In his playlet, Shaw had made his heroine, Mary Fitton, jealous, hot-tempered, violent (she boxes both Shakespeare's and Queen Elizabeth's ears in a fit of rage!) Now, in the Sonnets she has none of these qualities. As I have shown in my book, *The Man Shakespeare*, the best picture of Shakespeare's love is not to be found in the Sonnets, but as Cleopatra in *Antony and Cleopatra*, and there she is pictured as jealous, hot-tempered, and violent, for she strikes the messenger and hales him about by his hair.

Shaw had taken his Dark Lady, not from the Sonnets as he pretended, but from Shakespeare's Cleopatra, or from my proof that Cleopatra was the truest, most lifelike portrait of his Dark Lady. Mary Fitton, of course, he got from Thomas Tyler. She was a sort of left-over material when he tried his hand at improving Shakespeare by writing *Caesar and Cleopatra*, which, incidentally, was Mrs Shaw's favourite of all of Shaw's plays for years.

After this meeting I did not see much of Mrs Shaw. Consequently I should be the last person in the world to be picked to paint her portrait; but since no book of this sort would be complete without Shaw's wife, I have been guided by others who are more sympathetic in their character-drawing. I exaggerate; they minimise. But I can never get out of my mind the time I first saw them in daylight after their marriage. It was in Regent Street – Shaw gaunt and slender, Mrs Shaw comparatively short and well-nourished.

Whenever I have tried to describe her I have been cried down from all corners of my own household on charges of inaccuracy. I am immediately informed that she was not short, and not fat, but very fair of build and complexion, with a small face and white hair combed straight back; in short, a woman of pleasing, quiet ways, addicted to flounces and the kind of sweeping dresses that one associates with the statues of Queen Victoria. I am also credibly assured that she has dark brown hair and green eyes; that she is always well dressed in the latest fashion and is a strong advocate of short skirts; that her precise stature is five feet seven and her weight ten stone five pounds. Readers are now in a position to imagine her according to their own taste.

Nearly all visitors take pains to tell how charming Mrs Shaw is, and how, whenever they seek to draw her into the conversation, she purposely refuses to take her cue. She will not be interviewed nor photographed. For the most part she has been willing to stay in the background, but about twenty years ago she made a translation of Brieux's *Maternity* and added two other translations of his plays to make a book. But one of the three was *Damaged Goods* (*Les Avariés*) in Pollock's translation; and not a publisher in England or America would touch it. It was all about syphilis.

'Under these circumstances,' Mrs Shaw wrote, 'the plays were laid aside, apparently for ever. But four years later M. Brieux was made a member of the French Academy. This altered the case; for mud that may be thrown with impunity at a struggling reformer and propagandist must not smirch the robe of one of the Immortals, especially under the linked banners of the *Entente Cordiale*. So my husband's New York publishers, the Brentanos, took the book in America; and I was glad to arrange with Mr Fifield to bring it out here.'

Meanwhile she had secured a performance of *Maternity* by the Stage Society. Later on she translated Brieux's *La Femme Seule* as *Woman On Her Own*, and repeated her previous feat by procuring its performance by the Actress's Franchise League and its publication in another three-play volume. Both publications were successful, the first enormously so in America. Of it she naïvely says, 'my husband consented to write a preface'; as if all the King's horses could have kept him from it.

He went further than this. In an article on *La Femme Seule*, presumably written to domestic order, he tells us 'I once scandalised the French bellettrists by remarking that Brieux is their greatest playwright since Molière. They gasped, implying that the French biographical dictionary abounds with greater names. But when I asked them to mention one, there was no reply.' They might well be struck dumb on hearing an avowed propagandist placed, as such, above Beaumarchais, Voltaire, Victor Hugo, De Musset, and Dumas, *père et fils*.

Mrs Shaw has also edited *Selected Passages from the Works of Bernard Shaw*, some of which will be sought for in vain in any published book by him. It has now fallen behind the times, as he has talked and written a good deal since.

With the struggle against the censorship over *Damaged Goods* on the stage she was concerned only as a spectator. It began with the manufacture of an Authors' Producing Society, to stage plays 'of educational and sociological character hitherto unseen in London' (really, of course, to give a 'private' performance of *Damaged Goods*) and ended when the war made short work of the censor's scruples. The Cabinet was then only too anxious to educate the soldiers on leave on the subject of venereal disease.

Mrs Shaw has a proprietary air about Shaw – the 'my husband' complex, when he isn't 'the Genius' – but she has not his appetite for publicity, and seems to prefer the more quiet corners of their flat in London.

They live now at No. 4 Whitehall Court when in town, but when they lived for thirty years in the Adelphi Terrace flat, her name, and not his, remained on the door for a while. Their country place is Ayot St Lawrence, Hertfordshire, where they are well liked as gentlefolk who contribute to the Church.

Shaw has written millions of words on marriage, but he has only had this one marriage in his life. 'Until we sublimate the marriage relation,' he once wrote, 'the difference between marriage and Mrs Warren's profession remains the difference between union labour and scab labour.' Although he has never so much as thought of asking for one, he thinks divorce should be granted for the asking without any further reason. Another belief of his is that adultery never operates when it is the sole reason, which is sound realism.

'The vulgar, and consequently official, view of marriage,' runs another opinion of his, 'is that it hallows all the sexual relations of the parties to it. That it may mask all the vices of the coarsest libertinage with added elements of slavery and cruelty has always been true to some extent; but during the last forty years it has become so serious a matter that conscientious dramatists have to vivisect legal unions as ruthlessly as illegal ones. For it happens that just about forty years ago the propaganda of Neo-Malthusianism changed the bearing of children from an involuntary condition of marriage to a voluntary one. From the moment this momentous discovery was made, childless marriage became available to male voluptuaries as the cheapest way of keeping a mistress, and to female ones as the most convenient and respectable way of being kept in idle luxury by a man.

'There has also begun a change in public opinion as to the open abuse of marriage as a mere means by which any pair can procure a certificate of respectability by paying for it, which may quite possibly end in the disuse of the ceremony for all except fertile unions. From the point of view of the Church, it is a manifest profanation that couples whose only aim is a comfortable domesticity should obtain for it the sacrament of religious marriage on pretence of unselfish and publicly important purposes which they have not the smallest intention of carrying out.'

Mrs Patrick Campbell is authority for the statement that though Shaw wrote to her and talked to her as if no other person existed in the world except her, and no other interest except his literary and political work, actually his very well-regulated house came before everything. Whatever else might betide, Charlotte must not be kept waiting ten minutes.

Compare this with the interlude of *The Apple Cart*. This interlude has absolutely nothing to do with the plot. But it is not irrelevant to Shaw's private life, and that is how it absent-mindedly got into the play.

Observe this short scene, for instance, between the king and his favourite, whose relations with the king are, according to Shaw, 'strangely innocent':

MAGNUS   Impossible, beloved. Jemima does not like to be kept waiting.

ORINTHIA   Oh, bother Jemima! You shall not leave me to go to Jemima. (*She pulls him back so vigorously that he falls into the seat beside her.*)

MAGNUS   My dear; I must.

ORINTHIA   No, not today. Listen, Magnus, I have something very particular to say to you.

MAGNUS   You have not. You are only trying to make me late to annoy my wife. (*He tries to rise, but is pulled back.*) Let me go, please.

At another point, Shaw's hero in *The Apple Cart* remarks that his wife has her limitations and that he has his.

'Now, if our limitations exactly corresponded I should never want to talk to anyone else; and neither would she. But as that never happens, we are like all other married couples: that is, there are subjects which can never be discussed between us because they are sore subjects. There are people we avoid mentioning to one another because one of us likes them and the other doesn't.'

Or this scene:

> MAGNUS But my wife? the queen? What is to become of my poor dear Jemima?
>
> ORINTHIA Oh, drown her: shoot her: tell your chauffeur to drive her into the Serpentine and leave her there. The woman makes you ridiculous.
>
> MAGNUS I don't think I should like that. And the public will think it ill-natured.
>
> ORINTHIA Oh, you know what I mean. Divorce her. Make her divorce you. It is quite easy. That was how Ronny married me. Everybody does it when they need a change.
>
> MAGNUS But I can't imagine what I should do without Jemima.
>
> ORINTHIA Nobody else can imagine what you do with her.

In truth, I can't imagine how he could do without her, either. And, whether he could or not, the pragmatic point to remember is he hasn't.

16

Experiences with Actresses

In all my days I never met a man so eager to win women and so frightened out of possessing them as Shaw. He confesses as much himself. His relations with actresses may have been like those of Magnus and Orinthia, 'strangely innocent'; but though I am one who doubts men most when they boast of conquest, I often doubt them even more when they profess innocence. But in Shaw's case I don't know what to think. I can only say that if he is indeed one of the most virtuous men that ever lived, more's the pity. He protests against actresses being treated, police court fashion, as if they were in their private lives a separate species. They are human beings, he contends; and with human beings 'all the cases are different'.

Considering his innocence, Shaw's 'release dates' about such matters, to use a publisher's phrase which he, of all people, will understand, become more enigmatic the older he gets. His long delay in refusing to sanction the publication of his correspondence with Ellen Terry is an example of what I mean.

Among their letters, affectionate as they are, there aren't a dozen which would interest the tabloid journals of Bernard MacFadden, for whom Shaw used to write articles on physical culture.

Shaw says those who are privy to backstage manners and morals are honour-bound not to gossip about them, but I rather suspect fear of a woman's deadly aim and her notorious power over juries has as much to do with this reticence as anything else. When Ibsen's plays first invaded London, Shaw proposed to give some publicity to the movement by interviewing an American actress who was with the company. To his astonishment she replied, if he wrote a word about her she would shoot him.

'You may not believe here in England that such things are possible,' she said, 'but in America we think differently, and I will do it. I have the pistol ready.'

'General Gabler's pistol?' Shaw wanted to know.

But he didn't write the interview.

Perhaps this happened early enough in his career to show him that, while women were barred from the pulpit, the Bar, the political platform, and the army, they were a real power in the theatre, far more of a power than the actors.

Indeed, he remarks somewhere that the women who, if they were men, would have been cardinals, king's counsellors, or ambassadors, go on the stage, where they are more highly paid than men and enjoy an undisputed equality of opportunity and esteem with them. He sees, except for rare instances, that the male actor is at the bottom of the professions open to men, whereas the leading lady is at the top of those open to women.

In this age of women (which explains Shaw's popularity, for comedy flourishes in times when they are important whereas tragedy holds the stage in an age of men) it isn't just a question of honour which makes it impossible to kiss and tell, but fear of consequences.

Sir Henry Irving's refusal to take up with my *Saturday Review* critic as a playwright rankled Shaw, and he cracked Irving no end. Persons uninformed thought it was because he was jealous of Irving's attention to Ellen Terry. But Shaw couldn't be jealous of anybody. He was a philanderer – a male flirt, as he himself admits – and never felt half the lavish love phrases he so madly expressed – on paper.

Do I do him an injustice? Listen, then, to his own disavowal to Mrs Patrick Campbell as late as 1912: 'Shut your eyes tight against this blarneying Irish liar and actor . . . He cares for nothing really but his mission, as he calls it, and his work. He is treacherous as only an Irishman can be: he adores you with one eye, and sees you with the other as a calculated utility. He has been recklessly trying to please you, to delight you, to persuade you to carry him up to heaven for a moment (he is trying to do it *now*); and when you have done it he will run away and give it all to the mob.'

He then goes on and begs her not to cut him off utterly. He is really worth something, even to her. She must not harden her heart against him. She is too great a woman to belong to any man, he tells her; meaning that he is too great a man to belong to any woman. He warns her against himself with passionate regard for her – sincerely too, and yet knowing it to be one of his most dangerous tricks.

Trying to get at the bottom of Shaw's relations with actresses, and believing that Act 2 of *The Apple Cart* was from life, I sought the truth from him. At first he wouldn't reply to me. His relations with actresses were in camera, professional secrets not to be divulged in their lifetime. But I kept goading him about it.

Finally he let fly at me as follows. Estimated by contemporary standards of tabloid journalism his letter isn't much of a confession, but perhaps readers would prefer to judge that for themselves:

Malvern, September 18th 1930

DEAR FRANK HARRIS – What an impossible chap you are! You want stories about actresses. Don't you know that you might just as well ask a cardinal, whose life you were writing, to give you a few stories from the confessional as ask a playwright to give away the secrets of rehearsal? After Tree's death I wrote an essay on him in a memorial volume published by the family. In that I gave the public a very slight peep behind the scenes, the man being dead. But the rule is that nothing that happens behind the stage-door must get into the Press. The actor is entitled to his stage glamour. Not until Mrs Pritchard was dead had Johnson any right to let the public know that off the stage she called her gown her gownd, and that she had never read a word of *Macbeth* except her own part and its cues . . .

All the great actresses I have known could have talked Dr Johnson's head off and written it off too. Some of them were greater off the stage than on it. But I mustn't chatter about them in public.

Tree once, joking about my vegetarianism, said to Mrs Campbell, 'Let's give him a beefsteak and see what the effect will be.' 'Please don't,' said Stella; 'he is bad enough as it is; but if he eats a beefsteak no woman in London will be safe.'

Now, that story, which has been printed, and spoiled in the printing, is quite permissible, because it is extra-professional and might have happened if we had never been inside a theatre in our lives.

Here is another incident. I once said to Tree, 'Have you noticed all through these rehearsals that, though you and I have had twenty years stage experience, and have reached the top of our profession, you treat me as an amateur beginner and I do the same to you?'

Now, that story I should not be justified in publishing if Tree were alive. It is a criticism. If I published my producer's criticisms garnished with professional incidents behind the scenes, any actor or actress would be justified in refusing to rehearse when I was present;

and the fact that most of them couldn't afford to do it, poor dears, makes privacy all the more binding on me.

As to personal relations with actresses, the affectionate freemasonry of the profession makes it very difficult to let the public see it without misleading them absurdly. Morals and emotions are not the same on both sides of the footlights. Ellen Terry and I exchanged about two hundred and fifty letters in the eighteen-nineties. An old-fashioned governess would say that many of them were wild love-letters; and yet, though we were all the time within a shilling hansom-ride of one another's doors, we never saw one another in private; and the only time I ever touched her was on the first night of *Brassbound*, when I formally kissed her hand. For some time before the war I was on much the same intimate terms with Mrs Campbell as King Magnus with Orinthia in *The Apple Cart*. Yet I was as faithful a husband as Magnus; and his phrase 'our strangely innocent relations' is true. I may say that, from Ellen Terry to Edith Evans, all the famous actresses with whom I had any personal contact have given me their unreserved friendship; but only with one, long since dead, and no great actress either (she is hinted at in my preface to Archer's plays), had I any Harrisian adventures. From Lady Colin Campbell onward, I have been familiar with celebrated beauties, and with what is by no means the same thing, really beautiful women, without either of us moulting a feather of our integrity. I am, and always have been, an incorrigible philanderer, retaining something of the obsolete gallantry of the Irishmen of my generation; but you may count the women who have left me nothing to desire on less than the fingers of one hand. To these occasions I attach comparatively no importance: it is the others which endure.

Faithfully,

G. Bernard Shaw

He was then, or so he admits, on the same intimate terms with Mrs Patrick Campbell as Orinthia, the king's favourite, was with King Magnus in *The Apple Cart*. But as usual it was all a philanderer's bluff. The sober fact is that Mrs Campbell was all the time engaged to be married to a friend of both, who was a party to the whole business. The lady got married in the middle of it exactly as Shaw got married in the middle of the correspondence with Ellen Terry. Shaw can be a wonderful lover provided it is perfectly understood that nothing is to come of it. What woman would not entertain a 'great man' as her lover on such Safety First conditions?

Let us not forget that Shaw, the ex-cashier, is an economist. I suspect that the expense of maintaining several establishments would keep him straight more than any other factor. Indeed, the suspicion is beyond theory; for he says, with some truth from the Puritan point of view, but not from mine, that 'no man who has any real work in the world has time or money for a pursuit so long and expensive as the pursuit of women'.

Letter-writing is not so expensive a pursuit, I suppose, though some have found it led to breach-of-promise suits, which can be expensive enough. You have to know your woman in this case; and, so far, Shaw has always known his.

Some of his letters read like left-over copy from *Candida*, and not like the anti-romantic Shaw we all know. For him to write a woman not his wife, 'Remember that I am always your saint, and that my ecstasy will survive disembodiment. You must always sit enthroned in heaven for me,' reads to me like Eugene Marchbanks on a busman's holiday.

Still this isn't quite the note I want to strike in closing. I find another letter to Mrs Campbell more to my liking, and more, no doubt, to hers: 'The enclosed letter from Lucy [his sister] may please you a little,' he wrote to her on June 17th, 1913. 'This marble heart was most affectionately grateful to you for that visit. You are my friend and my darling, and I forgive you for not coming down today. The country was disappointed. The rabbits and fieldmice were waiting in the lanes for you; and when they saw it was only me on my reeking, snorting bike, they scuttled away in disgust. The heavens were furious: they thundered and hurled such mouthfuls of rain at me that the lanes became torrents in five minutes.'

It sounds a trifle lonely and sad. I rather like to think the superman in love can be that now and then. Without it we should never have had *Heartbreak House*, and without that play the springs of public sympathy for Shaw would dry before he was dead five months.

17

Shaw's Sex Credo

'What do you consider the greatest obstacle to the emancipation of women?' Louis Wilkinson once asked Shaw in a long questionnaire.

'Lust,' he replied.

In examining the document I come to a revealing conclusion: Wilkinson's more simple questions take Shaw pages to answer, but the problem of all problems he could answer in a word.

Many interviewers have tried to get at this side of Shaw, but most of them have failed to find out what he really felt, because they could not get below the surface. Having lived and loved much after the manner of normal men, I was never satisfied with Shaw's answers. I wrote him in the summer of 1930, and at last got back this unsatisfactory answer:

London, June 20th 1930

MY DEAR FRANK HARRIS – I had no love-affairs. Sometimes women got interested in me; and I was gallant in the old-fashioned Irish way, implying as a matter of course that I adored them; but there was nothing in it on my side; and you, as biographer, will have to face the very un-Harrisian fact that I lived on pictures and music, opera and fiction, and thus escaped seduction until I was twenty-nine, when an enterprising widow, one of my mother's pupils, appealed successfully to my curiosity. If you want to know what it was like, read *The Philanderer*, and cast her for the part of Julia, and me for that of Charteris. I was, in fact, a born philanderer, a type you don't understand. I am of the true Shakespearean type: I understand everything and everyone, and am nobody and nothing.

Ever,

G. B. S.

I was not satisfied with his answer, feeling sure the presence of a lady secretary had prevented him from expressing himself freely. He had not answered the modern reader's Freudian curiosity, much less my own, as to how he responded to his sexual urges.

He promised to write me in his own hand on the subject later, admitting it was a very wide and complex topic on which a mere record of copulations threw no light.

While awaiting that answer, and it came in time, I sought all possible data from other sources. George Sylvester Viereck told me that Shaw had told him that he had never refused any pleasure except the alleged pleasure of destroying himself.

'Everybody who does not live in a prostitute's bed and on a diet of cocaine snow is called an ascetic nowadays,' Viereck quoted Shaw as saying, adding, 'that an author of his sort must keep in training like an athlete'.

This amused me, and confirmed something which had surprised me very early in our acquaintance – Shaw's preoccupation with athletes, and his assumption that their method of living could contribute anything to ours. I thought there must be some psychological connection between it and his long virginity. It seemed to me to indicate some constitutional weakness or incompleteness in him which made him delight to dwell on complementary excesses of strength and vigour. His boxing novel *Cashel Byron's Profession*, his descriptions of the Carpentier fights, his friendship with Gene Tunney, seemed to me so out of character that I dismissed them as an elaborate masquerade to give him an air of the hardihood nature had denied him.

On the other hand, these writings of his showed a knowledge of the game; and one of Shaw's favourite clowning poses was to represent himself as a physical coward. 'Intellectual courage,' he boasted, 'is the courage of my profession; and I possess it in the highest degree; but when the shooting begins I claim the right to creep under the bed and leave the fighting to people whose lives, being of no value, are not providentially protected by a good sensible dastardly poltroonery.' I actually found that in his youth Shaw had a reputation as a pugilist. The late Henry Hyde Champion, who in his Socialist days knew Shaw well, and was the first publisher of *Cashel Byron's Profession*, inferred from the book that Shaw was a formidable boxer. Shaw laughed him to scorn. 'I know the moves,' he said, 'just as I know the moves in chess; but that is all.' He added, however, that it had been of some service to him to be conscious that he knew how to defend himself if he got into a row. Champion's grim reply was, 'It has been more serviceable to you than you think. You would have had your head punched pretty often if the comrades had not been afraid of you.'

The truth of the matter, as I discovered, was that Shaw, with the lack of initiative on which I have had to comment so often, and which made it so easy to push him into unlikely places, got pushed into boxing by his friend the late Pakenham Beatty, who published several volumes of verse, and had a passion for pugilism. He was, like all the gentlemen boxers of that day, a pupil of Ned Donnelly, who was the original of Ned Skene in Shaw's novel. Beatty went into training for the Queensberry competitions, and insisted on Shaw acting as his sparring partner, handing him by way of instruction a copy of Donnelly's excellent little book on the subject. As Shaw was greatly superior to poor Beatty in height and reach, and, being a vegetarian, was no more troubled with ring nerves than a cow, he found boxing with a straight left an easy and harmless amusement.

Shaw, after his manner, exhorted Beatty not to train, on the ground that the Donnelly ritual was pure superstition and only made its victims nervous. As a matter of fact it made Beatty so nervous when the fatal day arrived that Donnelly gave him a stiff dose of brandy before entering the ring, the effect being to paralyse and bewilder him completely. He gave up boxing in disgust; consequently Shaw gave it up too. Edith Nesbitt, poetess and fairy-tale writer, rather mischievously set him sparring once or twice with her husband, Hubert Bland, a really formidable heavyweight, who was fortunately merciful; and there is a record of a spar with Arthur Bonner, Bradlaugh's son-in-law, a lightning flyweight who was immediately all over the slower Shaw, but, if he had a knockout punch, was amiable enough to pull it. This appears to be the whole of Shaw's experience with the gloves; but, as Champion said, it served his turn. Nobody has ever called his pugilistic bluff, and now that he is halfway through his seventies nobody ever will. All that remains of it is his own wisecrack, 'It is superfluous to bluff: all you have to do is to strike the appropriate attitudes and leave the other fellows to do the bluffing and frighten themselves with their own imaginations.'

When I saw most of Shaw he was always tired, and learning to rest in some faddy fashion from Mrs William Archer or Annie Payson Call. He had no athletic interests and played no games, excusing himself on the ground that nobody who was at all keen could bear to play with him because he did not care whether he won or lost, and absolutely refused to count when he was amusing himself. Of late years on the Riviera one heard of his playing tennis with Albert Coates on the Lago Maggiore in a state of nudity; but as he maintained that competitive games are the ruin of English manners, and provoke all the worst anti-social feelings between friends and nations, he insisted on a Shavian version of the game in which the player who placed a ball in such a way that the other fellow could not return it with the same courtesy should apologise and consider himself disgraced. He allowed Coates's young lady visitors to snapshot him in his buff, until he found that they were filling the London pictorial papers with the results; and a final encounter with an American newspaper photographer at Antibes, who took a motorboat and caught him helpless in the water (he is fond of swimming), taking plate after plate in spite of the victim's protests, gave him a surfeit of exhibitionism. Nevertheless, like Dean Inge, he is very kind to the nudists, and once sat to Alvin Langdon Coburn for a portrait 'in the altogether'; for, he says, 'though we have hundreds of photographs of Dickens and Wagner, we see nothing of them except their suits of clothes with their heads sticking out; and what is the use of that?'

On the whole, though I cannot class Shaw as an athlete, my attempt to connect his sexual coyness with physical infirmity was a failure. He is certainly an open-air, morning worker; and his way of toning up his nerves by blinding about the Hertfordshire lanes on a motorcycle, his love of motor-driving, his swimming, and his striding walk, put him in the bodily active class among men of sedentary profession. The defect in him is not physiological: it must be psychological; and I must leave it to the psychoanalyst to run it to earth. That there is a defect seems to me evident. If Shaw is a normal man, then Frank Harris is an abnormal one.

Compare his private life with Shakespeare's. While Mary Fitton was banished from London, Shakespeare could write nothing but tragedies. That went on for five years. When the queen died and Shakespeare's dark lady returned, he wrote *Antony and Cleopatra*, his greatest love-story.

As nothing like that happened in Shaw's life we can only get a text-book, sexless, sort of plays.

When I ventured to hint this somewhere, Shaw repelled the charge very vigorously. He was astonished, he said, to find me falling into such an error, and he went on: 'Archer says, "Shaw's plays reek with sex," and he is right. I have shown by a whole series of stage couples how the modern man has become a philanderer like Goethe, and how the modern woman has had to develop an aggressive strategy to counter his attempts to escape from his servitude to her . . .

'In the tiny one-act farcical comedy I published the other day, I put the physical act of sexual intercourse on the stage . . .

'To conclude with a curious observation; though poverty and fastidiousness prevented me from having a concrete love-affair until I was twenty-nine, the five novels I wrote before that (novels were the only wear then) show much more knowledge of sex than most people seem to acquire after bringing up a family of fifteen.'

He denies that he ever said love was uninteresting, but insists that what he did say was that mere paper satisfactions are useless substitutes for real sexual adventures. He suffers under the delusion that art can flourish when sex is absolutely barred, and he quotes the Victorian literature, which produced Dickens, as an example – though I do not recall that sex was barred at the time: it merely did not go into books. If it had been barred, Shaw would have never been born, nor I have written about him.

With much the same false reasoning, he claims the modern drama, with its eternal triangle, proves that love can be the dullest of subjects, though he calls love 'adultery', so as to have the full support of the Puritans.

Finally he argues that the fleshly school of art is the consolation of the impotent, which must be a surprise to schoolboys, who are its greatest patrons.

I have no doubt he is sure that he has the sanest view in the world on sex; but the word 'imagination' plays such an important part in it that he opens himself to dangerous interpretations. In *Getting Married*, he has a girl refusing to marry because she cannot endure masculine untidiness, and she hints that her imagination provides her with a series of adventures that go far beyond the bounds of reality, as did the daydreams of Shaw's own boyhood.

This strikes me as getting perilously close to Lesbianism, and gets us to what all this sublimation nonsense of Shaw's may lead to – increased perversions. Men sublimate their sex urges in prisons, and I have yet to hear that the places are not hotbeds of all possible sexual vices.

I get the keenest pleasure watching Shaw squirm through a tabooed subject. He confesses he couldn't write words Joyce uses: 'My prudish hand would refuse to form the letters; and I can find no interest in his infantile clinical incontinences, or in the flatulations which he thinks worth mentioning. But if they were worth mentioning I should not object to mentioning them, though, as you see, I should dress up his popular locutions in a little Latinity. For all we know, they may be peppered freely over the pages of the lady novelists of ten years hence; and Frank Harris's autobiography may be on all the bookstalls.'

You will observe that he can find no interest in these matters, yet he appears to have read them all and remembers them pretty well; which would seem to belie his lack of interest in them. When I find no interest in a thing, I simply drop it and forget it, but Shaw is made of sterner stuff. Like reformers and censors and smut-hounds generally, he wallows in what he likes to call dirt, not from pleasure, but as a duty. This completely contradicts his simile that pornographic novels are like offering a hungry man a description of a dinner, and that, even if the description was very lifelike, it could not satisfy his hunger. All I can say in reply is that these descriptions seem to have satisfied Shaw's hunger, for he seems to have read them all and gone without his dinner.

Of course it is pretty difficult for any man who has ever tried to be an artist to find himself on the side of the censors, and Shaw, while he roundly thumps my belief in free language, will not join the other camp, even if by thumping me he is actually pushing himself there.

His own sole contribution to the restoration of Elizabethan English has been the use of the expletive 'bloody' in *Pygmalion*. He also says that one man's poetry is another man's pruriency, and puts down Sterne's *A Sentimental Journey* as prurient. He read it as a boy, and liked it; from which he concludes that he liked pruriency when it was well done, but from which I shall conclude that he has a pretty squeamish and over-refined sense of what the word means.

You get a little additional twist to his Puritan streak on this subject when you realise that crude sex, instead of being the most enthralling literary subject to him, is the dullest until a man like Brieux goes after it with a reformer's axe. Then Shaw's interest is as keen as mine in a prettily turned leg caught in a breeze. On such an occasion as Brieux affords him, Shaw is ready to toss his hat in the air and give three rousing cheers.

What disturbs Shaw and all Puritans is that you may exhibit seduction on the stage, 'but not its consequences in criminal abortion; that you can intoxicate young people with sexual appeal in the theatre, but must not utter a word about the diseases that follow prostitution and avenge the prostitute to the third and fourth generation of them that buy of her'.

Here you see Shaw writing from the writing of others and certainly not from knowledge, for if you should ask nine young blades out of ten where they contracted a sexual disease, you would find it was not from a prostitute at all, but from some nice young girl employed in a shop or from the country. But there would be no moral in that for this garrulously great man who falls so often perilously close to being an old maid.

Indeed, I never knew anybody who could talk more on less experience than Shaw, so it must appear that, however dull crude sex is, he must have been an omnivorous reader of this subject he affects to despise. Of course I have read a good deal too, but I never have read half as much as I have lived, and for good reason. I told de Maupassant, when he first tried to induce me to write, that I preferred life to any transcription of it, and I still do.

I remember Anatole France telling me once in the Avenue du Bois, when we met casually, that he preferred the popular quarters and the quays of Paris to the aristocratic quarter where, if you admired them, ladies never answered you except with disdain.

'The little *midinette*,' he went on, 'if you say what a pretty little figure she is as she passes, will turn round and laugh with delight at you, and if you ask her to lunch she is willing if she may bring a friend for protection. Harris: thirty years ago they never wanted to be protected from me, but now, when there is no necessity, they want protection. One of the tragedies of life!'

If you compare the writings of Shaw with those of D. H. Lawrence you discover how far apart the present generation is from the last on this question of sex.

Both Shaw and Lawrence wanted to be painters, and Lawrence actually did express himself in this medium, and bravely enough to have the gallery raided where his paintings hung, and so give them a passing notoriety. Shaw never painted anything. I know he tried to, but he could not believe in the results.

To the generation before the war, Shaw had tremendous meaning, but the younger men and women who have grown up since have other gods, and among these Lawrence is foremost.

Curiously, both these men were pre-occupied with their virtue when young, though Lawrence succumbed to the frailties of this world years younger than Shaw. Shaw, you will remember, held on to his unsullied manhood till he was twenty-nine. Sex seemed to give Lawrence a terrible time until he threw off its shackles and went as far, in *Lady Chatterley's Lover*, as possible.

Shaw on Lawrence is ineffable. He says *Sons and Lovers* is the work of a man of genius, but adds, if you please, that it is 'hard reading'. Of *Lady Chatterley's Lover* he highly approves – as a document! 'If I had a marriageable daughter,' he said, 'what could I give her to read to prepare her? Dickens? Thackeray? George Eliot? Walter Scott? Trollope? or even any of the clever modern women who take such a fiendish delight in writing very able novels that leave you hopeless and miserable? They would teach her a lot about life and society and human nature. But they would leave her absolutely in the dark as to marriage. Even Fielding and Joyce and George Moore would be no use: instead of telling her nothing they would tell her worse than nothing. But she would learn something from Lady Chatterley. I shouldn't let her engage herself if I could help it until she had read that book. Lawrence had delicacy enough to tell the best, and brutality enough to rub in the worst. *Lady Chatterley* should be on the shelves of every college for budding girls. They should be forced to read it on pain of being refused a marriage licence. *But it is not as readable as* Ivanhoe *or* A Tale of Two Cities'!!!

I now come to what has likely been the most eagerly awaited, and what is sure to be the most quoted, part of this biography – Shaw's letter to me in which he reveals his unabashed belief about this thing called love. I must preface it with an apology for one or two changes which Shaw has insisted on. He is eternally wanting me to edit things down, to emasculate them for fear of offending some remote old lady whose goodwill seems essential to him now, though it did not in the least seem essential to him forty years ago when his life was really a struggle and every friend counted like a crumb in a famine. I mean, asking me to take words like 'whore' out of the following letter to me, and substituting 'mistress'; with the remark that our language of the forecastle won't do on the quarterdeck. He even changed the word 'copulations' to 'gallantries'! He tells me that I must rehabilitate myself after my escapade with *My Life and Loves*, and not use a syllable that would shock a convent.

I wonder if he reads modern novels at all. Books come to me from America, and Germany too, that use old Saxon words more robust than the ones which got me prosecuted. The world has moved. Has Shaw stood still? Substitute 'gallantry' for 'copulations'! What squeamish nonsense! I cannot, in all conscience, do it without warning the reader of the corrections, so that he may restore the words which Shaw has ordered out, and thus give his letter the force which Shaw would rob it of if left to his own devices.

It is possible that this considerateness is shy Shaw returning to the habits of his childhood, but the editing is of such a nature as to make that hypothesis remote. It reads more like a fear of what people will say, like female editing, and in a man of Shaw's stature nothing at the twilight of his career could be more ludicrous than that.

I was enormously pleased to get his own confession, and even his emasculations could not destroy its value. For those who can read between the lines, the confession is complete enough and extraordinarily interesting. But here it is, and my readers can judge for themselves:

London, June 24th 1930

DEAR FRANK HARRIS – First, O Biographer, get it clear in your mind that you can learn nothing about your sitter (or Biograph*ee*) from a mere record of his gallantries. You have no such record in the case of Shakespeare, and a pretty full one for a few years in the case of Pepys; but you know much more about Shakespeare than about Pepys. The explanation is that the relation between the parties in gallantry is not a personal relation. It can be irresistibly desired and rapturously executed between persons who could not endure one another for a day in any other relation. If I were to tell you every such adventure that I have enjoyed you would be none the wiser as to my personal, nor even as to my sexual, history. You would know only what you already know: that I am a human being. If you have any doubts as to my normal virility, dismiss them from your mind. I was not impotent; I was not sterile; I was not homosexual; and I was extremely, though not promiscuously, susceptible.

Also I was entirely free from the neurosis (as it seems to me) of Original Sin. I never associated sexual intercourse with delinquency. I associated it always with delight, and had no scruples nor remorses nor misgivings of conscience. Of course I had scruples, and effectively inhibitive ones too, about getting women into trouble (or, rather, letting them get themselves into it with me) or cuckolding my friends; and I understand that chastity can be a passion just as intellect is a passion; but St Paul's was to me always a pathological case. Sexual experience seemed a necessary completion of human growth; and I was not attracted by virgins as such. I preferred women who knew what they were doing.

As I have told you, my adventures began when I was twenty-nine. But it would be a prodigious mistake to take that as the date of the beginning of my sexual life. Do not misunderstand this: I was perfectly continent except for the involuntary incontinences of dreamland, which were very infrequent. But as between Oscar Wilde, who gave sixteen as the age at which sex begins, and Rousseau, who declared that his blood boiled with sensuality from his birth (but wept when Madame de Warens initiated him), my experience confirms Rousseau and is amazed at Wilde. Just as I cannot remember any time when I could not read and write, so I cannot remember any time when I did not exercise my overwhelming imagination in telling myself stories about women.

I was, as all young people should be, a votary of the Uranian Venus. I was steeped in romantic music from my childhood. I knew all the pictures and statues in the National Gallery of Ireland (a very good one) by heart. I read everything I could lay my hands on. Dumas *père* made French history like an opera by Meyerbeer for me. From our cottage on Dalkey Hill I contemplated an eternal Shelleyan vision of sea, sky, and mountain. Real life was only a squalid interruption to an imaginary paradise. I was overfed on honey-dew. The Uranian Venus was beautiful.

The difficulty about the Uranian Venus is that, though she saves you from squalid debaucheries, and enables you to prolong your physical virginity long after your adolescence, she may sterilise you by giving you imaginary amours on the plains of heaven with goddesses and angels, and even devils, so enchanting that they spoil you for real women or – if you are a woman – for real men. You become inhuman through a surfeit of beauty and an excess of voluptuousness. You end as an ascetic, a saint, an old bachelor, an old maid (in short, a celibate), because, like Heine, you cannot ravish the Venus of Milo or be ravished by the Hermes of Praxiteles. Your love-poems are like Shelley's Epipsychidion, irritating to *terre à terre* sensual women, who know at once that you are making them palatable by pretending they are something that they are not, and cannot stand comparison with.

Now you know how I lived, a continent virgin, until I was twenty-nine, and ran away even when the handkerchief was thrown me.

From that time until my marriage there was always some kind lady available, and I tried all the experiments and learned what there was to be learnt from them. They were 'all for love'; for I had no spare money: I earned enough to keep me on a second floor, and took the rest out, not in money, but in freedom to preach Socialism.

When at last I could afford to dress presentably I soon became accustomed to women falling in love with me. I did not need to pursue women: I was pursued by them.

Here, again, do not jump at conclusions. All the pursuers did not want sexual intercourse. They wanted company and friendship. Some were happily married, and were affectionately appreciative of my ready understanding that sex was barred. Some were prepared to buy friendship with pleasure, having made up their minds that men were made that way. Some were sexual geniuses, quite unbearable in any other capacity. No two cases were alike: William Morris's dictum 'that they all taste alike' was not, as Longfellow puts it, 'spoken of the soul'.

I found sex hopeless as a basis for permanent relations, and never dreamt of marriage in connection with it. I put everything else before it, and never refused or broke an engagement to speak on Socialism to pass a gallant evening. I liked sexual intercourse because of its amazing power of producing a celestial flood of emotion and exaltation of existence which, however momentary, gave me a sample of what may one day be the normal state of being for mankind in intellectual ecstasy. I always gave the wildest expression to this in a torrent of words, partly because I felt it due to the woman to know what I felt in her arms, and partly because I wanted her to share it. But except, perhaps, on one occasion I never felt quite convinced that I had carried the lady more than half as far as she had carried me: the capacity for it varies like any other capacity. I remember one woman, who had a quite innocent sort of affectionate worship for me, explaining that she had to leave her husband because sexual intercourse hurt her physically, 'like someone sticking a finger into my eye'. Between this extreme case and the heroine of my first adventure, who was sexually insatiable, there is an enormous range of sensation; and the range of celestial exaltation must be still greater.

When I married I was too experienced to make the frightful mistake of simply setting up a permanent mistress; nor was my wife making the complementary mistake. There was nothing whatever to prevent us from satisfying our sexual needs without paying that price for it; and it was for other considerations that we became man and wife. In permanence and seriousness my consummated love-affairs count for nothing beside the ones that were either unconsummated or ended by discarding that relation.

Do not forget that all marriages are different, and that a marriage between two young people followed by parentage cannot be lumped in with a childless partnership between two middle-aged people who have passed the age at which it is safe to bear a first child.

And now, no romance; and, above all, no pornography.

G. B. S.

18

Technique

Though his technique in love may be pitifully incomplete, few people realise what a talent Shaw has for the technical side of stage direction and to what extent his success can be traced to this fact. It's hard enough to keep a play going when your drama is full of action, and for Shaw to have been able to keep his round table conferences on the move was little short of genius.

Recitation on a platform, with the spectators seated around the reciter in the medieval fashion, was long out of date before Shaw arrived, and yet he managed to use this minstrel-show idea in *The Apple Cart* without the audience walking out. He could only do this because his knowledge of stage technique and direction was as wide as anybody's, and if he didn't use the ordinary technique that a scene called for, it was not because he didn't know it, but because he had discarded the standard 'business' for something more to his taste.

A letter he wrote to Matthew McNulty, his old schoolfellow, has been published under the title *The Art of Rehearsal*. It gives his technical routine as producer in a couple of thousand words. He once asked Elgar whether there was any manual of musical composition worth reading. Elgar told him that the half sheet or so of tips which Mozart jotted down for his pupil Sussmaier, published in England as *Mozart's Succinct Thoroughbass*, contains everything that can profitably be handed on. Shaw's Succinct Play Producing may have been the result of that hint. His letter certainly looks as small beside the volumes on the subject by Gordon Craig and his school as Mozart's little memorandum beside the enormous literature of harmony and counterpoint; but it is useful in the pioneering camps of the drama; and it throws some light on his methods.

Shaw's manners were always ingratiating, his directions usually helpful, and altogether he carried an air of angelic sweetness while he sometimes undid the work of weeks of another man quite as competent as himself in the matter at issue. His manners alone saved him from being hit with an axe. He knew that the secret was to do things without making people nervous.

He steadily refused to keep actors up until three in the morning, and declared that plays would be much better produced if there were a stiff Factory Act limiting producers to three hours a day.

Some critics think Shaw's stage directions mostly superfluous and generally not important, but Shaw insists that the printed play must not only be readable but practicable as a prompt copy for producers. At rehearsal, however, an almost invariable incident with Shaw is his personal directions being met with 'But, Mr Shaw, the book says – ' and his reply, 'Oh, damn that book! it sets everybody wrong.'

Shaw shows the clear difference between novel- and play-writing. Novelists, he points out, do not write, 'A keen pain shot through the mother's heart, for she saw at a glance that her child had not many chapters to live.' Nor should playwrights inform the audience that 'part of the stage is removed to represent the entrance to a cellar'. He insists that 'a dramatist's business is to make the reader forget the stage and the actor forget the audience, not to remind them of both at every turn'.

Early in his dramatic career, Shaw developed a theatrical formula that he often gave – without extra charge – to aspiring playwrights. All one needed, Shaw would tell them, was 'an idea of a dramatic situation. If the playwright imagines it a splendid, original idea, whilst it is, in fact, as old as the hills, so much the better. For instance, the situation of an innocent person convicted by circumstances of a crime may always be depended on. If the person is a woman, she must be convicted of adultery. If a young officer, he must be convicted of selling information to the enemy, though it is really a fascinating female spy who has ensnared him and stolen the incriminating document.'

With such 'plots', he assured beginners, the success of the play may be regarded as assured, 'if the writer has any sort of knack for his work'.

Comedy was more difficult, he believed, because it required a sense of humour; but the process was essentially the same: the manufacture of a misunderstanding.

'Having manufactured it, you place its culmination at the end of the last act but one, which is the point at which the manufacture of the play begins. Then you make your first act out of the necessary introduction of the characters to the audience, after elaborate explanations, mostly conducted by servants, solicitors, and other low-life personages (the principals must all be dukes and colonels and millionaires), of how the misunderstanding is going to come about. Your last act consists, of course, of clearing up the misunderstanding, and generally getting the audience out of the theatre as best you can.'

As a rule, Shaw never follows the precepts he gives others, but so far as his advice for the writing of plays is concerned, he certainly has.

'I avoid plots as I would the plague,' he tells us. 'I have warned young playwrights again and again that a plot is like a jigsaw puzzle, enthralling to the man who is putting it together, but maddeningly dull to the looker-on.' So his plays are not really dramas in a legitimate sense, and even less in the backstage melodramatic sense.

They are quixotic, but his quixotism differs from that of the Spanish don in that it is too narrowly and self-centredly Shavian, even though he has ranged from the dentist's chair to the Inquisition, from a camp in the Wild West to the throne of Cleopatra, from a Salvation Army hut to 'as far as thought can reach'.

He warns us that the real process of his windmill-fighting is very obscure, but he is sure that 'the result always shows that there has been *something behind*, all the time, of which I was not conscious, though it turns out to be the real motive of the whole creation'.

He was heading in the direction of greatness in *Candida* and *Saint Joan*, but he always seemed to return to the dry comic or to poking in the desert sands of social reform and laughing to himself as the sand fell into the hole again. Not that way lies immortality, however skilled the technician. Great themes are in great tragedies; passing amusement in your comedies.

Shaw has somewhere said that it is not possible to train one to become a playwright or dramatist, unless nature has done ninety-nine per cent of the work. 'I know a good deal of stage technique which I did not know when I wrote my first play, but my first play held the audience as effectively as my last.'

Considering the lack of heat in his writings, it's surprising how Shaw can get so much go and gusto in his style. Like the London omnibuses that weave rapidly in and out of a maze of traffic, he gets to his destination with astonishing speed. This would indicate that, for all his wordiness, he does seem to know where he is going, since he gets there eventually.

His convictions are his style. To him the whole art of writing simply depends on assertion. The degree and quality of that power depends on the firmness and strength of your conviction. Since Shaw has nothing but convictions, his style ought to be sharply defined, and it would be if his convictions were not so contradictory. He is a Socialist, a Fabian, a pacifist, a vegetarian, a teetotaller, and many other things. He is the champion anti: he is anti-capitalist, anti-cannibalist, anti-smoke, anti-drink, anti-royalist, anti-democrat, anti-vivisectionist and anti-inoculationist, and many others. Moreover, he is pro and counter in many things at the same time, for he is pro-war and against war; he is pro-democracy and against parliament, pro-evolution and counter-Darwin, pro-nationalism and counter-patriotism, pro-prudery and counter-censorship, and so forth *ad infinitum*.

In short, our dear Shaw, a man of no principle, swears by many. These are often contradictory and even mutually exclusive. Is it any wonder, then, that his style often lumbers along like the London buses I have just used as a comparison?

In this matter of his stage technique and the comparison with Shakespeare, Shaw has given us a helpful document in a letter which Louis Wilkinson has passed on to me:

> *10 Adelphi Terrace, London, W.C.*
> *December 6th 1909*

DEAR SIR – I note in your syllabus the following sentence: 'Significance of elaborate stage directions. Reasons why these are not needed by the greater dramatists.' I should strongly advise you not to meddle with questions of practical stage management on the strength of a purely literary equipment. If you compare the Shakespearean stage with the modern stage, you will find two points which would be quite worth dealing with in a lecture by a practical stage-manager with a historical knowledge of his craft derived, not only from books and tradition, but by actual observation of performances, such as those at Oberammergau and elsewhere, in which the old conditions still survive. The first of these two points is the absurd extent to which Shakespeare was compelled to incorporate stage directions in his dialogue, making his characters tell the audience what they are supposed to be doing, because the physical conditions of representation did not permit them actually to do it, and because the imperfect differentiation of dramatic dialogue from epic and literary poetry prevented both the author and the audience from seeing anything absurd in Macbeth saying to Macduff, 'Before my body I cast my warlike shield,' although if in a modern melodrama the villain were to say, 'Forth from its pouch I draw my deadly pistol,' the whole audience would shriek with laughter.

The second point is the enormous loss we suffer because Shakespeare did not put into literary form the stage directions which he must have given to his actors, not so much as to the mere tricks of gesture, movement, pace, etc., as to the feeling with which the speech should be delivered. For want of these the most distressing misconceptions, not only of scenes from his plays, but of entire characters, have become traditional on the English stage. To conclude that Shakespeare was able to dispense with elaborate stage directions without suffering, merely because, as a matter of fact, he did dispense with them, seems to me, if you will excuse my frankly saying so, simply stupid. It may as well be said that because Mozart, though we know by tradition that he was rather exacting when he was conducting his own works, nevertheless left only the most slender and conventional written directions on his scores, the much more minute and elaborate directions of Wagner are superfluous. The practical result is that a really Mozartian performance is much rarer than a really Wagnerian one.

The reason my stage directions are more elaborate than Shakespeare's is that Shakespeare needed only a specification of dialogue for use in the theatre under his own personal direction, whereas when I began my career I had to give my plays a complete artistic existence as printed books, because I could not get my plays performed in England at all, and in America and Germany, where they first gained their hold of the stage, I could not superintend their production personally. And even if such personal superintendence had been possible, I should still have been warned by the experience of Shakespeare and Mozart not only to provide for future generations (which may not be concerned with my work at all), but also for the mass of readers who live too far from theatres to make the acquaintance of dramatic works by witnessing actual performances.

I have noticed that writers who have no practical experience of the art of producing plays – which is as much my profession as writing them – are fond of pointing out that my stage directions are really literary sallies and not stage directions at all. This is simply ignorance on their part. Nothing but actual experience can teach anyone what it is that an actor really wants over and above that purely technical instruction which is common to all plays and need not be set down. A stage direction need not tell an actor *how* to act: it should tell him *what* he is to act. There is only one effect to be produced; but there may be fifty different ways of producing it.

I hope I have said enough to convince you with regard to the passage I have quoted from your syllabus that in it you step on to difficult and dangerous ground – ground that can hardly be trodden safely by anyone who has not had a good deal of technical experience behind the curtain.

Yours faithfully,

G. Bernard Shaw

Wilkinson's point, though buried under Shaw's wordiness, was well taken. He maintained that a great dramatist incorporates his stage directions in his characterisations – completely. As the character becomes alive through his speech and action and the speech and action of other characters, what is the need of all this parenthetic 'reluctantly', 'rising brightly', 'striking himself on the chest', 'with magnificent snobbery', 'a pause', 'crossly, without looking around', 'encouragingly', 'powerfully', 'in consternation', 'peeping out', and all that rot?

The foregoing letter bears out Wilkinson's contention. Shaw can't draw characters for nuts. They all have his own weakness, except where he becomes a mere reporter, as in *Saint Joan*, and borrows almost wholly from the court record.

You will observe how he constantly drives his shafts at Shakespeare. That name has stuck in his throat for forty years. I shall tell now how it came about.

19

Greater than Shakespeare?

Bernard Shaw is known to everyone, but the world does not see him at all as I see him. To understand the perverse Puritanism of which Shaw is capable it is only necessary to remember that seriously he puts Bunyan above Shakespeare. He saw in Bunyan a manly acceptance of life as a serious and high adventure, whereas in Shakespeare he found nothing but a sort of disappointed voluptuary. Shaw will not understand that whoever climbs to the highest heights has need of an intenser will-power than those who remain on a lower level.

I have had numerous disputes with Shaw about Shakespeare. Again and again, when he was my critic on *The Saturday Review*, he referred in his theatre articles to Shakespeare, and I soon saw that he was using the ordinary English opinion on Shakespeare and had no definite views of his own, beyond the fact that he had adopted Tyler's theory that the dark lady of the sonnets was Mistress Mary Fitton.

I wrote to him once: 'You are writing so brilliantly on the weekly theatre-happenings, why on earth drag in Shakespeare always like King Charles's head, as you know nothing about him.'

I got an answer by return: 'What in thunder do you mean by saying I know nothing of Shakespeare? I know more about the Immortal Will than any living man,' and so forth and so on.

I replied: 'Come to lunch one day at the Café Royal, and I'll give you the weeds and the water your soul desires, and prove, into the bargain, that you know nothing whatever about Shakespeare.'

He came. I had a porterhouse steak, a generous lump of Limburger cheese, and a couple of liqueurs. Harold Frederic, who was present, had the same. Shaw had a penn'orth of macaroni and some Apollinaris. He soon finished, and sat contemplating us with the face of a judge at whose elbow lies the black cap. I wanted another porterhouse steak. So did Harold. But with that face fixed on us we lost our nerve. I began fencing with Frederic to make him speak first. He tried to put it on me.

We almost quarrelled. (We always almost quarrelled.) I forget which of us gave in. Whichever it was said feebly, 'If you will have another *entrecôte*, I don't mind if I do too.' I only know that we both had another, and that the elbow of the hanging judge moved nearer to the black cap.

In desperation I swallowed half a tumbler of neat brandy.

'You believe,' I shouted, 'that because Shakespeare left Stratford after being married a couple of years, and did not return for eleven years, he loved his wife – the wife whom he insulted by leaving her in his will "the second-best bed"! Aren't you ashamed of yourself? Here's Shakespeare, the most articulate creature that ever lived, the greatest lord of language in recorded time, unable in his will to express a passionate emotion so as to be understood. Why, had he even written "our bed, dear", as the common grocer would have done, we'd all have known what he meant. Shakespeare could never write "the second-best bed" without realising the sneer in the word and intending us to realise it as well. Besides – '

'My dear Harris' – it sounded like 'Prisoner at the bar' – 'the dowager always gets the second-best bed or the second-best room or the second-best house. The best belongs to the heir and his consort. Common form, Frank, common form, I assure you. No sentimental significance whatever.'

I would not be put down. I looked him in the face as steadily as I could after the brandy, and ordered another steak. If Frederic had not mercifully taken half of it I should not be alive now. I have never been quite the same man since that luncheon.

Poor Frederic's death was announced a few days later.

I then began my articles on Shakespeare, which afterwards grew into books; but Shaw kept writing again and again on the subject and always with a bias.

Shaw's explanation of his anti-Shakespearean campaign under my editorship is – Ibsen. Shaw had written his *Quintessence of Ibsenism* and was judging everything on and off the stage by Ibsen's standard. Many lesser men suffered by that standard; but, as Shaw says, Shakespeare was the most conspicuous victim.

'It is useless to talk of Shakespeare's depth now,' wrote Shaw; 'there is nothing left but his music. Even the famous delineation of character, the Molière-Shakespeare-Dumas-*père* novel, is only a trick of mimicry. Our Bard is knocked out of time. There is not a feature left on his face.

Hamlet is a spineless effigy beside Peer Gynt, Imogen a doll beside Nora Helmer, Othello a convention of Italian opera beside Julian.'

He was reluctant to admit Shakespeare's gentleness and his abandonment to passion; the fact that the loss of Lady Mary Fitton, the woman he loved, embittered Shakespeare and turned him from a writer of comedies and histories into a writer of tragedies, degraded him in Shaw's opinion and thus made me conscious of a British hardness in Shaw which came, I thought, from want of passion, from lack of feeling. Shaw was, too, impatient with weakness and parasites – anything but a lover of the underdog. I grew to think of him as a little obstinate, English in mind and not Celtic at all, and time has proved that theory to be correct.

He underrated the enduring fascination of the reckless wastrel type. Yet in one generation the dour Cromwellian veterans planted in Ireland all yielded to the charm of the Irish nature and became, as the saying went, more Irish than the Irish themselves. Even if one prefers the English rose to any other flower, still one may admire the bravery of daffodils dancing naked in the wind, or the magic of bluebells blushing in the copses. There is room surely in God's garden for every variety of flower.

There is no doubt, of course, that Shaw speaks the truth when he asserts that he is 'fond, unaffectedly fond, of Shakespeare's plays'. He recalls the days of the New Shakespeare Society, under F. J. Furnival, as bright spots of experience.

I want to put it down black on white, in justice to Shaw, that he fights hard for the performance of Shakespeare's plays in their integrity, and has succeeded in seeing about thirty of the master's plays performed on the stage. Yet that in no way altered his attitude to Shakespeare nor his conception of his masterpieces. He could see neither the deep psychology nor the humanity and wisdom of the Bard, and he insisted on emphasising only the musical quality of the plays. Thus he could write: 'It is not easy to knock this into the public head, because comparatively few of Shakespeare's admirers are at all conscious that they are listening to music as they hear his phrases turn and his lines fall so fascinatingly and memorably; whilst we all, no matter how stupid we are, can understand his jokes and platitudes, and are flattered when we are told of the subtlety of the wit we have relished, and the profundity of the thought we have fathomed. Englishmen are specially susceptible to this sort of flattery, because intellectual subtlety is not their strong point. In dealing with them you must make them believe that you are appealing to their brains when you are really appealing to their senses and feelings. With Frenchmen the case is reversed: you must make them believe you are appealing to their senses and feelings when you are really appealing to their brains.'

About 1910, when the National Shakespeare Memorial Committee announced *The Dark Lady of the Sonnets* as a new play by Shaw, I was moved to laughter, as I had been many times before by Shaw's presumption in this field of letters.

Fourteen years before, provoked by Shaw's nonsense, I had written my articles on Shakespeare, in which I showed in especial that Hamlet was a good portrait of Shakespeare, for the master had unconsciously pictured Hamlet over again as Macbeth and as Jaques, Angelo, Orsino, Lear, Posthumus, Prospero, and other heroes. With his usual quickness, Shaw proceeded to annex as much of this theory of mine as he thought important. In the preface of *Man and Superman*, for instance, he took my discovery and used it as if it were his. He wrote: 'He (Shakespeare) must be judged by those characters in which he puts what he knows of himself, his Hamlets and Macbeths and Lears and Prosperos.'

I mention this so that it may be placed opposite his remark in one of the letters which I have used as a preface, and in which I am roundly berated for the biographical method I used in arriving at a new portrait of Shakespeare.

I do admit that in *Three Plays for Puritans* he gave me a casual mention, remarking that 'all Shakespeare's genuine critics, from Ben Jonson to Mr Frank Harris, have always kept as far on this side of idolatry as I', but that is not saying I admit him in our class merely because he goes to the same school.

Some years later I wrote a play, called *Shakespeare and his Love*, for Beerbohm Tree. Shaw read it. Stopping me on the street one day, he remarked, 'You have represented Shakespeare sadder than he was, I think; but you have shown his genius, which everyone else has omitted to do.'

After all this, Shaw wrote *The Dark Lady of the Sonnets*. He even showers me with his kind of praise in his preface, remarking at one point, 'The only English writer who has really grasped this part of Shakespeare's story is Frank Harris; but Frank sympathises with Shakespeare.'

This is equivalent to saying that all the other parts of Shakespeare's story had been grasped by someone else, presumably by Shaw himself, and not by me. I likened it at one time to Mr Cook's saying: 'The only American who really knows anything about Polar exploration is Captain Peary, though he used his knowledge quite stupidly.' One can imagine that such testimony from such an authority would have been very grateful to Captain Peary.

I pointed out that Shaw's sole contribution to our knowledge of Shakespeare is the coupling of him with Dickens, which is very much the same thing as if he tried to explain Titian by coupling him with Hogarth. This, in my opinion, was Shaw's only original observation on the subject of Shakespeare, and its perfect originality I should be the last to deny to this day.

I seemed to have been a little indignant about it in 1910, for I recall asking, 'Is this the best Shaw can do with his astonishing quickness and his admirable gift of lucid, vigorous speech? Will he, who is not poor, always be under our tables for the crumbs? Why should he not make a feast of his own? Why does he not take himself in hand and crush the virtue out of himself and distil it into some noble draught?'

He once coolly asserted that he had my ideas ten years before, leaving it to be inferred that he, the most talkative of men, had concealed them carefully. The truth is I let him write himself out on the subject before expressing myself, and then in quite a contrary vein.

I had, perhaps, an extra piety of Shakespeare. I have still; but, unlike the dolts who put up saintly statues to him, I knew of his frailties and could forgive them easily, for I loved him much. The soul tragedy of Shakespeare is not the stuff for plays. Indeed, in my own case, my excessive love for the man has been a hindrance to me as a playwright. Shakespeare's glaring fault, Shaw insists, is his intellectual incoherency. He admits that Shakespeare is a great poet, humorist and storyteller, but he damns his studies of character and society as crushingly inadequate, flat and disappointing.

Shaw forgets that the Bard was concerned more with the individual than with the collectivity; indeed, exclusively so. Human character, the great universal species, man in his thousand psychical variations, was Shakespeare's theme. A theme universal and, for all we know, eternal, with its fundamental passions of love, jealousy, envy, the will to power, and so forth – passions as primitive as they are enduring.

Of course there were rich and poor in Shakespeare's time, and social problems, even if less consciously formed than in our day: indeed in Shakespeare you will find enough allusions to the sad condition of the disinherited of the world. He was aware of them. But to parade them on the stage was another matter – in those times.

You must remember in what small esteem actors and plays in general were held in Shakespeare's epoch. Their theatres were kept outside the city walls, like the refuse. Shakespeare knew that social problems could not be put on the stage. It would have served no purpose. It would simply not have been tolerated.

Poets had a far better standing, and Shakespeare as a poet had a standing above most. Yet, because the Queen of England exiled Mary Fitton from London for five years, Shakespeare never wrote a line of eulogy about the queen when she died. All the others said the conventional things in very pretty phrases, but Shakespeare would not even give lip-service to the dead he despised.

Now this act of omission of his took as much courage in Shakespeare's day as the most flagrant apostasy would have taken in wartime Europe in 1914. I contribute it here and beg you to consider it again when Shaw's war record is revealed, and then ask you just what basis Shaw has for his claims that he stands on Shakespeare's shoulders.

Of course, if Shakespeare lacked a social conscience he didn't lack personal courage. These reformers, these Ibsens, Tolstoys, and Shaws, see the earth as a vale of tears, and they burn with zeal to dry at least those that are caused by man's inhumanity to man. Viewed from that hilltop, all human effort is insignificant, even useless and often harmful, unless it serves the great cause of the Tolstoys and Shaws. All art, poetry and the drama included, is good or bad – from that standpoint – in proportion as it serves the cause. It is therefore that Tolstoy refused to recognise Shakespeare's greatness as in fact he condemned all art and literature that did not directly advance the gospel of human equality, and peace and love among men.

By what right, though, can Shaw apply the 'social consciousness' criterion to Shakespeare?

Perhaps by the right of superior dramatic achievement? For did he not himself declare, with Shavian modesty: 'If my play *Widowers' Houses* is not better than Shakespeare, let it be damned promptly.'

Their conception of moral values is fundamentally different, and, in that sense, Shaw considers his own work far higher than Shakespeare's. He amplifies his meaning by saying that 'the reason why Shakespeare and Molière are always well spoken of and recommended to the young is that their quarrel is really a quarrel with God for not making men better. If they had quarrelled with a specified class of persons with incomes of four figures for not doing their work better, or for doing no work at all, they would be denounced as seditious, impious, and profligate corruptors of morality.'

It is clear, then, that Shaw judges Shakespeare by the yardstick of the 'proletcult'. In other words, by the Socialist standard of value, the Marxist criterion of 'social usefulness'.

Bearing this in mind, it is not difficult to understand the difference in the portraits painted of the same person by Shaw and Shakespeare. Take Shakespeare's Cleopatra, for instance. I have always considered his sorceress of the Nile a most wonderful study, the most remarkable complex woman's portrait that was ever painted; a miracle of revelation and a miracle, too, of expression. This portrait of his love – for Cleopatra is, of course, the dark lady of the sonnets – will always rank in my estimation with his Hamlet.

But Anatole France has portrayed a Cleopatra too, and though Shakespeare makes her tall, Anatole France will have it that she was little, because that was his personal predilection. He wanted her *petite* and young, although he knew that she was nearly fifty. But he liked Parisian *midinettes*, so his Cleopatra had to be a Parisian *midinette*, *petite*, *très jeune*, and *très mignonne*.

Shaw, contrarily, has made his Cleopatra a heartless, soulless, cruel little cat. I am convinced that Shaw, Socialist Puritan that he is, could not conceive the real Cleopatra, who was neither.

Nor can he conceive Caesar. As the sensuous and seducing serpent of the Nile is only a prostitute to Shaw, so is the Bard's human – all-too-human – Caesar but a make-believe and weakling in Shaw's eyes.

Shakespeare's play is extraordinarily full-blooded and passionate; he is over-sexed, one would say, and this full tide of lust in him shows, not only in his hero's insane abandonment to his passion, but also in the superb richness of language and glow of imagery. His intellect is implicit, showing mainly in side figures such as Caesar and Enobarbus, and in regal magnificence of phrase:

> Age cannot wither her, nor custom stale
> Her infinite variety; other women cloy
> The appetites they feed, but she makes hungry
> Where most she satisfies; for vilest things
> Become themselves in her.

Shaw's work in comparison is thin and bloodless; intellectually very interesting, but the colour is subdued, it is all in cool greys and dark shadows like a Whistler, or Franz Hals in his old age.

'Caesar was not in Shakespeare, nor in the epoch, now fast waning, which he inaugurated,' Shaw argues. 'It cost Shakespeare no pang to write Caesar down for the merely technical purpose of writing Brutus up. And what a Brutus! A perfect Girondin.'

Excellent criticism, but it does not do justice to Shakespeare. Shaw's Caesar is Bernard Shaw, and his contempt for Cleopatra's wiles is very amusing, and his intellectual appreciation of his position and his duties is quite admirable, but I do not find in Shaw's Caesar either the ruthlessness of the Roman or the will-power and dignity of the world conqueror. Plutarch's Caesar gives us a far better picture of a man. Who can ever forget young Caesar dominating the pirates and daring to tell the chief to his face that he would hang him after paying him his ransom? I find more of the real Roman emperor in Shakespeare than in Shaw. When Antony challenges Augustus to fight, the second Caesar's answer is soul-revealing.

> Let the old ruffian know
> I have many other ways to die; meantime
> Laugh at his challenge.

The master of the world has nothing but disdain for the 'sworder'. And when his deserted sister weeps, and he has to tell her that Antony has gone back to the serpent of old Nile, he adds:

> Cheer your heart . . .
> But let determin'd things to destiny
> Hold unbewail'd their way.

There is no line in all literature with so much of Rome's majestic domination in it.

Greatness of insight and soul is revealed again and again in Shakespeare's Romans.

It has been justly said that the critics of Shakespeare have made him in their own image, as man has made his gods. However much I might deny it in my own case, for I worked thirteen years before I got hold at last of *The Man Shakespeare*, whereas striking him off in my own image would have been a month's job, I believe the criticism is true of

Shaw. Indeed, he admits as much. 'I am convinced,' he writes, 'that Shakespeare was exactly like myself.'

It was clever of Shaw, of course, never to have attacked the great Elizabethan poet on any point except 'voluptuousness' and lack of 'modernity', for only in these virtues could Shaw pretend to be 'greater'. Virtues which are, as a matter of fact, Shaw's fatal weaknesses.

He could not attack Shakespeare's gift of words nor his stagecraft, but merely what he considered Shakespeare's limitation of ideas, bound by the limitations of his time. A modern battleship may be greater than an Elizabethan man-of-war, but I doubt if Admiral Jellicoe had more brains than Drake. I apply the scepticism with greater force to any comparisons between Shaw and Shakespeare.

Considering Shaw's early career as a clerk, it might be amusing to record a story about Shakespeare in this connection.

One Henry Morley, professor of the University of London, happened to be moved by my assertion that Shakespeare had had a nervous breakdown about 1608 or 1609 and had never really recovered from it. His later works, I pointed out, were all replicas of earlier ones. And these later productions lacked the passion and love of life which made his earlier works memorable.

The London professor was struck by this, and in an essay set forth my conclusion, but naturally he wanted to justify it in a new way, and the way that suggested itself to him was to say that the breakdown was manifested in Shakespeare's shaky handwriting! This *gaffe* amused me.

Some 'varsity man wrote to me at the time, asking me if I would contribute an article on Shakespeare to *The Cambridge Review*. I used the occasion to hold the professor up to ridicule, and incidentally to tell the truth about Shakespeare's handwriting.

I pointed out that Shakespeare's writing, good or bad, had nothing whatever to do with his nervous breakdown. I myself frequently write with a shaking hand at ten and a mighty steady one after the noonday luncheon coffee and liqueur. That might have been Shakespeare's case too, though it happens it wasn't, for he has taken the pains in *Hamlet* to tell us the truth about his writing.

In Shakespeare's day, as in our own, it was a convention of Englishmen of the better class to write badly; only clerks were supposed to write legibly, and so all persons who wished to be considered gentlemen were apt to write badly as Shakespeare did.

Here is what he tells us in *Hamlet*:

> I once did hold it, as our statists do,
> A baseness to write fair, and labour'd much
> How to forget that learning; but, sir, now
> It did me yeoman's service . . .

In other words, Shakespeare had as a boy learned to write well – had no doubt been proud of his good writing, and then in London probably had met this tradition that only clerks wrote legibly, and so did his best later to forget his learning and tried to write badly. Anyone who studies his signature will see that his German script has excellently formed letters.

Shaw tells us how he had to discard his boyish straggly sloped handwriting for a straight-up, clear, well-formed hand, when Fate kicked him from his junior clerk's stool to an abhorred eminence as chief cashier. Had he known of this scorn among gentlemen for well-rounded letters he might have gone Shakespeare in his twenties, though I doubt it, because snobbery was almost imperative in Shakespeare's time, whereas today we have something of a choice.

I was asked where was the proof that Shakespeare was speaking of his own handwriting and not of Hamlet's. The proof is simple. 'Statists' in the foregoing quotation stands for statesmen. Statesmen like Essex and Southampton, whom Shakespeare met on the stage of the Globe, were very important persons indeed to the little actor-dramatist; but statesmen would not have been important people to Prince Hamlet, so that clearly Shakespeare is here talking in his own person.

Now, never before, so far as I know, had this interesting little piece of Shakespeare's biography been published, but since then it has been used by all sorts and conditions of men from Bernard Shaw down.

One word more about Shaw on Shakespeare and I have done. He has praised my work on Shakespeare time and again in his prefaces, and notably, as I have shown, in the foreword to *The Dark Lady of the Sonnets*, but his greatest praise came at a dinner once with Sir Sidney Lee, the chief academic critic and biographer of Shakespeare in the late Victorian era, and incidentally I may say the best of the band. Asked about my book on Shakespeare, Sir Sidney Lee tried to praise it: 'A remarkable study,' he began, 'but the Shakespeare is Harris himself, of course.'

The old formula, you see.

'Good God,' cried Shaw, 'think of what you are implying. To have discovered Shakespeare in his work after three hundred years is praise enough, but if you say that Harris has created Shakespeare out of himself, you make Harris the greatest man that ever lived. Do you really mean that?'

20

Fights and Friendships

I know little of Shaw's friendships, as I did not frequent his cliques. He avoided literary society purposely, declaring once that when he first came to London he lunched with a friend at the Savile Club and, having 'listened to them all taking in one another's washing', resolved to avoid meeting men of letters as carefully as the Duke of Wellington avoided meeting soldiers. But he remains outside not only literary society but all society as such. You do not see him at clubs nor at at-homes. He pays no social calls. He is not a diner-out. I doubt whether he has used a hundred visiting-cards in his whole lifetime. He does not ride, hunt, shoot, row, golf, play tennis or cricket, or do any of the things that bring men of his means into contact with one another. The luncheons which are his wife's only form of hospitality have nothing of the routine promiscuity of a tit-for-tat visiting and entertaining list. The only way to know Shaw is to be on a committee with him or to be concerned in his incessant work. His amusements have been defined by himself generally as 'anything except sport' and particularly as 'showing-off'.

In London I did not gather that he was popular in his profession. But as he was too coolly economical to waste time in quarrelling, as so many literary men do, and for the same impersonal reason was helpful on occasion, it was almost impossible to be his active enemy without behaving badly. His friends, notably H. G. Wells, could let their spleens get the better of them and make the most furious attacks on him without exhausting his exasperating patience. There was a good deal in that jibe of Oscar Wilde's about none of Shaw's friends quite liking him.

Shaw and Wilde understood each other, though they met scarcely ten times in their lives. They both were after the same thing, and used, as I have said in my introduction, the same self-exploiting methods to attain their end.

But Shaw is the better man. Far kinder, though he hates any reference to that. By formula it brings abuse from him on the head of anybody who says it. He's so frightfully afraid all the beggars in Europe will read it and come crawling to his doorstep, stripping him little by little until they have him as poor as themselves. And he once knew poverty and is in mortal terror of knowing it again. So he isn't as great as he himself supposes. Still I consider him, as I say, a finer personality than Wilde, and think that, as a personality, Shaw will endure – at least much longer than his works.

As earlier related, Sir William Wilde, Oscar's father, operated on Shaw's father to correct a squint and botched the job so badly that the elder Shaw squinted in the other direction for the rest of his life.

Later in London, a passing fancy of Oscar's for Shaw's sister, whom he heard singing somewhere, led to Lady Wilde inviting Shaw to her At Homes during those lean years spent as an unsuccessful novelist. At these At Homes Shaw met Oscar and they were always over-polite to each other. This social stiffness continued to the last time they met, which was at the tragic luncheon of mine at the Café Royal.

Oscar was present once when Shaw delivered an address on Socialism. Robert Ross pleased Shaw by telling him that Shaw's address had inspired Oscar to write *The Soul of Man under Socialism*.

They also once had a chance meeting at the stage-door of the Haymarket Theatre, a meeting which Shaw remembers for its typical over-cordiality, just one more proof to him that they never could get on.

Still he does remember a pleasant meeting with Wilde, when both dropped their guard. It was at an exhibition in Chelsea, which was so unsophisticated that the mere idea of their both being at it amused them enormously. This was Shaw's first experience of Oscar as a story-teller. Shaw had not to talk, but simply to listen to a raconteur. Wilde was dressed, like Shaw, in tweeds instead of a frock coat. They got on splendidly.

The only other meeting Shaw remembers was at the Café Royal, when Wilde's liberty was in danger; in fact, on the eve of his case against the Marquis of Queensberry, I was urging Wilde to skip to France, as he had not a chance of winning his suit.

This meeting was embarrassing because Shaw, who had praised Wilde's first plays, had criticised *The Importance of Being Earnest* as a really heartless play. Shaw thinks now that this weakness in the play represented a real degeneracy produced at the time by Oscar's perversion, of which, however, Shaw, like many other of Wilde's acquaintances, and even some of his intimate friends, was entirely ignorant until the Queensberry affair made it public. There were a few words between them, but they didn't quarrel over their difference.

When Wilde was sent to prison, Shaw drafted a petition for his release. On meeting Willie Wilde, Oscar's brother, a journalist, at a theatre in St Martin's Lane, Shaw spoke to him about the petition. Shaw said that nobody would sign it except himself and Stewart Headlam, and that as they were both notorious *frondeurs* their signatures would do more harm than good. Willie assented. So the petition fell to the ground; and what became of Shaw's draft Shaw himself doesn't know.

When Wilde had done more than half of his inhuman sentence, he was reported to be in bad health, and I busied myself to get him released before his time. The head of the Prison Commission, Sir Evelyn Ruggles-Brise, told me that if a dozen literary men of distinction would sign the petition for Wilde's release on the ground that the sentence of two years' hard labour had been condemned by a Royal Commission as too severe, he had no doubt that the Home Secretary would advise the Queen to remit the rest of Wilde's sentence. I have told in my *Life and Confessions of Oscar Wilde* how I tried to get Meredith to sign the petition and failed. After various other failures I asked Shaw: he shook his head and said: 'Oh, I'm not the right person; get respectable signatures.'

Still later, when Wilde after his imprisonment lived as an exile in Paris, Shaw made it a point to send him inscribed copies of all his books as they came out. Wilde did the same to him. The real thing they had in common was that they both were considered as court jesters and they both resented it. Thus they treated each other as distinguished and important personalities.

Now and then they touched a common chord, as in the case when they agreed they were both more than witty triflers in words. When the Chicago anarchists were sentenced to death (I wrote a novel, *The Bomb*, about them afterwards), Shaw tried to get up a petition for the release of the imprisoned men. Of all the courageous rebels (in parlours) he got only one signature. That was Oscar Wilde's. It won Wilde Shaw's consideration for the rest of Wilde's life.

They took issue on many things. Shaw didn't like Wilde's Protestant insolence to the Catholic T. P. O'Connor. In the end this meant nothing, for Wilde died a Catholic in a state of grace and is buried at Père Lachaise, consecrated ground, in Paris.

William Morris, when he was slowly dying, said he enjoyed a visit from Wilde more than from anybody else, and Shaw tells me that he can understand me when I write that I would rather have Wilde back than any other friend I ever talked to. And at this point, Shaw makes an excellent analysis of Wilde, declaring that Oscar was 'incapable of friendship, though not of the most touching kindness, on occasion'.

He records a *gaffe* made by Willie Wilde. In defending Oscar to Shaw after Oscar's imprisonment, Willie remarked with maladroit pathos, 'Oscar was *not* a man of bad character. You could have trusted him with a woman anywhere.'

Shaw also saw through Oscar's art pretensions – a holdover from his Oxford days. Raised in a family where music and painting were like bread and butter, Shaw looked on Wilde as a humbug when he talked of art.

In this I never took issue with Shaw, for I had already marked it down that Wilde continually pretended to a knowledge of music which he did not possess.

Shaw shrewdly sees, however, that Wilde was so in love with style that he put up more style than the subject-matter would carry, whether it was in his clothes, his manners, his plays, or the harsh realities of life.

Well believing that the gates of heaven have not been shut against Oscar, he being far too good company to be excluded, Shaw nevertheless had that old Puritan dislike of Wilde's air of leisure.

'The first thing,' Shaw once wrote to me about Oscar, 'we ask a servant for is a testimonial to honesty, sobriety, and industry, for we soon find out that they are the scarce things, and that geniuses are as common as rats.'

I pointed out to Shaw that this was the English shoddy in him. Genius is the rarest thing on earth, whereas nine human beings out of ten have honesty, sobriety, and industry beaten into them by life.

'If so,' he replied, the crafty expert that he is in repartee, 'it is the tenth that comes my way.'

But Shaw had little real sympathy for Wilde; did he not write of him as 'ending his life as an unproductive drunkard and swindler'?

How he hates drinkers!

I concede, however, that Oscar was pretty careless with the money of his friends. You couldn't say the same about Shaw under any conditions.

I recall trying to get Shaw's co-operation for a film of Oscar Wilde which was under consideration in 1921. The moving picture was to be based on my book about Oscar, to which Shaw had added his copyrighted impressions.

The producers wanted Shaw's co-operation, and were willing to pay him six hundred pounds for this service. I had my wife in London drop in to see him and cabled him to telegraph his approval. But any time you urgently cable Shaw, you're almost sure to be answered by a postcard. This time, however, it was a letter:

June 1st 1921

DEAR FRANK HARRIS – I write in the middle of this mess about Mrs Harris's mission. I have cabled you that I do not understand the proposal, and that Mrs Harris is helpless without a scenario. You have replied that you are sending one, adding at the end, 'cable'. But I have nothing to cable until I receive the scenario. I am, however, so apprehensive of a disappointment for you that I had better write and say certain things that you may not know.

First, I can, by lifting up my finger, get ten thousand pounds for an Oscar Wilde film by Bernard Shaw, or with the name Bernard Shaw in the advertisement of it. I have in my desk offers to guarantee me twenty thousand pounds a year for five years if I will release two films per year during that time. Anybody can get it if he can secure my name, which is all that is wanted. Not a month – sometimes not a week – passes that some hard-up literary hack does not come to me and plead that I can rescue him from a desperate situation by writing a preface to his book or letting him make a comic opera or a film out of one of my plays. If, therefore, the offer you have had involves the announcement of my name as collaborator, or in any capacity whatever, there is nothing in it: it is really an insult to you and a thank-you-for-nothing attempt to sidetrack me.

Second, I am a married man; and my wife is a member of the firm. We have arranged our domestic affairs in such a fashion that she has put a good deal of money into my business by spending her income on the house whilst I do the saving. The ten thousand pounds that my name is worth on a film is an asset of the firm; and I am not free to give it away with a Cyranesque gesture, even if I could afford it.

Third, though I have copyright in the words of what I have written about Oscar, I have none in the events of his life; consequently a film representing the life and adventures of Oscar needs no authorisation from me, even when the events represented have been narrated by me for the first time, unless I prove that they are fictitious, in which case I should be proving myself a liar and impostor. Therefore my refusal to allow my name to be used, or to give any authorisation in connection with the film, will not prevent you from introducing all the scenes I have described into your scenario. Nothing that I can do can prevent Frank Harris from filming his Life of Oscar Wilde, and getting the full value of his work. What I can do is to prevent the film firms from throwing in the value of my name as well without paying me for it. I may add here that, though the firms are right to secure the attraction of my name if they can get it, they will, if they cannot help themselves, pay just as much for the film without my name as with it, however loudly they may protest the contrary.

Where I foresee the possibility of a disappointment is in the danger of representing real persons on the screen without their consent. You can make up a movie-actor as Oscar, and another as old Queensberry, and another as yourself; but what about Carson and all the other still living actors in the tragedy? If you avoid this by calling them Smith and Jones, and not making up the actors like the originals, you put a good deal of water in the brandy. Film firms (not to say American business men generally) never foresee these things until they break their shins over them: I am constantly receiving the very maddest proposals of moral, legal, and even physical impossibilities from America. I think it is quite a good and feasible notion to take advantage of your biographical reputation to make a series of films, calling them educational, of lives of famous men by Frank Harris; but the more contemporary they are the greater will be the difficulty. Suppose one of them anticipated you with a Wilde film in which an actor posed as Frank Harris in His Cell and so forth, what would you do?

As far as I can see, what can be done is this. The film can begin, after the usual lists of everyone employed in the film company, from the office boy upward, with a portrait of F. H., followed by extracts from *The Times Literary Supplement*, the *New Statesman*, etc., and a sentence from one of my letters, to the effect that F. H. is the greatest biographer since Plutarch or the like. No authorisation is needed for these; but there must be at least three or four of them from various sources; and there must be no reference to them in the announcements: if the film people attempt to use my name, I shall be down on them instantly with all the legal thunderbolts I can throw. You must use this threat to prevent them pushing you off the stage and putting me in the centre, which they will certainly do if you or I let them.

Now you know how the case stands with me. I await further information.

In great haste,

G. BERNARD SHAW

P.S. – The six hundred pounds was unacceptable because it is far beneath my market rate.

That ended our efforts to feature Oscar in seven reels. It might have been doomed to failure even if we had completed the project; in which case, Shaw would have learned, ten years sooner than he did, how roughly critics of the cinema could handle a great man.

I've had my fights with Shaw, and one was because he publicly characterised me as a ruffian. I didn't know then that he was paying me the homage a serf pays his hero. He wrote me a long letter to show he too was a ruffian, but of an inferior strain.

It is a curious confirmation of Shaw's view that, when I first read the story which Shaw tells of Beethoven's independent gesture and of Goethe's subservience, I became impatient at hearing Goethe praised; Beethoven's attitude pleased me the more.

Here is Shaw's letter:

July 14th 1918

MY DEAR FRANK HARRIS – You must not take my comments on your personal characteristics as sneers and disparagements. If you do, you will find me an impossible man to have any relations with. I tell you you are a ruffian exactly as an oculist might tell you that you are astigmatic. I will tell you now more precisely what I mean – if I have done so already you have brought the repetition on yourself.

Somebody in London society who likes interesting people meets you and invites you to dinner. He asks you to take in a bishop's wife. You entertain her with deep-voiced outpourings of your scorn for the hypocrisy and snobbery of the Church, finishing up with a touch of poetry about Mary Magdalene and her relations with Jesus. When the poor lady escapes to the drawing-room and you find yourself between the bishop and Edmund Gosse, you turn the conversation on to the genius of Rops, and probably produce a specimen of his work, broadening your language at the same time into that of the forecastle of a pirate sloop.

And if you observe the least sign of restiveness or discomfort on the part of the twain, you redouble your energy of expression and barb it with open and angry scorn. When they escape upstairs in their turn, they condole with one another. Gosse says, 'My God, what a man!' The bishop says, 'Oh, impossible; quite impossible!'

Now, though this particular picture is a fancy one, it is not founded on any lies that people have told me. I have seen and heard you do such things: I have been condoled with, and have had to admit that you are a monster, and that, clever as you are, it is impossible to ask anyone to meet you unless they are prepared to stand anything that the uttermost freemasonry of the very freest thought and expression in the boldest circles can venture on. Poor old Adolphe Adam used to run away from Beethoven's symphonies crying, '*J'aime la musique qui me berce!*' You would have run after him with a trombone blaring Beethoven's most challenging themes into his ears.

Now, intensely disagreeable as this was to our Adams and snobs and conventional people in general, it was not at all disagreeable to me. It was quite genuine and natural, like Beethoven walking truculently through the Court group with his hat thrust down on his eyebrows, when Goethe stood aside politely, hat in hand like a good *Geheimrath*. When Beethoven's brother put *Landbesitzer* (Landed Proprietor) on his visiting-card, Beethoven put '*Hirnbesitzer*' (Brain Owner) on his. All this was ruffianism on Beethoven's part; but it was an assertion of real values; and the man who asserts real values cannot be passed over by nobodies, or disliked by somebodies, merely because he asserts them in a ruffianly way. And your ruffianism was, on the whole, of this description. If it had been aristocratic insolence and impatience of self-restraint like that of Randolph Churchill, it would have been intolerable. As it was, I liked it.

But – and here is the point of insisting on it as I do – it damaged you socially. It must have agonised Wilde, not merely because he was a snob and could hear Shakespeare saying, 'Harris, with his teeth ever in the plump calf of prosperity', but because he shrank from seeing nice and innocent people wounded and scorned merely because they were not geniuses. But Wilde did not greatly matter socially: what did matter was that, though one could ask you to meet Julia and Jessica, one could not ask you to meet Mrs Humphry Ward. You may say: 'God be praised for that! I never wanted to meet Mrs Humphry Ward.' All the same, you cannot have a career in London as a journalist and politician unless you can be trusted to take Mrs Humphry Ward in to dinner and leave her under the impression that you are either a very respectable or a very charming man.

You may say that this may be true, but why rub it into you now that you are out of London? Well, you are out of London; but you have left a reputation there, part of which consists of vague impressions that in some way or other you made yourself impossible and had to go off to Monte Carlo and then to America, where you publicly shook the dust of London from your feet. People whose curiosity is roused by your writings ask, 'What was wrong with Frank Harris? Wasn't he a Jew, or a financial blackmailer-journalist, or another Verlaine, or a German spy or something?' It is necessary to reply, 'No: he was simply the most impossible ruffian on the face of the earth,' and explain in the sense in which I have explained above. As to myself, of course I am a ruffian. Set a ruffian to catch a ruffian. But I am only ruffianly nor'-nor'-west. Though it be ruffianism, yet there's method in't.

Yours ever,

G. BERNARD SHAW

Shaw is quite right about himself; he offended English convention only on one or two points. He was on the British side of the Boer War, and he is never tired of declaring that the Irish were as much to blame for the impasse in Ireland as the British.

Besides – and this is the most important point – he always observed the Puritan convention in regard to writing and to speech, while I am always chafing against a prudery that fetters the spirit and debases literature. I want to reinstate the broad humane tradition of France or of the spacious days of great Elizabeth, and I am certain that the modern scientific spirit will yet sweep away all corseting restrictions as unhealthful and ridiculous. The future must judge between Shaw and myself in this respect, and I'm not afraid of the verdict.

But, in one respect, Shaw is mistaken. It is quite true that Mrs Humphry Ward, and the upper middle class she represented, disliked me and tabooed me; but I never wanted to know them, nor did they ever stand for English Society or, indeed, for anything inspiring or interesting.

England is the land of anomalies. The so-called smart set, the coterie which was grouped round King Edward in my days, included all the rich cosmopolitans in London and was as free in thought and as outspoken in words as the best Society in Paris or Rome or Madrid. Lord Randolph Churchill hardly exaggerated when he once said on a public platform that the best class in England and the lowest were united in the bonds of a frank disregard of all conventions. The members of these classes in London forgive everything to talent, and, provided they are amused, put no restrictions on those who interest them.

Shaw has described me as a veritable monster, unfit for 'good society', too frank of speech and too direct of thought to be tolerated by the Mrs Humphry Wards who are the bulwark of respectability in every age.

Could I have any better credentials, as a biographer, for painting a frank and honest portrait of my friend Shaw, who is only ruffianly nor'-nor'-west? To remove all doubt let him be his own witness even further:

November 11th 1915

MY DEAR FRANK HARRIS – Your book reached me sometime in September when I was in Torquay. I have a friend there, Carlos Blacker, who was a friend of Oscar Wilde's; and he pounced on the book at once. As others followed his example, and as anything I don't do at once is generally either not done at all or horribly delayed, John Harris has had to wait until this month for the book.

Has it been published in England yet? I have seen one review of it, and a few patriotic imbecilities about it; but I forgot to note whether the review referred to an English edition or to the one you sent me. The allusions remind me very much of the conventional allusions to Rousseau. You disconcert the whole of Europe. It is a sort of criticism that began, ironically, with Hamlet. The world most potently and powerfully believes, but holds it not honest to have it set down.

But there are two things worth saying about these *Contemporary Portraits*. First, when you tackle a great man you really do know the sort of animal you are dealing with, which I suppose establishes your claim (if you make it) to be one of the species yourself. Second, they are not like anybody else's attempts at the same kind of things. They are really much more like what used to be called Characters than the sort of stuff we do nowadays. I doubt if any of our Savile Club scribes would venture to defend them. Neither would they venture to defend the memoirs of St Simon, which means that you can draw the bow of Ulysses and they cannot.

I am called away and must break off suddenly.

Yours ever,

G. B. S.

On more than one occasion he described me as a monster; and his ground was 'Frank Harris adores literature with a large L and yet can write: that is, he combines the weakness of the amateur with the strength of a genuine vocation.'

That is true enough, I suppose; I share with Shakespeare and Doctor Johnson that weakness of the amateur which delights in the feast of reason and the flow of soul among my literary compeers, and my betters if I can tempt them to sit with me. But you will remember how Shaw saved his soul, when he came to London, by resolving, after his first glance at the Savile Club, that he would never be a literary man or consort with such. 'I might have spent my life sitting watching these fellows taking in each other's washing and learning no more of the world than a tic in a typewriter if I had been fool enough,' he says.

I tried to cure him of this by inviting him to my *Saturday Review* luncheons at the Café Royal; but it was no use. He came a few times, being sincerely interested in the café, in the waiters, in the prices, in the cooking: in short, in the economics of the place; and he concluded that Harold Frederic and I ate too much meat, and that it was a waste of money to pay Café Royal prices for his own plateful of macaroni, which he could obtain elsewhere for tenpence. The fact that I paid for it made no difference whatever to him: he objected to a waste of my money just as much as his own.

Many times since, I have wished that other people were equally considerate. But Shaw's consideration amounts to an interference with one's private affairs. One of his hostesses said Shaw was a most dangerous man, and, on being asked how and why (in the hope of eliciting some scandal), explained, 'You invite him down to your place because you think he will entertain your guests with his brilliant conversation; and before you know where you are he has chosen a school for your son, made your will for you, regulated your diet, and assumed all the privileges of your family solicitor, your housekeeper, your clergyman, your doctor, your dressmaker, your hairdresser, and your estate agent. When he has finished with everybody else, he incites the children to rebellion. And when he can find nothing more to do, he goes away and forgets all about you.'

All attempts to make Shaw be sociable are wasted. He's only available to committees. But, though I have never sat on committees with him, I have seen enough of him during the long years of our friendship. He rarely goes anywhere unless he has business there. He used never to pay social calls, but now makes exception to persons at the moment in the limelight, anything from tennis champions to polar fliers – for all the world like a White House incumbent with his perpetual hand-shaking before news photographers.

Years ago he was not so eager to please. He knew how to make enemies, which is the gift of the great. He says: 'Treat your friend as one who may some day be your enemy and your enemy as one who may some day be your friend.'

He knows human vanity, being one of its high priests, and he is a fighter who appreciates a worthy antagonist.

'Beware,' he warns us, 'of the man who does not return your blow: he neither forgives you nor allows you to forgive yourself.'

Shaw is modest on his own account. He gives himself away freely. Good manners alone, he imagines, prevent him from doing as much for his friends. This consideration for them robs them of their revenge and forces them to pay him tribute when they feel at heart they have been victimised.

Shaw objects that it 'is difficult to class as vain a man who gives himself away even to the point of making himself ridiculous'.

What complicates the matter is that Shaw brags about his intellect until it seems quite clear he is pulling your leg. He thinks people like this, and advances as proof that they love Cyrano's eagle-beaked bragga-docio and 'hate the modest cough of the minor poet'. Praise Shaw's books in his presence and you will be overwhelmed with his own chorus, in which all the blurbs on the covers of his book are outdone. After that you cannot get a word in edgewise, so that there is no chance of your withdrawing a particle of your praise.

All this play-acting has its base in the belief that what people say for and against him cannot be half as true as what he knows of himself, and he therefore throws out all charges of vanity or modesty.

One of the fine things about Shaw is that being placed on a pedestal and flattered beyond measure has not increased his arrogance. On the contrary, it has rather diminished his self-assertion and increased his kindliness. So long as men denied him the position he was conscious of deserving, he demanded it loudly in and out of season; but as soon as they treated him as one of the Immortals and paid him honour, he became more considerate of others and less inclined to stand on the extreme verge of his claim. Like Meredith, he can see that too much honour is not good for a man who has to live his life and do his work. Measured by high standards, Shaw withstands the tests of eminence triumphantly, and what a delight it is to be able in all sincerity to say about a contemporary writer that his character is at least as noble as his best work.

Because Shaw writes with such vehemence when treating general subjects, persons meeting him for the first time prepare themselves for any insult and go in with all their armour on. He always astonishes them by his charm, and his explanation is that part of this is due to the fact that 'no human being could possibly be so disagreeable as they expect me to be. I have only to be commonly civil to seem quite charming.'

It is true everybody tells of being put at ease on a first meeting by Shaw's brisk, cheerful manner and his, to them, simple, unaffected charm. He used to affect a vitality of body to match his brain, but the fact was, as I have related, his work frequently exhausted him and he had to lie down or collapse. He throws away a good deal of physical energy, as he talks to you, by continually crossing and uncrossing and recrossing his legs, putting his hands in and out of his pockets, sitting on the edge and then far back in his chair, stretching out full length in his chair – in short, anything but the phlegmatic philosopher of legend.

He can talk on for hours, quickly breaking his phrases with a short laugh and going on again in his faint brogue. He finds the world a far more pleasant place, judged by his daily pleasures, than when he sits down to abuse it for its social and economic wrongs.

If you do not meet Shaw for a long while and are forced to draw on him only through print, all your original dislikes may return. This explains why, sometimes, persons pour out bitterness and violence against him which, as he says, must have been rankling in them for years.

Someone has said of him, 'He has a heart of gold which he carefully conceals.' I remember when he lent to the Durham coalminers thirty thousand pounds for the construction of cheap dwelling-houses. When the journalists came to ask why, he said: 'Six per cent,' and he could not be drawn out beyond that.

I know also this type of Shaw humanism from personal experience.

I have told about the fine way he acted when I wanted him to stay on till I could sell *The Saturday Review*. Years later, in referring to this again, he wrote:

November 11th 1915

MY DEAR FRANK HARRIS – In your letter you allude to an article in the *Smart Set*. I didn't see it; but I know too well the incredible things they still do in America to accept anything that is put forward, even over an individual signature, except on overwhelming evidence of style, sentence for sentence. It was perhaps, however, as well that they smudged out your generous reference to my pecuniary loss. The truth is, I didn't lose anything in the long run. When the paper changed hands, I came upon the scene as a creditor, but not a pressing one, as Harold Hodge conveyed to me that if I could possibly hold on for a time it would make matters easier for him and for everybody else; so I said there was no hurry, and took no further steps until a longish time after – it may have been a couple of years, when I saw that the paper had passed into the hands of a gentleman who was quite well able to pay his way. I then wrote to Hodge and asked him whether I could put in my claim without affecting him in any way. He said I could; and it was then paid. So you may write that off your conscience. The delay never really cost me the slightest inconvenience. From 1894, when I ceased to live from hand to mouth and began to draw money from the theatre, I always had more money at the bank than I wanted; consequently the debt, which was no great matter after all, never reached me: my banker had so much the less to play with: that was all. In 1898, my play *The Devil's Disciple* made quite a lucrative success in America. Also in that year I got married to a lady who was considerably more than self-supporting. So you see there really was no pecuniary loss at all, nor even the most momentary inconvenience.

Yours ever,

G. B. S.

I wouldn't have you believe I was the only friend Shaw had in the world. Indeed, there must be thousands who consider themselves closer to him. The late Cecil Chesterton, then unknown, has written of meeting Shaw, already famous, who received him on terms of boyish equality. Shaw's explanation of this is that he makes no mistakes about men or manners.

Backed by this social ease, Shaw generally does not care what he says, or does. He can be callous, and likes to have you in doubt as to what line he will pursue, no matter what the subject is. 'That,' he confesses, 'is not a receipt for a reassuring or popular personality, though it may be for a provocative one.'

Most critics of Shaw have said that he has made enemies because of his Socialism. I think they are wrong. I rather believe that there is nothing in Shaw's political and social programme, not even all his talk about absolute equality of income and its dissociation from every kind of personal industry or virtue, which could disturb a sleeping dog. On committees he is known as 'safe', and his tact certainly helped the Fabian Society over the fights that have broken up all the other Utopian organisations.

Incidentally, speaking of the Fabian Society, Sidney Webb, now exercising his democratic ideas as Lord Passfield, exerted tremendous influence over Shaw in their early days. Shaw himself gives unstinted credit to Webb as the real formulator of the Fabian policy. Webb was the very reverse of Shaw in character and temperament, yet these two leaders of the Fabian Society got along most amicably.

'We are in perfect contrast,' Shaw has said, 'but we complement one another; and that's useful to us both.'

While speaking of these friendly influences in Shaw's life, I want to refer to William Morris, the great English poet and craftsman. Shaw has said that he once found to his surprise that Morris had been reading, in an obscure magazine, the monthly instalments of one of Shaw's unsuccessful novels. 'But that only proves,' someone added, 'how much easier it is to please a great man than a little one, especially when you share his politics.'

On the strength of this, some of Shaw's commentators claim that Morris exercised a certain influence over Shaw. He certainly did, though the poet disliked the Fabians. But after trying hard to knock some sense into his group of 'Communist Anarchists' he dropped them and left the Fabians to make the best of things in their own way. He was far too able in practical matters to be an Anarchist, or to mistake the 'comrades' of the Socialist League for capable administrators; but he also divined what Shaw and the Webbs did not see until later on, that Socialism could not be established by our parliamentary party machinery. Shaw always knew the poet's value, and said 'We can flummox him in debate; but he is fundamentally right.'

Shaw often offended critics by exposing their stupendous and un-ashamed ignorance, which, in truth, often exceeded his own. Recall his *First Aid to Critics*. With those worthy of his steel, however, he always remained understanding and a friend at heart, regardless how fierce the combat while it lasted. Take, for example, Shaw's attacks on Pinero and his praise of Jones. Shaw has later said that he left Archer to praise Pinero and looked after Jones himself; for Pinero was a good friend of Archer, and Shaw and Jones were personal friends also. In after years Jones quarrelled frantically with Shaw over the war, but on his death-bed scribbled a few broken words to say that he had no personal enmity. Pinero, to whom Shaw had been 'admirable and detestable', has now long been good friends with him. And it is a fact that it was Shaw who urged the Prime Minister (Asquith) to confer knighthood on Pinero, which he did.

Detractors of Shaw have charged him with unkindness and even downright brutality when, on the contrary, he was being merely honest and frank, and at the same time trying to be funny. A case in point is his quarrel with Henley, whose great love was Mozart, and whose poetry so extolled the he-man's captaincy of his own soul.

As Shaw thought he also knew Mozart's value, Henley asked him to write on music for his paper, then called the *Scots Observer*. Shaw wrote perhaps half a dozen articles but found Henley an impossible editor.

'He had no idea of criticism, except to glorify the masters he liked, and pursue their rivals with quixotic jealousy. To appreciate Mozart without reviling Wagner was to Henley a blank injustice to Mozart. Now, he knew I was what he called a Wagnerite, and that I thought his objection to Wagner *vieux jeu*, stupid, ignorant, and common. There-fore he amused himself by interpolating abuse of Wagner into my articles over my signature. Naturally he lost his contributor; and it was highly characteristic of him that he did not understand why he could not get any more articles from me.'

Only recently Gordon Craig wrote a letter to, I think, *The Observer*, in which he said: 'Mr Bernard Shaw has ever been the sincere enemy of English art and artists, and while this offends many of us, we must not forget that he is, after all, a foreigner, and, as such, always entitled to our sufferance. He tickets us all off as this or that: the great ones he insults, but he is kinder to the smaller fry – for example, he merely dubs me "spoilt child". A moment's glance at his bankbook and at mine would show which of us is the spoilt one. Mr Shaw came down to destroy our theatre. Let us turn to what he wrote to Ellen Terry in 1897: "If I were to let the public see that I have private reasons for destroying Henry Irving, I should never be allowed to criticise him again without suspicion of partiality." '

These were his words, Craig thought. 'If I have a comma wrong, we can correct it as soon as the Ellen Terry and Bernard Shaw letters are published.'

Shaw, to whom a proof of Craig's letter was submitted, wrote: 'This letter is such a perfect gem of Craigery that it leaves me speechless. The public must await the publication of my correspondence with Ellen Terry to appreciate the audacity of her son's quotation from it.

'I was not "allowed" to settle in England. I came without leave. I am not a refugee here: I am a conqueror.

'Mr Craig is the last of the rebels: I should be sorry to see him surrender. Like the empress in my play, I want him for my museum.'

The letters are now published, making it clear that the 'private reasons' came to nothing worse than Shaw's old-fashioned Irish gallantry, which obliged him to pretend to be jealous of Ellen Terry's devotion to Irving.

The doctrine of *aut nihil aut bonum de mortuis* (either nothing or good of the dead) is a mawkish sentiment unworthy of honest men, and I see no reason why Shaw was so roundly condemned in the case of his obituary notice of Sir Henry Irving. Speaking frankly, passing literary opinions without much fear or favour is the greatest virtue of Shaw, and saying his say caustically and with much wit is his forte. To help out, he lacks the pettiness of ill-will, and bears even his most unreasonable critics no great grudge.

I have seen Shaw remain superior and calm under the most virulent attacks. Whether these came from the medical profession full of personal abuse for Shaw's anti-vivisection and other heresies, or from other antagonists, Shaw always replied with that complete composure that enables him to ridicule or annihilate an adversary by the shafts of his cool logic and wit. How often had Henry Arthur Jones, for example, shouted 'traitor', 'blackguard', 'viper', at him from *The Morning Post*. But Shaw smilingly assured Jones that his friendship and regard for him remained unchanged.

And yet, why go so far afield? I have myself accused Shaw of plagiarism and underhand dealing, but he has continued to eulogise me and we have remained the best of friends.

I am happy to note that these traits in Shaw's character have exerted a salutary influence upon the world of letters, outweighing the bad effect of his conceited self-advertisements.

Shaw ordered a special copy of *Oscar Wilde: His Life and Confessions*, a book of mine which seems destined to outlive many which I consider its superiors.

Like everything else I write, once it gets into Shaw's hands it stirs him into telling what *he* thinks, and creating a row between us.

Still, I can truthfully say that, with the single exception of Bernard Shaw, the men of my own time have made it as difficult for me to do my work as they could. Time and again I had fought for the underdog, for the Irish, the Egyptians, the Hindus, and the Boers, when all men knew that my attitude was directly opposed to my self-interest. When I tried to state the case of the enemy fairly in the world war, English writers didn't hesitate to ascribe to me unworthy motives. Shaw was alone in defending me, a very Abdiel, 'faithful he among the faithless, true amid innumerable false'.

A *just*, even if not a solemn, attitude to men and critics is one of the main characteristics of Shaw. I think that most of his critics believe it deep down in their hearts, whatever their public protestations. From this I should except, perhaps, his French critics.

He has reason to remember the French critics who coldly received his *Candida*, in 1908, *Mrs Warren's Profession*, in 1912, *You Never Can Tell*, in 1913, and *Pygmalion*, in 1923; and that, ten years ago, the Paris publisher Calmann-Lévy began and then dropped a complete edition of his works. It was not till later that Aubier undertook to publish his plays in the Hamon translation.

It is because Shaw remembers these things that he struck back in the *Temps* in 1925. Henri Bernstein, the well-known playwright of the boulevards, had declared that the success of *Saint Joan* in Paris was achieved in spite of Shaw, as every stroke of Ludmila Pitoeff's acting contradicted every line of the text. Shaw made fun of Bernstein to his heart's content; but later on, when he had seen Ludmila's performance, he confessed that Bernstein was the one critic who had said exactly the right thing. The two met in London, and parted on the best of terms. Shaw never leaves an enemy behind him if he can possibly help it. He prefers them, he says, in front.

Shaw's translators have been great fighters in his behalf, but he hasn't always treated them with the consideration they deserve. Siegfried

Trebitsch, who introduced Shaw into Austria and Germany, and did wonders for him there, is a case in point.

Trebitsch wrote a tragedy and Shaw translated it, making it a comedy. This is funny if you happen to see the world wholly from Shaw's comic window, but when the Pitoeffs treated Shaw's *Saint Joan* in their own manner he resented it, though they did nothing so ruthless as he did to Trebitsch.

Max Reinhardt annoyed him even more by pornographising parts of *The Apple Cart*, and incidentally giving it the far better title of *The Emperor of America*. When it comes to tampering with the chastity of his plays, Shaw is absolutely furious, which means, I suppose, that though he has endless wit he really has no sense of humour. As proof of this distinction I might cite the case of George Sylvester Viereck. He sent me a batch of letters, from which I extract these samples.

Viereck had been expelled from some idiotic authors' league in America during the war, and Shaw had rushed to his aid by pointing out that any literary society which expelled a member because of his political opinions was not a literary society at all: on the contrary, it became a political party.

In reply he received this pearl of great price from somebody I never heard of before or since in the field of letters.

It ran:

> *23 East 41st Street, New York*
> *February 17th 1919*

DEAR SIR – I beg to acknowledge an ukase from you, under date of the tenth of January last, relative to the expulsion of members of literary societies.

I am living in the United States of America, and in the affairs of an American society I see no warrant on the part of an Anglo-Irishman to intrude either his counsel or command.

Literature, Art, and Science are not 'free of frontiers', as you imagine. There is one frontier which cannot be violated with common decency, and that is an intrusion on the part of an alien into the domestic affairs of an independent people.

Yours truly,

CONDE B. PALLEN

Shaw could no more have neglected pricking this bubble than he could neglect to breathe. He replied:

10 Adelphi Terrace, London, W.C.2

DEAR SIR – Your letter of the 17th February fills me with a wild hope that you may be able to recover for me the considerable sums I have paid into the United States Treasury since 1913 as income tax. As the United States were founded on the principle of No Taxation without Representation, it seems to me that if you can succeed in establishing your contention that I have no rights in America, I shall get my money back.

Until I do, you may depend on it I shall take advantage of the position its payment confers on me to express my opinion, and to issue what you call my 'counsel and command' in American affairs with the utmost freedom.

By the way, are you an Englishman? Your epistolary style is almost comically British.

Faithfully,

G. BERNARD SHAW

To be sure he would fain have the world believe that he nurses secret vices. I remember, for example, the incident when a London lady invited him to lunch. While coffee was being served his hostess offered him a cigarette.

'I don't smoke,' Shaw declined.

'Oh, I forgot you have no vices,' she remarked.

'None that I let the world know about,' Shaw retorted.

One of the most amusing quarrels of recent times has been between C. R. W. Nevinson, the painter, and Shaw, as the result of Shaw's advice to a very clever flower painter, Gertrude Harvey, to call a then forthcoming exhibition of her pictures 'a Woolworth Exhibition', and announce that any picture in the room could be bought for five pounds. He actually wrote the catalogue for her; and Mrs Harvey sold all her pictures triumphantly.

Nevinson, taking Shaw to mean that no picture is worth more than five pounds, and being greatly offended by his claim that the Woolworth plan would 'eliminate seedy artists, starving artists, and drinking and drugging artists', declared that a frame alone cost roughly five pounds, and 'a good frame, as all artists know, can sell a bad picture, just as a good actor, as Mr Shaw knows, can often save a bad play'. He advised Shaw to stick to the safety of learning to fly, rather than rush into print and advise young artists on how not to make money, and ended, 'If Shaw will reduce the prices of his theatre below cost, even I would be prepared to sacrifice sixpence for a stall.'

Now, Shaw can say those things about himself, does say them often, but for anybody to hint that he is slightly senescent arouses his ire. The proof, however, of how old an old man he is came the next day, when he replied, 'If we walked down Bond Street, people would take me for Nevinson's son.'

This left his chin completely exposed, and Nevinson hit it with, 'I have no doubt of it, his arguments are so childish.'

Can you imagine Shaw twenty years ago leaving himself open to such a counter-attack? Alas, time slows down all of us, as his friend Gene Tunney, after fourteen seconds on the floor, would have been the first to tell him.

During the war, Shaw wrote a pamphlet called *The Last Spring of the Old Lion*, which James Douglas described as 'The Last Grin of the Old Clown', and it was Nevinson's opinion that if Shaw had stopped there, Shaw's career would have had a more ennobling effect on the younger generation instead of being the sorry thing it is – 'going around chasing young Englishmen with a painted red-hot poker'.

The worst abuse I have ever read of Shaw was by Benjamin de Cassères, and all of it had its roots in Shaw's ill-timed humour on the occasion of Arnold Daly's death by fire in a hotel room. Daly, who drank a good deal, posed as the founder of Shaw's fortunes in America. The real founder was Richard Mansfield; but that is hardly any reason why, when poor Daly was horribly burned to death, Shaw's verdict should have been spontaneous combustion. This is a dull enough witticism, perhaps, for a wet Senator to make about an Anti-Saloon Leaguer, but it seems hardly the sort of thing that passes between civilised people on any occasion. Shaw's callous defence was that it gave the catastrophe an artistic turn which Daly would have liked!

Whether the funerals of the Dublin Shaws set up an early association in Bernard's imagination between death and humour, or his Irish blood carries in it that delight in mischief which Father Keegan rebukes so bitterly in *John Bull's Other Island*, certain it is that death seems to exhilarate Shaw. His Don Juan, meeting Doña Ana in hell, says, 'You may remember that on earth – though of course we never confessed it – the death of anyone we knew, even those we liked best, was always mingled with a certain satisfaction at being finally done with them.' St John Ervine reports Shaw as setting the table in a roar by describing how an old man's first sadness at seeing his contemporaries drop round him one by one soon changes to diabolical exultation in seeing another one go down. This impishness is not *Schadenfreude*, and not altogether his usual clowning. In his hurry for the Superman, or for that next creation with which he advises God to supplant humanity altogether, Shaw tends to regard himself and us his poor fellow-creatures as provisional make-shifts, and our deaths as clearances of scrapped material. This is the best explanation I can give of his heartless macabre pleasantries. An explanation, but not a defence.

Shaw often infuriates people with his amusing air of superiority – he the parent, you the child – that rankles in the end. You can go through almost all his friendships and find this streak running through it. He usually remarks that your wife is more competent to handle the matter, or that he looks to her to keep you in order on the point of dis-agreement between you and him, or some such phrase. It gives your wife an excellent sense of how important she is in your literary life, and to have Shaw on her side is the last word in the matter.

That you think she doesn't really matter in the least is Shaw's laugh at the expense of both of you.

I have seen him escape through such a trap-door frequently, and the fact that I have seen him do it is sufficient proof that it didn't fool me, even where I was a victim of it. What it actually did was to reduce Shaw's stature by several inches every time I saw him try it.

Another stunt of his has been to try to smile through a knockout blow by saying it wasn't a knockout blow at all, and that you hadn't delivered it, really, but the office boy. You will see more of what I mean in this letter:

> *September 27th 1919*
> (*posted from Kerry on the 30th*)

DEAR FRANK HARRIS – Your letter of the 14th July is still unanswered; so here goes.

I may be quite wrong in this or that detail as to your career in London journalism after *The Saturday Review* passed out of your hands. For instance, your letter is the first intimation of the screaming joke which you mention so seriously: to wit, that you were once the editor of *Hearth and Home*. I feel that I may see you editing the *Leisure Hour* and *Good Words* before I die.

But I read *The Candid Friend*, because you sent it to me from the office, and because Lady Jessica, who knew my wife, tried to get hold of me when she was editing it for you. After the first two numbers I don't believe you wrote fifty lines in it all told until it expired.

Your *Vanity Fair* never came my way except when the Press Cutting people sent me its invariably scurrilous references to me. I did not suspect you for a moment of writing them, not on sentimental grounds, but because you could not have written so badly if you had tried for a year. At last there came a surpassingly bad article, apparently written by the office boy, signed F. H. I was not surprised at your leaving the editing to the office boy; but when he actually used your signature (which you seldom used yourself) I concluded that you had become utterly reckless. That article has long since been collected by the dustman: I cannot tell you the date of it; and it may very well be that the paper had passed out of your hands, and that some Freddy Hicks or Frank Hodges was airing himself in it. But there the article was, anyhow: and it was quite in the style of the things that had been coming to me during the time when you were the reputed editor.

Then came that ridiculous action you took against some candidate for whom you had written speeches, and who, I suppose, irritated you by some *gaucherie* or other. Finally there was the *Modern Society* affair in which at last someone to whom you had abandoned your functions let you in for a criminal prosecution. All this time you talked freely about Ernest Terah Hooley in a manner which showed that you were more interested in him than in literature; and it was current gossip in journalistic circles that it was a common practice with financial journals to write articles exposing shady promotions, and make them buy off the insertion: blackmail, in short. You were suspected of this method of making papers pay: on what grounds I do not know; but it was clear that *Vanity Fair* was no more like *The Saturday Review* than *The Mystery of a Hansom Cab* was like *Hamlet*, and that you were living mostly in Monte Carlo. The conclusion was that either you were leaving your newspapers to be edited by anybody who happened to be on the spot, and not even troubling to keep the standard up to Lady Jessica's or Blanchamp's, or else you had fallen off as a literary hand to an extent that could only be accounted for by utter demoralisation, and that your character had collapsed with your talent. As I came across you a few times, and saw that the latter was not the right explanation, I fell back on the former.

But you suffered also from your personal style. Like everyone else, I took you to be much more of a man of the world than you really were. As I told you, it was Julia Frankau who first opened my eyes to the fact that the buccaneer of Monte Carlo, the pal of Lord Randolph, the impressive editor of the *Fortnightly* and the *Saturday*, the financier who gave tips to Hooley, and the scorner of the transparent and trivial West End, was a romantic boy and even a sensitive child without the ghost of a notion of the sort of society he was living in and the people he was up against. You were so surprised and indignant at finding that England was England, and human nature human nature, and so hurt by the knocks that seasoned adventurers in London soon cease to feel, and, what was worse for you, so absurdly unconscious of the shock and jar of your *Anschauung* against that of Eton and Oxford, and of the Savile Club's resentment of your scale of literary values, which reduced most of its members to pigmies, and piffling pigmies at that, that you never really knew where you were, or what you might say or do with impunity. You often seemed to be brutally and truculently outraging susceptibilities which no doubt would not have existed in a community of Napoleons and Maupassants, but which are the whole life of the London you had to steer through. Instead of teaching that poor devil Runciman manners, which were really all that he lacked to make him a first-rate critic, you taught him to drink; and he died prematurely and miserably in consequence. I don't pretend that you were responsible for his ruin: men have to save themselves: the point was that you did not know what was the matter with him. When he was stupid enough to be insolent to Hubert Bland, Bland knocked him down, to his great astonishment; for he had no idea that insolence was not the normal thing in intercourse with people whom he happened to dislike. But when he was insolent in your paper to Mackenzie, and let you in for damages, thereby getting *you* knocked down for his bad behaviour, you agreed with him on the fundamental point that people who are not geniuses of the first order have no right to common civility. Your theory of manners was the same as his: the practice varied only as the climate of South Shields (or whatever the barbarous place was in which Runciman was allowed to tumble up, an unlicked cub) differs from the climate of Ireland. I have an eye for these things because I had to learn manners myself; I, too, in my nonage, was occasionally wanting in respect to people of cruder tastes and blunter wits than myself.

Now, it is hard enough on other people to know that you think you know more than they do. It is not possible for the most vigilantly considerate man of high talent to go through the world without moving those who feel at a disadvantage with him to furious moments of hatred and envy; but when you openly scorn these victims, and wipe your boots on them publicly, you sow dragon's teeth in all directions. You certainly sowed a great many in London: but you did it naïvely and unconsciously to a much greater extent than anyone could have guessed from your style, which was that of a man who knew every corner of society and human nature, and did nothing without knowing it. Whereas, as I say, I believe that Julia was right and that half the time you had not the least idea of the pain you were causing or the fierce animosity you were rousing.

Publishing your books at your own expense, as I have done for many years in England, is the price you had to pay for your independence.

Pearson's proves my case as regards the papers you didn't edit. *Pearson's* is quite obviously edited by Frank Harris. Whenever you really edit a paper, there is no mistake about it. And when you don't edit it, there is no mistake about that either.

What you say about Rhodes is very interesting. Why did you not sell yourself to Rhodes? If I had been Rhodes I should have said, 'Why not sell yourself? You have the reputation of being a man without conscience, a city-article blackmailer, a reckless libeller, a pirate in finance and journalism. You have no right to a reputation you have not earned. Come and earn it. If you refuse, nobody will give you the least credit: they will only say, "He couldn't get on even with Rhodes." '

Your quotation from Andrea del Sarto is apt; but it was not by stealing the King of France's money to spend on his worthless slut of a wife that Andrea learnt how to take a bit of chalk and correct the arm that Raphael mis-drew. Raphael might with more force have said: 'Let some perfect draughtsman make my two hundred friends. Let him try.'

And could Andrea have put a mother's protecting hand on a child's back as Raphael put it in that pencil study for the 'Incendie' which is in the print-room at the British Museum? He could find the *plein air* school in his frescoes 300 years before it became the ambition of all the Paris studios; and Raphael never did anything half so clever. All the same Raphael was the divine Raphael, a prince among painters; whilst Andrea, with an opportunity from Francis I as great as the Pope could offer Raphael, used it to become a thief.

You are quite right about the German respect for art and intellect as distinguished from the English contempt for it and respect for money and acres and push. But that is called education! However, I have said my say about that in two immortal prefaces. Let it suffice.

Your ignorance of Dickens is a frightful gap in your literary education. He was by far the greatest man since Shakespeare that England has ever produced in that line. Read *Little Dorrit, Our Mutual Friend,* and *Great Expectations.* Until you do, you will not have the very faintest notion of what the name of Dickens means. *Barnaby Rudge* is mere boy's work in comparison. He did not come of age until Ruskin and Carlyle probed his social conscience to the depth, and he made a beginning of his great period with *Hard Times.* But when it came, it *was* great.

I don't know what you mean by my book of musical criticism. I have never printed my musical articles. There is nothing but *The Perfect Wagnerite* . . .

I cannot send you a portrait, because pictures have been so ingeniously used for enemy communications that they are now barred by the censorship. What have you done with the Rothenstein drawing you had? There is a book of sayings from my works compiled by my wife, with a photogravure picture of Rodin's bust of me which I might perhaps get through. I believe the publisher can send it if he is prepared to guarantee that he picked it at random out of a thousand copies, and can certify that it has not been tampered with. I will have a try, anyhow.

I got the story about the madman safely. Why have you always been so curiously shy of publishing your stories in your own papers and writing your name well across them? I believe you suffer from the sort of neurosis that prevents certain actors from ever becoming anything more than 'character actors'. They are adepts at disguise, and can act very effectively in a disguise; but if you ask them to 'play straight', as one must do in the grand school or in 'leading business', they are paralysed with stage fright immediately, and simply cannot do it. There are journalists, too, and even authors, who can write with the greatest impudence as 'we' without a signature, or over a *nom de plume,* but can hardly be persuaded to write a letter for publication because it involves the first person and the name and address. Thus Brodribb makes a great reputation as Henry Irving, Miss Evans as George Eliot, Duval (or whatever it was) as Victor Hugo, Arouet as Voltaire, though as Brodribb, Evans, etc., they would have been as awkward as an actor making a speech before the curtain. Even Oscar Wilde shrank from Fingal O'Flahertie and hankered after Sebastian Melmoth. I wonder whether you would have made yourself more widely known as Ferdinand Hohenstaufen. You are, like most of us, a mass of contradictions. You sail the Spanish Main with the blackest of flags, the reddest of sashes, the hugest of cutlasses, and the thinnest of skins.

I am writing all this drivel on the coast of Kerry with nothing visible in the grey but the white horses on the waves and a blanket of incessant rain zenith high and horizon far. However, you deserve it. You seem to extract what Ibsen calls a salutary self-torture from making me hold up the distorting mirror of London before you. What an amusement!

Ever,

G. Bernard Shaw

In the summary of opinions about him by his friends and enemies I think next to Wilde's was George Moore's. Moore put Shaw down as 'the funny man in a boarding house'. Huneker said he was 'a wingless angel with an old maid's temperament'. De Cassères classified him as 'a fifth carbon copy of Voltaire who could never be great because his humour is not tragic'.

As Ireland reared him and America discovered him, it may be presumed these opinions say about all there is to say on Shaw. No English opinion has anything like the same sting to it. There, for the most part, he is surrounded by sycophants – from people like Sir Barry Jackson, who introduced *Back to Methuselah* and *The Apple Cart* to English audiences, to transients like Charlie Chaplin, who only stay in Shaw's smiling circle long enough to answer the demands of flashlight photographers.

21

In War and Peace

For years I suffered, along with many others, under the delusion that Shaw's war attitude was courageously independent, but later developments seem to have taken a little glamour off St George's shield. These new facts move him, I think, a good deal nearer the gallery of British war heroes. His public utterances stirred a lot of Englishmen into considering him as an enemy within their gates, but in point of fact he was 'safe', and the Government always knew he was safe. They even took him on a personally-conducted tour of the battlefields, and you do not do that exactly with spies.

More than that, there is evidence that he was a party to documents – one in particular, 'An Epistle to the Moors' – that were circulated to fool the Arabs, or at least to prevent them from revolting against the Allies. He played the same trick on his own countrymen to induce the Irish to take up the War Loan and to see the world outside their own country by emulating *O'Flaherty, V.C.* Of course, it might be argued that, after all, Arabs are Arabs, and using them one way or another is not to be considered too seriously in the issues of life and death; and, after all, German bombs did crack Shaw's windows at Adelphi Terrace to give him a realisation of how close to home angry words can bring the shrapnel of war.

I don't mean to say he did not strike out against abuses, and his *Common Sense about the War* was certainly used by the Germans as propaganda to prove that the English were not guiltless in bringing about the world catastrophe. But who but a fool thought they were? All the parties suffered from degrees of guilt, and, if the Germans had the most blood on their hands, the others were not free from minor stains. All this was known before and during the war, and afterwards.

A few years ago the publication of Lord Morley's letters proved beyond a doubt that Viscount Grey and others in London were about as culpable as the men around the Kaiser.

Now Shaw must have had inner knowledge of these things in 1914, as all great men have access to the information denied the gentry; but I do not see that he used it to blow up the whole mean business, and so bring the world either near a complete ruin or real peace. He compromised here, as I have shown he compromised in his plays, and if he were in good company, that doesn't forgive him in my eyes. I can respect opinions like Chesterton's, who had fixed ideas about Huns before the war, during the war, and after the war. Shaw is not of this type. I don't mean to imply that he was a chameleon placed on a Scotch plaid and therefore driven nearly to distraction, but I do intend that the world shall understand that he changed colours all too easily, and became not merely pro-Ally, which would be narrow enough, but a part of England's civilian home guard, which kept the War Office and the generals in the field safe.

He is protesting in 1924 that he never attacked the Government at all: 'The danger of discouraging enlistment during the voluntary period and of weakening the national *morale* was,' he argues, 'too serious. I did not let myself go until the war was over.'

And he assures us that the British Government fully knew that he was on their side. He tells us that: 'I still find Americans, and Englishmen who were in America at the time – Henry Arthur Jones, for example – under the impression that I was what the French called a "Defeatist". It was lucky for me that the British Government knew better, or I should have been shot.'

This moral support of Shaw's was so well understood by Whitehall that it explains why, whatever his writings or interviews, no attempt was ever made to put him behind the bars. Many others were imprisoned in all countries – from Liebknecht in Germany to Debs in America – but Shaw, if he suffered any inconveniences, suffered none greater than those of other civilians without conscience anywhere in Europe between 1914 and 1918.

Only a Freudian could dissect such a confused mind and ascertain the specific pre-natal and other influences that enable the man who 'hates slaughter, whether in war or in the butcher's back-yard', to write: 'As a matter of fact, I myself should not like to sail far into Socialism without a powerful Army and Navy and a highly susceptible patriotic sense of nationality.'

Imagine coupling that with a social creed the aim of which was to abolish all national boundaries and national feelings, and the war-cry of which was: 'Workers of the world, unite!'

After this it is small wonder that Shaw is to be found either on the one side or on the other of warring armies, just as any patriot. He is a Fabian, a Socialist, in time of peace. The moment war breaks out – or threatens to – he forgets his peaceable philosophy.

Recall, for instance, his attitude on the Boer War. To the amazement of most of his admirers, Shaw declared himself on the side of the British, and, though he explained his position with perfect sincerity, he only convinced me that, Briton-like, he mistook English Imperialism for the cause of humanity. Here is his defence to me. To some it may appear satisfying:

March 5th 1918

DEAR FRANK HARRIS – In the South African business I was not a pro-Boer. I never got over Olive Schreiner's *Story of an African Farm*. Some few years before the war, Cronwright Schreiner came to London. I asked him why he and Joubert and the rest put up with Kruger and his obsolete theocracy. He said they knew all about it and deplored it, but that the old man would die presently and then Krugerism would be quietly dropped and a liberal régime introduced. I suggested that it might be dangerous to wait; but it was evident that Oom Paul was too strong for them. During the Boer War, a curious thing happened in Norway. There, as in Germany, everyone took it for granted that the right side was the anti-English side. Suddenly Ibsen asked, in his grim manner, 'Are we really on the side of Mr Kruger and his Old Testament?' The effect was electrical. Norway shut up. I felt like Ibsen. I was, of course, not in the least taken in by *The Times* campaign, though I defended *The Times* against the accusation of bribery on the ground that it was not necessary to pay *The Times* to do what it was only too ready to do for nothing. But I saw that Kruger meant the seventeenth century, and the Scottish seventeenth at that; and so, to my great embarrassment, I found myself on the side of the mob when you and Chesterton and John Burns and Lloyd George were facing the music. It is astonishing what bad company advanced views may get one into.

Today something of the same kind is happening. I stand with Balfour and against Hertling in contending that the Balance of Power is not obsolete. This is a Balance of Power war between Democracy and Plutocracy, and also an experimental test as to whether modern war can settle anything except the hash of the combatants. It must be fought out, either to a stalemate, which means the defeat of war as an institution; or to a result sufficiently decisive for either Wilson or the Kaiser to impose their terms. I do not believe in the least in the efficiency of the German governing class. If the German army had been efficient and ready, it would have gone straight to Paris. It missed its rush, and practically lost the war, because it came to Liège without siege guns and had to turn tail almost at the gates of Paris because Von Kluck dashed on without food. The first year of the war proved abundantly that old Liebknecht was right when he so implacably ridiculed the legend of German education and efficiency. The Prussian system delivered Germany into the hands of the lieutenants and the generals who made themselves agreeable to Wilhelm, and the result was that even Kitchener and French were able to bluff them and stall them off until we improvised an army.

Yours,

G. B. S.

Again and again I shall have to show that this Bazarof, like Molière, is full of the milk of human kindness; but, even as Turgenev's Nihilist hero, Shaw fails just at the moment when a critical situation, in the world or in his plays, demands the drastic action of his revolutionary *credo*.

No doubt of Shaw's kindness of heart. On learning of the death of a friend's son in the late war, he could not restrain his real feelings, usually well under leash, about the universal slaughter. Under date of January 7th, 1918, he wrote to Mrs Patrick Campbell about the death of her son.

Never saw it or heard about it until your letter came. It is no use: I can't be sympathetic: these things simply make me furious. I want to swear. I *do* swear. Killed just because people are blasted fools. A chaplain, too, to say nice things about it. It is not his business to say nice things about it, but to shout that the 'voice of thy son's blood crieth unto God from the ground'. No, don't shew me the letter. But I should very much like to have a nice talk with that dear chaplain, that sweet sky-pilot, that . . .

No use going on like this, Stella. Wait for a week, and then I shall be very clever and broadminded again and have forgotten all about him. I shall be quite as nice as the chaplain.

> Oh, damn, damn, damn, damn, damn, damn, damn, damn, DAMN.
And oh, dear, dear, dear, dear, dear, dearest!

G. B. S.

But if he didn't take the stand of an internationalist toward the World
War, as such, he at least bitterly condemned the savage treatment of the
conscientious objectors; and, indeed, the treatment of all of us who did
not share the madness of war.

I have personal reasons to congratulate myself on Shaw's kindness
of heart, for when I left France and went to America, and told what
Shaw and others have since proved to be the truth about the war and
England's partial responsibility for it, I found that I was being treated
in England as a sort of traitor because I preferred to be loyal to truth
rather than to English interests. The baser sort howled at me in
every newspaper, and even men like the late Arnold Bennett, who
had followed me with praise for years, were not ashamed now to hint
at corruption in order to explain my incomprehensible admiration of
certain German virtues. But when I was attacked in *The New Statesman*, Shaw defended me in his own way, with the old kindliness. He
and I have been able to differ about the war without impairing our
friendship.

This reminds me of Shaw's attempt to excuse his unorthodox stand
on the war: perhaps to allay the pangs of his Specialist conscience. At
the end of his preface to *Heartbreak House* he tries to justify himself for
having written pamphlets on the war instead of plays. He says: 'You
cannot make war on war and on your neighbour at the same time.
War cannot bear the terrible castigation of comedy, the ruthless light
of laughter that glares on the stage. When men are heroically dying
for their country, it is not the time to show their lovers and wives and
fathers and mothers how they are being sacrificed to the blunders of
boobies, the cupidity of capitalists, the ambition of conquerors, the
electioneering of demagogues, the Pharisaism of patriots, the lusts
and lies and rancours and bloodthirsts that love war because it opens
their prison doors and sets them on the throne of power and popularity.
For unless these things are mercilessly exposed they will hide under the
mantle of the ideals on the stage just as they do in real life.'

I differ, of course, and all history proves Shaw wrong in this. It is
what you preach to the people in a crisis that influences their actions.
Sunday sermons have no effect. Everybody is pretty good on Sunday:

it's weekday goodness (pacifism in wartime) that the world needs. In a World War, Sunday sermons only heighten the tragedy.

For fifty years the German Socialists had been preaching to their followers 'international brotherhood'; but, when the Kaiser demanded financial sinews for war, they immediately voted it, and the Socialists throughout the world – with few exceptions of truly courageous and convinced internationalists, like Liebknecht, Debs, Russell, and Rolland – followed their example.

Shaw simply forgot what he himself had written about those who seek to justify every outrage and infamy with the cry of 'On principle.' Listen to him in *The Man of Destiny*: 'There is nothing so bad or so good that you will not find Englishmen doing it; but you will never find an Englishman in the wrong. He does everything on principle. He fights you on patriotic principles; he robs you on business principles; he enslaves you on imperial principles; he bullies you on manly principles; he supports his king on loyal principles, and cuts off his king's head on republican principles. His watchword is always duty; and he never forgets that the nation which lets its duty get on the opposite side to its interests is lost.'

Why didn't he remember that in 1914, he who knew that war was a crime and that 'soldiering is the coward's art of attacking mercilessly when you are strong, and keeping out of harm's way when you are weak'?

Why didn't Shaw ever smash out against the whole mean business? It had to be left to the young Remarques, Barbusses, Stallings, and Hamiltons to show the realism and madness of war. Shaw only showed its chocolate-eating soldiers, and medal-wearing Irish privates.

That he knows the whole truth, and is able to tell it, he proves to the hilt. Listen to this: 'In spite of a Liberal Revolution or two, I can no longer be satisfied with fictitious morals and fictitious good conduct, shedding fictitious glory on robbery, starvation and disease, crime, drink, war, cruelty, cupidity, and all the other commonplaces of civilisation which drive men to the theatre to make foolish pretences that such things are progress, science, morals, religion, patriotism, imperial supremacy, national greatness, and all the other names the newspapers call them.'

Someone has said that Shaw protests against war *generally speaking*. How tragically true! But, *particularly* speaking, we find him right in the midst of the Great War – and on the safe side at that. The very same side against whom, he tells us, he 'warned our patriots and emphasised the fact that the militaristic morality of Lord Roberts and Mr Winston Churchill was precisely that of the German militarists'.

Could any sane and reasonable man, then, choose between the two? Not to speak of a peace-loving Fabian? Perhaps I'm old-fashioned; it may be a mark of Shaw's genius that he can divide the indivisible and thus square the crooked circle.

He confesses England's direct if partial responsibility for the war.

'For three hundred years,' he tells us, 'it has been a fixed principle in British diplomacy that no military power of any magnitude shall occupy the continental shores of the North Sea . . .

'Therefore it is true that the invasion of Belgium by Germany was the provocation on which England declared war, having prepared for this contingency since 1906.

' . . . As balance-of-power diplomacy was neither popular with, nor indeed comprehensible by, the man in the street (who was presently to be the man in the trenches), it was camouflaged with a mass of nonsense about our disinterestedness, our unpreparedness, the sacredness of neutrality and of a long extinct treaty, and all the rest of it.

'This went down in America until the Germans occupied Brussels and found all the records of our secret military arrangements with the Belgians. They blew the gaff by circulating facsimiles of the documents on an enormous scale. I guessed that this would happen, and set to work to disclaim the camouflage to the Americans I met, and to set our case on a genuine footing. Senator Beveridge gave the publicity I desired to my disclaimer; and of course the Germans eagerly quoted me to show that the moral case against them was a trumped-up one, which it was. But they made very little effective play with it, because their intelligence service was remarkably un-intelligent – nothing like so cunning as ours.'

I lacked Shaw's talent of choosing and championing the 'right' side in a quarrel of two scoundrels whose aims are identical. Therefore I felt myself compelled to attack Shaw and his position during the World War. In the March 1919 issue of *Pearson's*, a magazine which I published in New York at the time, despite ceaseless sniping by the United States Government, I exposed the falsity of Shaw's attitude as well as his numerous public misstatements. I wrote exposing how the British Lion crowned himself with American laurels!

'After discounting all blunders and all reserves,' Shaw had written, 'we can say now that Germany was not only hopelessly blockaded, but out-witted, out-prepared, out-generalled, out-fought, overflown, out-gassed, out-tanked, out-raided, out-bombed, and finally brought to her knees at England's feet, more abjectly than Philip or Louis or Napoleon, or any of the old rivals of the British Lion.

'It has been an amazing and magnificent achievement of which the English themselves will not become conscious until some eloquent historian a century hence tells them what to think about it.'

I pointed out to him the early disorganisation of the British at Mons, and told him of the English soldiers I saw in Paris who admitted they had been driven out of all discipline and run off their feet. I reminded him that when Balfour travelled to America in 1917 he made no bones about admitting that Great Britain was at the end of her resources.

It isn't any credit to America; it's simply a fact that she won the war. She won it, as a young and fresh halfback, thrust into a game in the closing minutes, wins the contest by a great run which scores the deciding point. The veterans who have played all through the game saved it from being lost, but the newcomer won it. That's the yardstick by which victories and defeats are measured – the sporting yardstick – and why people resent using it in this instance is beyond me.

Anybody interested in those things must know that what 'eloquent historians' will say will be that the German achievements were the surprise of them all, and that America, lucky as always, turned the tide at Belleau Wood and St Mihiel. The French, English, and a dozen others fought the war: the Americans won it. That's the historic truth. Anything else is just national pride parading as history.

Observe how Shaw, when you riddle his lapse into jingoism, escapes to safe ground:

March 1919

MY DEAR HARRIS – Your article on 'How the British Lion Crowns Himself with American Laurels' does not really affect the truth of my general statement of the position. The British Empire has smashed the German Empire: that is the point to be seized. That she did it with French troops, with Russian troops, with Italian troops, with Portuguese troops, with Irish and Indian troops, and finally with American troops, only enhances the demonstration of her amazing instinctive war craft. If it could be shown that the British Navy did not exist, and that not a single English soldier had been under fire, the demonstration would be all the more imposing: indeed, it would be miraculous.

The question of personal prowess is for schoolboys. For grown men the interest of the actual fighting lies in the absurd vicissitudes of the campaign. All the armies won glorious victories and incurred crushing defeats; but none of them seemed to matter. Napoleon at Waterloo and Pompey at Pharsalia suffered only trifling reverses in comparison with Gough in the rout of the Fifth Army and Cadorna at Caporetto. Yet these were the preludes to victory. The French ought to call it the war of the *à peu près*: Paris nearly taken, Verdun all but captured, the channel ports only just not reached, St Quentin and Cambrai on the verge of falling, Rheims morally if not militarily stormed, Jutland 'a damned near thing' (Jellicoe's book implies your verdict on it), and the decision, after everyone had given up all hope of a decision, achieved with appalling completeness by Famine. There were moments when all seemed lost; yet nothing happened. At the first gas-attack four miles of our line vanished in strangulated terror and left the way to the sea open; and the result was no worse than if it had been held by fifty million troops. When we suddenly changed from taking less than our share of the line to more than we had men for, and the collapse of Gough was followed by a warning from Haig that the Germans were through, the panic here was so utter and shameless that the Government frantically abandoned the harvest and conscribed Ireland (on paper); yet the upshot was more triumphant for us than when Haig exploded nineteen volcanoes simultaneously on the Messines Ridge, and seemed in full flood towards Berlin. The Turks drove us into the sea at Gallipoli; sent our fleet flying from the Straits; and gathered Kut and General Townshend like daisies. They might just as well have made us a present of Constantinople and Bagdad without striking a blow.

The American Army was so farcically inexperienced at first that it had to be brigaded with the French Army; and the moment it was cut loose and left to itself its lines of communication jammed and it was left without food and munitions for two days, during which it was at the mercy of the Germans (if they had only known); yet the American Army wiped out the St Mihiel salient and saved Colonel House from having to send General Pershing home to be run for the Presidency as a consolation prize.

I asked a British war correspondent what his grounds were for saying that the British Army could knock the American Army into a cocked hat. 'Well,' said he, 'it is like this: In your communication lines, on which the whole thing depends, you order the men to drive to the right. The English soldier drives within a foot of the right. The French soldier drives within two feet of it. The Belgian soldier drives within three feet of it. The American soldier asks who in hell you suppose you are talking to, and makes up his mind that no bloody staff car is going to pass his lorry if he can help it. And that is why the sheep-like Englishman can beat the brave American bullyboy every time when it comes to scientific soldiering.' I dare say there is enough truth in this picturesque summing-up to be worth repeating. The way in which the American boys slaughtered and defeated themselves by rushing on machine-guns without tanks while Haig's men, who had learned their lesson, got off with a tenth of the American casualties, was heart-rending to hear about.

Do not encourage the Americans to underrate the British as warriors. Like all the Allies, they have had plenty of staggering reverses. They have been beaten by the Turks and by the Germans in engagements which will fill glorious pages of Turkish and German history, and not be mentioned in English history at all. They have been stampeded on occasion with a comic completeness that would not let down a Chaplin film at its wildest. But, as they say themselves, what of it? At the battle of Waterloo the British artillery ran away so flagrantly that the Iron Duke would never allow an official history of the battle to be written. But the British came out on top. In 1914 the French Army, as Joffre told it bluntly in the face of Europe, disgraced itself by its headlong retreat from Namur. The Portuguese Army, after holding a frightful position for several days, apparently with unquenchable valour, achieved a record skedaddle. But for the resulting intervention of the British General, Lord Cavan, the Italians who surrendered at Caporetto would have been starved to death after the armistice by their own commanders. I will assume, as I am writing this to America, that no American ever blenched, ever ran, ever sat down and cried like a child, ever ceased posing for his picture in the next number of *Life*. But the American soldier's heart knows its own bitterness; and it is for him to tell his countrymen the truth when he hears them explaining how the American Army won the war when all the Europeans were whipped to a frazzle.

When everyone has owned up, England remains the most formidable single fighting Power in the world. I have insisted on that of set purpose; and I insist on it still, not as a mere Jingo brag of how Von

Kluck has pleaded in his own defence that in the retreat from Mons the British soldier, even when the British Army was running away at a speed which sometimes worked out at eight miles an hour, had an incredible and impossible quantity of fight left in him (perhaps from lack of imagination), but because the most dangerous mistake that could be made in the world now is the mistake of America under-rating England as a fighting power.

I do not think there is much danger of the converse mistake being made. England knows fairly well that she could not have won without America. The supplies from America before the States came formally into the war, and the staggering demonstration of their ability to send men by the million across the Atlantic at a time-rate which nobody had believed possible, had an effect far beyond that of their actual feats in the field; for the American Army had not had time to learn its business in that department, and its exploits can give no measure of what it would be capable of in full training. It took the British and German Armies years to shape with any sort of efficiency; indeed, the French Army, in spite of its initial collapse, was probably the best trained at the start, though perhaps I am influenced in saying this by my own observation and comparison of the passing glimpses I got before the war at Treves and Toul, of the daily work of the German and French soldiers.

Of course, the Germans fought splendidly; but then, so did every-body. Heroes and Thermopylaes were six a penny in Europe before the war had lasted three months.

I rejected your Paris information as to the British having promised an army of a quarter of a million to the French, because Haldane's figures are precise, and are confirmed by the Brussels documents, whereas the size of the old British Army, which was known to the French, made an offer of 250,000 men impossible. French gossip, which always assumes that other countries have conscription and millions of men to play with because France has them, might easily invent such a story; but it could not have come from a military expert.

As to the panic in which Mr Balfour appealed for American help, it prevailed all through the war. There were moments during the sub-marine campaign when it was excusable; but much of the funk was chronic and contemptible. Civilian and parliamentary England often reminded me of a certain prizefighter who flourished when I was a boy. His skill and power were such that he was always victorious at his weight; but he was so nervous that they had to keep a mirror in the ring to shew him his face between every round to disprove his piteous pleas that his features were obliterated and that they must throw up the sponge for him, as he would surely be killed if he went on. People of his kidney, with howling rage and terror, denounced as 'pro-German' all who ventured to express the slightest doubt that the Germans were irresistible and that England was at her last gasp. One well-known author [Henry Arthur Jones], at a moment when England was playing the very devil with the enemy, told me that England was his mother, and that I had 'kicked his dying mother on her deathbed', because I told him that Germany had not a dog's chance of winning, and the British Lion was never going stronger. On the other hand, the retreat from Mons was bragged about as if it were a masterpiece of victorious strategy. We were, it was said, luring the Germans into a trap. Nothing that you can say of the demoralisation wrought by the war among the civilians can be too severe; but is anyone in a position to cast the first stone?

You can tell the Americans from me that they have seriously compromised the credit of republicanism throughout the world by their outrageous repudiation, at the first shot, of all the liberties the Declaration of Independence proclaimed. When they began by sentencing a George Washingtonian colonel to imprisonment for life, and followed that up by a series of persecutions which culminated in the ridiculous sentence on Debs, they disgraced their country, disgraced Wilson, and gave Germany, which had tolerated an avowed traitor like Liebknecht for an incredible time before at last sentencing him to only four years' imprisonment, the right to claim that even under the Kaiser she was much freer than the United States under its boasted democracy. As a republican I am ashamed of the American-patriots; and you may tell them so with my compliments. I have had to stand up for Wilson, not as an American, but as a great man of whom his country is apparently utterly unworthy. Heaven knows we did abominable things here when we could not go to bed without fearing that we should be wakened by a bomb coming through the roof; but at least we raised our War Loans without the help of highwaymen.

That is all I have to say about the Laurels. Let the British and American Jingoes scramble for the leaves to their heart's content: I take it that your business and mine is to uproot the tree and cast it into the bottomless pit.

Ever,

G. BERNARD SHAW

In his divination of what our business is, Shaw is correct. I only hope, however, that 'an eloquent historian of the future' can prove he did try to uproot the tree and not merely clip off a few branches.

The time has come when most sensible people agree with what I had been saying for years in regard to the World War. It was, as I have claimed all along, the inevitable outcome of the gospel of wealth preached assiduously by all capitalists and economists for the last century or so. 'Every man for himself', was the new commandment given by Adam Smith, Malthus, and Ricardo. And about the middle of the nineteenth century this gospel was rounded off with the phrase, 'Every nation for itself', which resulted in the seizing of Egypt and the partition of Africa – Britain taking the lion's share as always.

Now this gospel still remains in force. It has not been rescinded yet, nor discredited, whether by individuals or by nations. On the contrary, it is now being applied relentlessly to Germany by the victors, just as it was applied by Germany to Russia at Brest-Litovsk.

'Like causes produce like results', is immutably true. If France, Britain, Italy, as other Powers, pushing their selfish interests as far as they can, be not restrained, another furious war of nationalities, which is now being prepared, may certainly be expected before long, especially when the generation which has suffered through the last war shall have died out.

This is and was my view, and, as the reader must see, I have acted up to it.

And this is also Shaw's view. It is, therefore, a permissible question, 'Has *he* acted up to it?' As a humane man, a peace-loving man, a Fabian, even a vegetarian, what has he done to help stop wholesale human slaughter?

Assume that he had tried his best to stop the war, as far as lay in his power. Such an example by the greatest living man of England would have exerted a tremendous influence upon the minds of men in every country. And who can foretell the effects of a strikingly idealistic and courageous example? It is like a stone thrown into water – the ripples spread, multiply, and agitate the whole sea. There are enough examples in history of courageous men who, by standing boldly up against the storm of general viciousness or madness, have changed the whole current of history. Jesus, for instance, was such a man. Socrates was another, and though both had to die for their love of justice and truth, yet they live for ever. In our own times, men like Tolstoy and Gandhi have by the courage of their convictions gained millions to their cause. Many similar instances can be found that illumine the otherwise dark pages of human history. They are the bright spots, the beacons of light and hope for the future. Their names are those of the really *great*.

Is Shaw great in this sense, the *only* sense indeed in which human character can be called great? Can we niche him among the illustrious of the world?

Let Shaw speak for himself: 'After a speech of mine at Stourbridge, in support of the late Mary McArthur,' he tells us – after he exposed the fake claims of the alleged 'war to end war' – 'a soldier said to me: "If I had known all that in 1914, they would never have got khaki on *my* back." My reply was: "That is precisely why I did not tell you in 1914." '

Yet he pretends to have tried all his life to enlighten people on the evil, folly, and infamy of war. He dealt in his numerous tracts with it, he wrote long essays and plays about it – when there was peace, of course. But in 1914 – that is, when a critical moment came that called for real men to speak out – Shaw pocketed his true opinions.

He issued his famous *Common Sense about the War*, which was certainly worthy of Shaw, the great comedian, but which a Tolstoy, who took the commandment 'Thou shalt not kill' seriously, would have considered a betrayal of his Master.

What it may be asked, of his *Common Sense about the War*? Nothing but a one-sided militarist appeal in the best Shavian manner. No wonder it failed of all effect, except to induce some old-women-men's clubs to pass commendatory resolutions. When Dr Henderson asked him what were the results of his appeal, Shaw truthfully replied: 'None beyond selling 75,000 copies.'

Apparently it is true that 'evil bringeth its own punishment'. For the only result of *Common Sense* was to accuse Shaw of having taken sides with the Kaiser. Again it was proven true that you can't sit between two stools: you can't abhor war and at the same time participate in universal slaughter.

'It ought to be plain to a child of three,' he says, 'that, in any newspaper friendly to the Allies, *Common Sense* should either have been published all in one piece or not published at all. It was designed very

largely for American consumption; and it began by a complete disclaimer of all the pretexts for the war which the Germans could and did
prove to be invalid, and which must have seemed in America merely
hypocritical . . . Then I gave the real reason why German Imperialism
had to be smashed. To allow it to triumph would, I said, be "to shut the
gates of mercy on mankind".'

The New York Times published part of it, and left it 'to be continued in
our next', without a hint of the nature of the sequel. America took
the first section to be a pro-German manifesto, and never read the
remaining instalments, Shaw insists. 'I could do nothing: it had not
occurred to me that such a blunder was possible.'

But it was not a blunder on the part of the *Times*. It was a crime on
the part of Shaw. The blood madness of the war mania had hushed the
voice of the great prophet of peace. *After* the war he remembers again
his *credo* and 'courageously' – alas, too late! – declares: 'If ever you go to
war again, shoot all your red-hot patriots first thing.' Not, however,
because they are bellicose. Solely because they get into the way of the
soldiers, and diminish military efficiency!

It may be protested that Shaw's failure to stand by his guns in a
critical time does not affect his place as writer of great dramas. It
doesn't – theoretically speaking. But, in my estimation, no art has any
value whatever unless it is sincere. To be great, to live, it must be that,
above everything else. What effect can mouthings of peace have in the
mouth of a soldier about to rip open his antagonist's belly? I do not
exaggerate, I hope. I think I am justified in applying this to Shaw, for at
heart he agrees with me.

He didn't conceal his contempt for the people who had taken the
frightful slaughter of soldiers in Flanders as if it were a cinema-show
got up to please their patriotism, but who went stark raving mad when
the *Lusitania*, one of their favourite pleasure-boats – actually with first-
class passengers on board – was blown up.

I fear it will be equally hard for the impartial future historian to
conceal his contempt for the preacher of peace turned patriot in time
of war.

Is my charge that Shaw played the rôle of war-drummer and round-
them-up sergeant, exaggerated? Let him support me in his own words:
'I may say once for all that on every occasion – and there were three or
four – when I was asked to do a literary job to help the authorities
during the war, I did it to the entire satisfaction of those who asked me.'

Too late, Shaw realised that the war to end war was not the blessing he had painted it before the Armistice. Asked whether he thought the effects of the war, on the whole, beneficial to mankind, Shaw replied in his characteristic manner: 'Do *you* think the effects of the San Francisco earthquake have been beneficial to California as a whole? It demonstrated the stability of steel-framed sky-scrapers and shook down great numbers of rotten and unsanitary buildings, besides removing many people who have not been perceptibly missed. Well, the war shook down Tsardom, an unspeakable abomination, and made an end of the new German Empire and the old Apostolic Austrian one. But if we can be reformed only by the accidental results of horrible catastrophes,' he went on to ask, 'what hope is there for mankind in them? The war was a horror; and everybody is the worse for it except the people who were so narrowly selfish that even a war improved them.'

I despair of finding Shaw clear – with himself, I mean – on any question whatever. His practical knowledge of men seems to me no better than his application of Fabian tenets to life. It has always especially amused me how he berated me in May 1919 for my criticism of Wilson, and how later he denounced him as an apostate.

On May 24th, 1919, I had the following letter from Shaw:

DEAR FRANK HARRIS – Be careful about Wilson. There is a case against Wilson: but it is the case of Tom Paine against Washington; and I think you will admit, in the perspective of history, that Paine got his values wrong. Wilson has had an impossible task; and years will elapse before his success or failure can be estimated. Even those who are behind the scene, who alone know the secret understandings by which the parties have squared each other, cannot place him as we can now place Washington or Lincoln. What is certain is that he succeeded in making himself the spokesman of the right side when he entered the field; and I backed him accordingly, and shall continue to do so until I find a better man to back. Don't raise an alarm of damp sheets when there is a fire to be put out.

Ever,

G. BERNARD SHAW

But later on, Shaw seemed to come nearer to me in my approximate estimate of Wilson's character and weaknesses. By 1924 he had discovered that the moment Wilson realised that Clemenceau and Lloyd George had no intention of making good his fourteen points, and were out simply for plunder and for abuse of victory, just like the North after Lincoln's death, he should have shaken the dust of Europe off his feet and withdrawn the United States from the settlement. Most unfortunately, at that moment Wilson caught war-fever, and to the utter consternation of his admirers (that is, G. Bernard Shaw *et al.*) he began to talk of German guilt and so forth.

The 'tin Jesus', whom Clemenceau ridiculed behind his back, suddenly became a raving Jingo. 'The purely pathological nature of this disastrous change was proved by the breakdown in Mr Wilson's health which followed. It was a tragic calamity. Whether history will ever forgive him for his apostasy at a moment when all the remaining hopes of the half-despairing goodwill of the world were centred on him I cannot tell.'

This from Shaw, who has faith in treaties! At least, he says in *Saint Joan* that 'one good treaty is worth ten fights', though he declares in almost the same breath: 'When wolves combine to kill a horse, the death of the horse only sets them fighting one another for the choicest morsels. Men are not better than wolves if they have no better principles; accordingly, we find that the Armistice and the Treaty have only landed us in a race of armaments towards the next war.'

Somewhere else Shaw has said that unfortunately the earnest people get drawn off the track of evolution by the illusion of progress.

I am afraid that Shaw himself has, all through his life, been one of those 'earnest people'. But do really earnest people mistake the quarrels of international capitalists and imperialists for a struggle 'to end all wars'? And do really earnest persons, who have their wits about them, even if only Fabians, confound punitive treaties with progress?

No wonder that Shaw finally came to see *such* progress as illusion. Socialist prophet that he aspired to be, he should not have been drawn off the track of evolution. He should have realised instantly that 'winning the war' was only an illusion of progress.

But Shaw remains true to himself in a certain sense. I mean, true to the psychical Babel that *is* Shaw. No sooner had he come to see that 'the Armistice and the Treaty have only landed us in a race of armaments towards the next war', than he took a fresh breath and declared for a League of Nations, thus confounding the confusion.

'If the diplomats win,' he added, 'the fight for the balance of power will go on, and the peace they will negotiate will be only the interval between the rounds.'

Astonishing wisdom, indeed, and an uncanny power of divination amounting to genius. The genius of Babel, and I am afraid 'tis the only sign of genius I can find in Shaw on questions of peace and goodwill.

I don't like to be hard on any man who has done the least service for humanity, least of all to Shaw who, when I went to America in the beginning of the war and was attacked in the British Press as pro-German, defended me with unique humour, as only he can defend. 'If you don't think Harris a genius,' he wrote, 'at least everyone admits he is a very clever fellow. But for a very clever man he is the most short-sighted possible. From the beginning he has defended Ireland against England, and surely money and reward were on the other side. Again, he defended Egypt and India against England, and again money and reward were on the other side. Now he has been defending Germany against England. In every single case, Harris brings his pigs to the wrong market, which is a strange trait in a man recognised as extremely clever. Perhaps, after all, the truth is that he has convictions and not selfishness to satisfy.'

To have convictions is dangerous in this world of ours, and 'bringing my pigs to the wrong market' is a result that matters little. At least to me. But it is significant that Shaw points *this* out as vital.

Shaw can say with Byron that it is not difficult to die, and enormously difficult to live: that explains why, at bottom, peace is not only better than war, but infinitely more arduous.

This applies with equal force – I think even with greater – to the individual as to the nation. And I believe Shaw supports my view when he declares: 'The truth sticks in our throats with all the sauces it is served with: it will never go down until we take it without any sauce at all.'

Why, then, not take it without any sauce at all? And whose business is it to give it to us in that natural form if not Shaw's?

As I have shown, Shaw more closely approximated a Government decoy than an enemy within during the war. Chesterton, whose book on Shaw is the only one that has ever proved interesting reading to me, says most people say they don't understand Shaw or they don't agree with him, and that he understands him, but doesn't agree with him. If my well-nourished friend can understand Shaw's war attitude he can take the trophy without any protest from me. Chesterton's own position is clear; he was pro-British and anti-German. But Shaw, invited by Romain Rolland to *planer au dessus de la melée*, replied that he had no wings; and that in a shooting match one must stand by one's neighbours and shoot those who are trying to shoot them. Heine's camp of God's spies who fight the war for the liberation of humanity and have no time for other larger-screened but less important international quarrels is not in question in vulgar shooting matches. Besides, both sides claimed to be God's spies.

While the war was at its height, I received this letter from Shaw, after he had completed his visit to the western front. One sentence in it is characteristically Shavian. It deals with Russia. I cannot help quoting it:

DEAR FRANK HARRIS – Good news from Russia, eh? Not quite what any of the belligerents intended, any more than Bismarck intended to make France a republic in 1870; but the Lord fulfils Himself in many ways. It is probably not the least surprise He has up His sleeve for us.

Yours ever,

G. BERNARD SHAW

22

Religion

Shaw's conception of the Supreme Being is what he calls 'Life Force', and I have spent half my days trying to find out what that may mean.

'I say that Life Force is God,' he declares, 'but the Englishman objects to this. He says that Life Force is a foreigner, while God is an Englishman. That is where we disagree.'

Amusingly Shavian, winning the world's support at the expense of his cardboard Englishman, but hardly revealing; on the contrary, confusing.

He tells us that he was baptised a member of the Irish Church, and was freed, with the help of an unbelieving world about him, from all church-going by the time he was ten. While still in his teens he became an atheist, and after that, Narcissus-like, worshipped his own wit. Still he strove to be broad-minded.

He realised that 'the Roman Catholic priest could be as agreeable and cultured a person as a Protestant clergyman, and that the notion that the courtly distinction of Dublin society corresponded to any real human distinctions was as ignorant as it was pernicious'.

Though he thought he had rid himself of theological superstitions, he has all his life remained a religious man, and religion has been the subject on which he has written perhaps more than on any other theme after Socialism; which I suppose is only another façade of the same temple.

But Shaw's religion has very little in common with the orthodox and generally accepted idea of it. 'If religion is that which binds men to one another,' he says, 'and irreligion that which sunders, then must I testify that I found the religion of my country in its musical genius and its irreligion in its churches and drawing-rooms.'

Having arrived at a ripe age, he now declares: 'This much I know, looking at life after seventy: men without religion are moral cowards, and mostly physical cowards, too, when they are sober.'

To Shaw the religion of Socialism represents a very definite ethical influence in the lives of men, though it seems to me that his claims are wildly extravagant. His sweeping belief that it gives one moral and physical courage may well be questioned. Where, then, was the courage of the Socialists of the world during the late war? Had they had the courage of their convictions they would have refused to slaughter each other. It seems to me they didn't show much greater courage than the believers in the orthodox Christian God: they followed the command of their officers rather than the precepts of Jesus.

And Shaw himself, the zealous apostle of the Socialist religion? Did he do any better than the rest of the patriotic and jingoist weaklings? The claims of Shaw for the courage-giving qualities of religion – by whatever name he may call it – do not seem to be borne out by the actual facts of contemporary history.

Here again our vaunted realist proves to be romancing. No doubt conscious of it, he attempts to explain away his confused ethics by switching from the religion of Socialism to that of 'Creative Evolution'. He must do it, because he knows that by no stretch of reason or imagination can a programme of economic and social reorganisation of society be converted into a religion, properly speaking. Religion is essentially spiritual; its fountainhead is man's longing to decipher the riddle of life, to learn the purpose of his being, to comprehend the universal motive and aim. It is, in short, the expression of man's need to identify himself with powers bigger than himself, and thus get into a soul-satisfying relationship with them.

What has Socialism to do with that? At best it concerns only man's physical relationship to his fellow-men and to the collectivity. However international its brotherhood, it does not, cannot, reach out beyond the earth. It must find all its chance for growth in the soil and sewer systems of this planet.

So Shaw has to turn from Socialism, as a religion, to something else. That something else, more embracing and universal than Socialism, is Creative Evolution. This, he insists, is such a religion. 'It is my religion. It is the religion of the twentieth century.'

But to me this 'explanation' still further mystifies the matter. Even if you spell this creative evolution with initial capitals, it does not explain things, though it may assume greater dignity thereby. Furthermore, the fact, or alleged fact, that this creative evolution is the religion of the twentieth century adds nothing to our understanding of it, nor does it prove its inner truth.

We do, indeed, believe that evolution is a law of the universe and we may assume that it is a creative evolution. But it is not clear in what way belief in our descent from lower forms of life can instil in us the spirit of moral courage and fill us with the 'courage and morality of religion'.

Yet Shaw still insists: 'Creative Evolution is religion; but, I repeat, it is also science, as every religion must become if it is to survive nowadays.'

There is the real Shaw for you, the eternal compromiser. He must harmonise religion and science, as he had harmonised peace-loving Fabianism with war-partisanship.

Thoughtful readers of Shaw have noticed the final note of his mysticism in such plays as *John Bull's Other Island*, *Major Barbara*, *Getting Married*, *Back to Methuselah*. It is the mark of weakness to seek spiritual aid outside of oneself.

Shaw's religion fails to give him the true meaning of life, and so he tries to find it in some superior will. 'This is the true joy in life,' he says, 'the being used for a purpose recognised by yourself as a mighty one; the being thoroughly worn out before you are thrown on the scrap-heap.'

Great indeed is the difference between Shaw and the really great. A far cry to Goethe, for example. For Goethe invests life with joy by making the individual himself work consciously for the highest purpose.

It is the Puritan in Shaw, 'who missed the *Mayflower* by five minutes', that defeats him. For his Puritanism is today not less than that of the first British refugees to the American colonies. He would fain call things, as he himself says, 'by their right names and not drape our expression of the will-to-live with moral tags'. But only too often his courage fails him at the last moment.

It is curious how a man even of Shaw's brains can dupe himself. Does the great Supreme Power need *his* help? Does Creative Evolution need it? Not in the least. Yet Shaw must persuade himself that he is 'serving a higher purpose'. Alas, I fear he knows at heart that even Socialism does not need his services, however valuable he may think them. For hasn't Marx, his teacher, declared once for all that 'triumph of Socialism is inevitable when the shell of Capitalism bursts', at the point of its highest industrial development? It will go off then without Shaw's compromising aid. It has gone off in several countries, but never in one where Shaw lived.

But Shaw has to play some rôle in the universe, and therefore the 'Great Power is neither all-powerful nor all-knowing'. It is trying to become both by the help of its own creations. Here, then, is Shaw's great opportunity. His Supreme One must be subject to error, and Shaw quite seriously instructs us that his 'God makes mistakes'.

Lucky devil, this Shaw. He found his vocation: correcting God's mistakes.

Having examined Shaw's religion, I may well ask: 'What logical and practical deduction does he draw from his conception? What is his view of the Church, of Christianity, and particularly of Jesus? In short, what is the final result of the evolutionary struggle of Shaw's religious consciousness?'

The Church is condemned unreservedly and he would welcome its abolition.

'I can hardly imagine,' he grieves, 'how it has the face to exist after its recreancy during the Great War.'

True belief in God is independent of the Church, he believes, and belief in a Supreme Force is both necessary and easy to the modern man.

But his God, the God who is still struggling with the work of Creative Evolution and using us as His labourers, having created us for the purpose, and proceeding by the method of trial and error, needs help.

But what of the Saviour? Is there room for Him in a religion whose God is 'still struggling with the work of Creative Evolution'? Shaw has written of Jesus, and in his preface to *Androcles and the Lion* he deals with the Nazarene as a man, as a reformer and a thinker.

Shaw recognises the Nazarene's influence on the world, and concedes that Christ is still a living influence in modern days, with notably more people at present who feel that in Christ is the only hope for the world than there ever were before.

But Shaw's real conception of Jesus and his attitude to Him I learned from my correspondence with Shaw on this subject. I had been studying the Master for years with the object of writing a book about Him, but the subject proved too overpowering for me and I resolved never to publish the work, unless it bettered my best. I was deep in the work while the rest of the world was spewing hate and slaughter in 1915. I happened to mention what I was trying to do in one of my letters to Shaw. Thereupon, I received from him the following reply:

10 Adelphi Terrace, November 11th 1915

MY DEAR FRANK HARRIS – It seems to be my destiny to dog your footsteps with apparent plagiarisms. The Shakespeare effort was bad enough, but you now tell me that you are doing the life of Jesus. I am doing exactly the same thing by way of preface to *Androcles and the Lion*, which is a Christian-martyr play. So you must hurry up.

They tell me that what I have gathered from the gospel narratives and the rest of the New Testament, which I have read through attentively for the first time since, as a boy, I read the whole Bible through out of sheer bravado, is much the same as Renan's extract. I do not know whether this is true; for I have never read the *Vie de Jésus*, though I will look it up presently.

Anyhow, it is rather significant that you and I and George Moore should be on the same tack. The main thing that I have tried to bring out is that modern sociology and biology are steadily bearing Jesus out in his peculiar economics and theology.

Your most interesting book will be your autobiography. People often ask me to tell them about Frank Harris: who he was, where he came from, was he an American? was he a German Jew? was he a Welshman? was he an Irishman? was he an Englishman? and I have to confess that, though I am as interested as they are, I have not the remotest idea of what the answers to all these questions may be, and that when I first met you you were an accomplished, unaccountable, and amazing fact, totally obscuring your past by the intensity of your present and the awestruck speculations suggested by your future.

Yours ever,

G. B. S.

In reply I wrote that, plagiarism or no plagiarism, I should be extremely interested in reading what he had written, and would let him know what I felt about it as soon as I received it. I was greatly struck with Shaw's essay on Jesus, and I wrote a review of it in which I set down my first thoughts on the work. 'Shaw's essay on Jesus,' I wrote, 'gives the message of Jesus and shows that it might well be adopted today.' Here is his analysis:

1 The kingdom of heaven is within you. You are the son of God; and God is the son of man. God is a spirit to be worshipped in spirit and in truth. We are members one of another: you cannot injure or help your neighbour without injuring or helping yourself. God is your father: you are here to do God's work; and you and your father are one.

2 Get rid of property by throwing it into the common stock. Dissociate

your work entirely from money payments. If you let a child starve you are letting God starve. Get rid of all anxiety about tomorrow's dinner and clothes, because you cannot serve two masters: God and Mammon.

3 Get rid of judges and punishment and revenge. Love your neighbour as yourself, he being a part of yourself. And love your enemies: they are your neighbours.

4 Get rid of your family entanglements. Every mother you meet is as much your mother as the woman who bore you. Every man you meet is as much your brother as the man she bore after you. Don't waste your time at family funerals grieving for your relatives: attend to life, not to death: there are as good fish in the sea as ever came out of it, and better. In the kingdom of heaven, which, as aforesaid, is within you, there is no marriage nor giving in marriage, because you cannot devote your life to two divinities: God and the person you are married to'.

The Communist Reformer Jesus is the ideal that Shaw idolises, but when Jesus speaks of Himself as the Christ, and predicts, not only His death, but His resurrection in three days, Shaw will have none of it.

Like a good many others in this time, Shaw has always been obsessed with the idea of reforming the world, remoulding it nearer to the heart's desire, and from first to last he has shown a fairly rational consistency of thought.

Where he and I differ is that he believes in a driving power behind evolution but makes an open question of the existence of Jesus, whereas I see no first cause in the universe, but am absolutely sure that Jesus lived, worked, and died among us. 'Christian doctrines would have been preached and practised,' Shaw says roundly, 'if Jesus had never existed.' This is possibly true, though we know no one in these last nineteen centuries who could have taken the place of Jesus or done His work. Still, in time, no doubt, humanity would have produced another man of similar insight and sweetness. To Shaw 'it is the doctrine and not the man that matters'. He proceeds to say he is no more a Christian than Pilate was, nor you, gentle reader; and yet he is ready to admit, after contemplating the world and human nature for all these years, that he sees no way out of the world's misery but the way which would have been found by Christ's will if He had undertaken the work of a modern practical statesman.

Sound thinking, in my opinion, and stamped with a high sincerity. Naturally, Shaw goes on to tell us that he knows 'a great deal more about economics and politics than Jesus did', and this superiority of his is based apparently on the fact that he has no sympathy with 'vagabonds and talkers' who would subvert the existing social order in the delusion that the end of the world is at hand. He then ends up by asserting that it does not matter whether Jesus ever existed or not. Always the nonsensical note, you see.

Let us look at this assertion of his in terms of another art. There are half a dozen pictures attributed to X, who has been classed for centuries as probably the greatest of painters. Shaw looks at them, sees they are all by the same hand, admits that they have not been equalled in two thousand years, and yet doubts whether the master ever existed really, 'any more than Hamlet'.

One gasps at such a lame and impotent conclusion. 'Who, then, painted the pictures?' we ask. And Shaw replies that one symbol is as good as another, that Confucius said certain things before Jesus; yet admits that for some reason or other, the imagination of white mankind has picked out Jesus of Nazareth as *the* Christ, and attributed all the Christian doctrines to him. 'Let us leave it at that,' he adds implicitly.

Fortunately or unfortunately, this seems to me not a theory, but a demonstrable fact. The pictures proclaim the painter, one single creative mind; and Jesus, if we can get to know Him, is more important than His teachings or parables, just as Shaw, when we get to know him, is more important than his plays or even his prefaces.

Curiously enough, another dispute Shaw and I had over Shakespeare crops up again in his criticism of Jesus. He objected strenuously to the gentle, loving, humane, melancholy, philosophising thinker and poet as the man Shakespeare, or rather he accepted all the epithets, while protesting that the 'gentle' was overdone. He has exactly the same quarrel with Jesus. He is in the Ercles vein; he cries: 'Gentle Jesus, meek and mild, is a snivelling modern invention, with no warrant in the Gospels.'

This assertion made me doubt my eyes. Did not Jesus advise us to turn the other cheek, and to give the cloak to the robber who had taken our coat? Did He not teach that you should do good to your enemies? How does the Sermon on the Mount begin?

'Blessed are the poor in spirit: for theirs is the kingdom of heaven.'

And to leave you in no doubt, Jesus strikes the same note again: 'Blessed are the meek: for they shall inherit the earth.'

This gentleness, this meekness, this forgiving of injuries, this loving-kindness 'a snivelling modern invention'!

Shaw, Shaw, why deniest thou Me? It is as certain as anything can be that it was just this gentleness, this meekness, this loving-kindness of Jesus that caught the imagination of humanity, and won for him the passionate idolatry of men. Shaw, a combative Anglo-Saxon, may find himself more easily in the Jesus who blasted the barren fig tree and scourged the money-changers out of the Temple; but that was not the spirit men love and reverence in Jesus. Paul could have done all these things, or Judas Maccabaeus or any of ten thousand brave Jewish rebels who threw their lives to a protest, or minted their souls in a curse. But only One could have done what Jesus did.

The instinct of humanity that has chosen Jesus – 'for some reason', as Shaw remarks – is profoundly right; forgiveness is nobler than punishment, and loving-kindness more soul-subduing than any tyranny. It is just the gentle, loving Jesus that takes the spirit like the fragrance of a flower or the innocent loveliness of a child.

Jesus was the first to discover the soul, the first to speak of it with certainty, and because of the divination He is throned in the hearts of men for ever: 'It is more blessed to give than to receive.'

I attach great importance to the personality of Jesus for many reasons which it would require too much time and space to set forth here; but one reason may be indicated. If one studies the personality of Jesus, one can perceive, I venture to say, a certain growth in His mind, certain moments of development which bring Him nearer to us and make Him clearer. It was Lecky, I believe, the author of *The History of Rationalism*, who first said that long after Christianity had perished as a creed, Jesus would live as an ideal. If he had said as an influence, I should have agreed with him; the influence and spirit of Jesus are certain to endure for hundreds of centuries to come; but no man can be an 'ideal' to us, even Jesus cannot fill the horizon; the time has come to see Him as He was, the wisest and sweetest of the sons of men, whose high place in the Pantheon of Humanity is assured for ever. His surpassing quality makes it unnecessary to prove His existence by the testimony of Paul, or by the references to His crucifixion in Tacitus and Josephus. It is impossible to study Rembrandt's pictures chronologically without realising Rembrandt's growth, impossible to read Shakespeare and not see his personality passing from flower to fruit; in the same way we cannot deny Jesus or ignore the Son of Man who become in truth for us the Son of God. Yet Shaw has ventured to declare that Jesus went mad when Peter said, 'Thou art the Christ,' and that this becomes quite clear when the searchlight of the stage is turned on His trial, as it has been by Masefield.

Three or four of His parables or short stories are the finest ever written; a dozen of His sayings come from a height of thought and feeling hardly reached by any other man; He was at once saint and seer and artist of the noblest, and the way He was treated by the world is symbolic of the fate of genius everywhere. His life showed (as He was the first to see) that a prophet is not without honour save in his own country and amid his own kin; His death established the dreadful truth that, in measure as one grows better than his fellow-men, he incurs their hatred. The highest genius in this world was beaten and scourged and finally crowned in derision with thorns. Crucifixion is the reward given by men to their supreme guides and teachers.

Shaw spends a hundred pages or more in a very fine and fair criticism of the four Gospels: he establishes, I am inclined to believe, several truths which more learned commentators have failed to perceive. He says that Luke has added sentiment and romance to the story told by Matthew and Mark, and declares that 'it is Luke's Jesus who has won our hearts'. He believes, on good grounds I think, that John's Gospel was written by the beloved disciple himself, and must be brought within the first century.

The old question as to the credibility of the Gospels Shaw declares unimportant: 'Belief is merely a matter of taste.'

And so he comes back to his beginning: 'Jesus remains unshaken as the practical man,' and we stand exposed as 'the fools, the blunderers, the unpractical visionaries'. For the root fact remains: our system of distributing wealth 'is wildly and monstrously wrong. We have million-dollar babies side by side with paupers worn out by a long life of unremitted drudgery. One adult in every five dies in a workhouse, a public hospital, or a madhouse. In cities like London the proportion is very nearly one in two. This distribution is effected by violence pure and simple. If you demur, you are sold up. If you resist the selling up, you are bludgeoned and imprisoned. Iniquity can go no further . . . Democracy in France and the United States is an imposture and a delusion. It reduces justice and law to a farce: law becomes merely an instrument for keeping the poor in subjection. Workmen are tried, not by a jury of their peers, but by conspiracies of their exploiters. The Press is the Press of the rich and the curse of the poor. The priest is the complement of the policeman . . . and, worst of all, marriage becomes a class affair.'

Never was there such a root-and-branch condemnation of human society. And the remedy is as sweeping. Shaw states it briefly: 'We must begin by holding the right to an income as sacred and equal, just as we now begin by holding the right to life as sacred and equal. The one right is only a restatement of the other . . . Jesus was a first-rate political economist.'

Now, it would not be difficult to show that this wholesale indictment of the existing social order is almost as one-sided and extravagant as the eulogies of an Individualist of the Manchester school; the bomb is not the best answer to the multi-millionaire, though it is a very natural one. The truth is, both Individualism and Socialism must find a place in modern life; just as analytic and synthetic chemistry both find their place.

My review of Shaw's *Androcles and the Lion* started a long correspondence between us on the subject of Jesus. Some of the letters add some more light on the problem, and so I reproduce two here:

January, 1917

DEAR FRANK HARRIS – Your review of my *Androcles* preface is very interesting reading, as all your stuff is; but on the subject of the mildness of Jesus you must fight it out, not with me, but with St Matthew. The Sermon on the Mount, even if we could accept it as a genuine open-air speech and not a very obvious collection of 'Sayings', would not afford the slightest presumption that Jesus himself was the sort of person he exhorted his hearers to be.

There is an old story, told sometimes about Mazarin, sometimes about Richelieu, of a Minister's antechamber hung with pictures; those on one side being all idyllic landscapes and scenes of domestic sentiment; those on the other, scenes of battle and blood and torture. The Minister, when he wanted to size up a new man, watched how he took the pictures. If he clung to the battle pictures, the Minister knew that he was a timid man of peace, for whom action and daring were full of romantic fascination. If he wallowed in cottage sentiment and the 'Maiden's Prayer', he was immediately marked down for military preferment and dangerous jobs. Have you ever known a sportsman who was ferocious? Have you ever known a humanitarian who was not ferocious? You are yourself so in love with the Sermon on the Mount, and with all aspects of gentleness and pity that people who have never met you possibly imagine you as a Christ-like, dove-eyed figure. But has anybody who has met you personally ever described you as 'Gentle Francis, meek and mild'?

The apparent contradiction of your pity for Sonia and Oscar Wilde by your buccaneering manners and occasionally frightful language is a familiar natural phenomenon.

Suppose I had declared that the Gospel of Matthew was incredibly inconsistent because the haughty and vituperative Jesus whom he described could not possibly be the preacher of patience, kindness, and forgiveness. Surely you would have found such a criticism hasty and shallow, and reminded me that the Shelley who wrote *Prometheus Unbound* and *Laon and Cythna* was the same Shelley who poured the fiercest invective on Castlereagh, on Eldon, and on his own father, not to mention the entire tribe of old men. Would you say that Herbert Spencer must have been a lazy man because he warned people so earnestly against the gospel of hard work? On the contrary, you can see very plainly that he gave the warning just because he had himself been unable to keep his industry within prudent bounds, and over-strained himself permanently in working at his *First Principles*.

Almost everyone who is interested in Jesus has a pet conception of him, and protests against my preface for not reproducing it. But my preface has nothing to do with any modern conception of him. I go to the Bible and I find there four biographies of Jesus. Three of them are called synoptic because they agree roughly as to the course of events in his life; and two of them are at least not contradictory as to his character. The fourth describes a different career and a different man – so different that if he were not named and had not been crucified by Pontius Pilate at the demand of the Jews, he might have been classed as an apostle or even as the leader of a great heresy. The world has mixed these three Jesuses into one Jesus. The great painters have painted the three kings in the stable with the shepherds: an impossible combination which would have scandalised Matthew and irritated Luke.

Matthew was a man of books, a chronicler. Luke was a sentimental romancer. John was a man of the world and a politician with a turn for magic and metaphysics, not unlike Paracelsus. Matthew took it for granted that Jesus belonged to the haughty classes; had socially correct views as to the Gentiles; and was offensive, as a matter of course, to those who disagreed with him. Luke made an operatic tenor of him and gave him charming manners. Neither Matthew nor Luke write as eye-witnesses or like men who had ever taken part in political life: they do not know how politicians and priests really talk and behave, viva voce. John, on the contrary, writes both as an eye-witness and as a man who knew what people are like on committees and at political and religious demonstrations, according to their classes. The difference is like that between Anthony Trollope and a provincial novelist who represents the King as always wearing the crown and being addressed by the Prime Minister in private as 'Your Majesty'. In the end, you feel pretty clear as to the sort of man Matthew was, and Luke was, and John was. You even have a distinct notion of Mark. But Jesus eludes you, because, though nothing could be more definite than the type of man chronicled by Matthew, you perceive that Matthew had no eye for character, and did not understand originality or even unconventionality. Luke's portrait, though good fiction, is too obviously Mozartian to be credible as a bit of realism. And John is making up a figure of the higher Freemasonry and never takes you behind the scenes of his temple-theatre.

Out of all these I have picked some scraps of doctrine common to the four, and some traits of Bohemian life in which the four records confirm what would be deduced from the circumstances. And I have given the only explanation as yet discovered of the otherwise unaccountable going like a lamb to the slaughter. Beyond this I could not go without dropping into fiction. You can project your ideal Christ on the pages of your next book, just as Burne-Jones has projected his Christ on the window of Speldhurst Church. This Christ is not a bit like Holman Hunt's 'Light of the World'. And Holman Hunt's Christ is not a son of Blake's God in Job. Your Christ will not be like Farrar's or Marie Corelli's. The ideal Christs are of all sorts, from tailors' dummies to reincarnations and revelations; but when you come to the documents you come back to my preface.

The so-called higher criticism is a bore, because it cannot see the man behind the Gospel. It does not even tell you that Matthew and Mark were *chiffoniers*: it insists that there were no such persons, and that the wind blew the *chiffons* into a heap and thus produced a Gospel. That is only the useless part of the truth: I have sifted the heap for the cinders, not for the dust.

Yours ever,

G. BERNARD SHAW

To which I replied:

DEAR BERNARD SHAW – You told me in a previous letter that my life-story was full of incident and change, and therefore interesting, while yours was humdrum; consequently, you said it was incumbent upon me to write my autobiography, but not incumbent upon you to write yours.

In the same way I might answer your letter by saying you are the most brilliant of living controversialists, while I detest controversy. I hate fighting and see no good in the conflict of wits. I am always seeking for the modicum of truth in the other man's arguments and trying to harmonise his view with my own in some higher synthesis which shall include both.

But when I read this letter of yours with this purpose in mind I was a little put out because you appear to me to contradict yourself. Your cut and thrust is so bewilderingly rapid, your swordplay so dazzling that you seem never to be in the same place for two seconds together and one is at a loss to know what you want beyond applause for your brilliant fencing. The story you tell of Mazarin or Richelieu and the inference you draw from it are alike excellent, and the fun you poke at me is just as good. But do you not contradict yourself? You say that 'Jesus eludes you'; that everyone interested in Jesus has a pet conception of Him, and that His sermons and sayings do not 'afford the slightest presumption that Jesus Himself was the sort of person He exhorted His hearers to be'. Yet you tell us you know Matthew, Mark, Luke and John from what they say, and you proceed to describe them. Their personalities and shortcomings are all clear to you, but Jesus eludes you, and you imply that He cannot be known. Surely this contradiction ruins your main contention. Let me see if I can throw any light on your perplexity.

You know Matthew, Mark, Luke, and John, and their peculiarities of viewpoint and vision; they have all written about Jesus, and three of them, Matthew, Mark, and Luke, have said much the same things about Him. All these accounts, if written by eye-witnesses, were yet written, it is believed, from thirty to sixty or seventy years after the death of Jesus, yet the outlines of the portraits are so similar that some commentators believe that all three Evangelists have borrowed from a common original. Besides this, one has an earlier account – the account of Paul, who did not know Jesus, but knew of His teachings.

Now Paul was a man of eminent capacity, a really good brain and great heart given to passionate enthusiasms, a man capable, that is, of understanding even the highest.

Paul was a historic character, and we know Paul intimately; and Paul tells us of Jesus; nevertheless, you say, 'Jesus eludes you'. Paul's chapter in Corinthians on 'faith, hope, and love' has been accepted by fifty generations as giving the very spirit of the teaching of Jesus; it is in intimate accord with what Jesus Himself, according to His other biographers, gives as His final word: 'A new commandment I give unto you, that ye love one another.'

All His teaching is but an exemplification or exposition of this text. His deepest words all flow from this fount; in this spirit He rebukes the accusers.

'He that is without sin among you, let him first cast a stone.'

'Much shall be forgiven her, for she loved much.'

Now, Shaw, you know all this as well as I do; you know that Jesus at His best does not elude you; yet, desiring above all things controversial victory, you say in effect that this gentle, loving Jesus may have been a hothead revolutionary, full of desperate resolves, a pirate or bully delighting in cruelties.

In other words, a man may be the exact opposite of what he preaches; he usually admires most, you say, the virtues alien to his nature. I think he admires most what he has a little of and would like to have more of.

You know that a man reveals himself in his work infallibly. All the new magical words of Jesus are words of love and pity. Paul was a born fighter; his worth to us comes from the fact that he has imbibed a full measure of the sweet loving-kindness of Jesus; the conclusion seems to be inevitable. The real Jesus is the traditional Jesus, gentle, mild, with more of the milk of human kindness in Him than in any other man.

It is quite easy, I believe, to determine whether Bernard Shaw, for example, is a sardonic Mephistopheles, contemptuous of all conventions and disdainful of all traditions, or a man whose mental equipment is that of an intellectual swordsman, but who at heart is considerate and compassionate beyond the ordinary, and devoted passionately to all high causes, especially, perhaps, to the highest of them all, truth.

That conception of Shaw reconciles all his contradictions, both in actions and in teachings; and yet there are extraordinary contradictions in Shaw which are almost inexplicable even to those who love him and seek to know him by love.

There is the Shaw who berates the English in and out of season; who tells them the murders in the Denshawai affair in Egypt were brutal and stupid; who calls them hypocritical self-seekers and despises their blind patriotism, and yet who declares that they must be victorious in war and invests twenty thousand pounds of his savings in their War Loans in order to help them.

I say that here is no contradiction. Shaw knows the English; he has always seen them from the Irish angle with refreshing clearness; but he does not know the Germans at all; consequently he mis-sees and underrates them, and honestly believes that the Allies deserve to win.

Here is another point: if he did believe that the cause of the Germans was the higher moral cause, he would be a pro-German tomorrow, and would not hesitate, even in England, to declare his faith. He is a soldier and servant of the truth, and not to be misled by shy fear. So that if he is now on the wrong side we can only forgive him in Christ's phrase because of his ignorance.

In the same way, Shaw, it is possible to reconcile all the apparent contradictions in the actions and teachings of Jesus attributed to Him by His biographers.

Your writing on the subject has done some good: you say, in spite of all the foolish learned commentators, that John is of the time and just as much to be trusted as Matthew. You say, too, that the Sermon on the Mount is 'a collection of sayings'; was not one discourse, that is, but a collection of little discourses, and you have held fast to one of the main truths in the teachings of Jesus, that there should be equality in the distribution of necessaries among men and women; that our present system of distributing wealth by giving hundreds of millions to one man and a few cents a day to another is shameful, and even more hurtful to the multi-millionaire than to the beggar.

Evidently you know a great deal about Jesus, and Jesus does not elude you nearly as much as you would have us believe.

Yours ever,

FRANK HARRIS

23

The Saint Joan *Row*

Few plays of Shaw have met such acclaim as *Saint Joan*. Indeed, I seem to have been the only one who has criticised it severely, or pointed out its historical errors, dramatic weaknesses, and general defects. All others have lauded it without stint. Archibald Henderson, Shaw's academic biographer, has even declared that '*Saint Joan* is the greatest play in English since Shakespeare', which is enough praise to make Shaw's vanity reel for the rest of his natural life.

Though I consider *Saint Joan* good enough to survive most of Shaw's other plays, I did not like his portrait of the Maid, and don't now. He makes of this peasant girl a Shavian female whose argument with the captain in Vaucouleurs consists of a few quips and jokes of questionable wit. She is a too modern flapper in her interview with the Dauphin, whom she addresses as 'Charlie'; which, as I pointed out, is about as likely as a girl of our day calling the King of England 'Georgie'.

When I first read the play I was greatly disappointed. He was dealing with one of the strongest and most dramatic figures in history. Her end was a medieval murder trial, a natural tragedy. It was easy to write, Shaw himself has bragged. Why then didn't he do better by her? Because he didn't know that great tragedies are far from easy to write.

'Most other writers,' he says with that cocky confidence of his which is half his charm, 'made Joan an operatic heroine – a grand-opera stunt. What she really was did not interest them. Schiller made Joan of Arc a German heroine of romance, Mark Twain made her a Virginian young lady in long skirts, surrounded by Babbitts.

'And Anatole France? His effort was the absurdest until I came along.'

Shaw has often said that his didactic assertions and constant repetitions of his own greatness have at last persuaded the world to take him at his own valuation. That certainly applies to his *Saint Joan*, for the play is historically untrue, and would have been slated for its *gaffes* if an unknown hand had offered it to the critics.

I think I know Joan at least as well as Shaw, for I studied her life and personality for years, and, indeed, once wrote a play myself around her tragic fate. Shaw didn't like my play, and that, you may be sure, quite obviously influences my judgement of his *Saint Joan*.

In the spring of 1925 I sent Shaw a copy of my play, and in reply I received the following letter:

> *Ayot St Lawrence, Welwyn, Herts*
> *May 20th 1926*

DEAR FRANK HARRIS – *La Romée* has arrived. And first I ask how you could be so unbusinesslike, when I had just reopened the medieval theatre market for saints, and proved it to be an extremely lucrative one, as to come into that market with the one saint in whom I had made a hopeless corner.

However, the impulse was evidently an artistic one, though you misunderstood its nature. I always want to make a drama of a subject, the bigger the better. You always want to make a short story of it, the shorter the better. My making a drama of Joan outraged your instinct; you felt that you must do something quite different with her; but you did not understand that the something was a short story and not another drama. The result is a shocking hybrid. Why not throw it into the fire and write your story? You have emptied out the Middle Ages and the Church and the Inquisition and the feudal system, and reduced the subject to a story of a young Virginian female, a few dullards, two crooks, and a very modern American executioner cheeking an English lord and snapping his fingers at the Holy Office (which would have burnt him in a brace of shakes for his heresy). Just like O. Henry, with the Harrisian style superimposed.

But when you have done it, it won't have been worth doing. Joan's history is the wrong material for O. Henry and De Maupassant and for you. Stick to the nineteenth century. Even a long-story man of genius, Anatole France, was beaten by the Maid: his *Vie* was the absurdest *gaffe* in modern literature until you came along with your idiotic *La Romée* and took the fool's cap from him. Be not deceived by people who don't want to quarrel with you; there is nothing to be done but drop the thing into the wastepaper basket with a good-humoured laugh, and apologise to posterity for the surviving copies.

You will remark that I have become perfectly reckless as to your feelings or anyone else's, and just shoo you off my grass as if you were a tramp. The explanation is that my health has given way at last; I have been ill for two months, and have only half-recovered, the pre-seventy part of me being as dead as a doornail. I am a ruin, and you may discount my opinion accordingly.

My handwriting is not fit to be inflicted on you.

Yours, half alive,

G. BERNARD SHAW

My answer to him didn't err on the side of tenderness either. I wrote:

May 27th 1926

MY DEAR SHAW – Your letter on *Joan La Romée* has reached me. What an extraordinary letter for you to write to me! I remember the shock I had when I read in your criticism of my Shakespeare that you annexed my discovery that the Countess of Rousillon was Herbert's mother, Sidney's sister, and coolly said that I wouldn't have it, though my words were, 'I think Shakespeare had this fine model in mind when drawing the old Countess of Rousillon.' You went on to poke fun at me and pretend that I said that Shakespeare had his own mother in mind – all pure invention.

Now this criticism of my Joan is just as astonishing. It is the pre-seventy part of you at its worst which still exists. I had written my play before I saw yours, and Joan had been in my head for twenty years with Jesus; and it wasn't until I saw from the bottom of her garden at Domremy that she could see the church that a glimpse came to me of the way her soul grew. But you see nothing of my work at all except that my Executioner is a very modern American because he dares to cheek an English lord and disagree with the Holy Office.

You talk of the 'Joan ground' as being yours, and you would shoo me off this grass. This inspires me to tell you something of the truth about your play in your own vein. In the interminable four hours of it there were only two moments in which you tried to realise Joan. You make the peasant girl speak to her King as 'Charlie' in open court – an anachronism as glaring as your epilogue; and you make Joan tear up her renunciation, which is contrary to the historical fact but which is a fine theatrical gesture; so much for your attempt to realise the heroine; but your Chief Inquisitor gets a speech of fifteen hundred words, which an actor can make effective by giving it his own individuality and character but which otherwise simply makes one yawn to hear. Then you place three men at a table to tell all you know about France in the beginning of the fifteenth century for thirty-two intolerable minutes by the watch, and they say nothing of any value to any human soul; and yet you call this your drama!

Your idea of a drama is to make Jesus call Pilate 'old top' and give two hours of conversation to Caiaphas and his compeers. Our disagreement, you see, goes to fundamentals. You think the Cauchons and the Inquisitors and all ordinary persons worth depicting at length, but these, like the poor, you have always with you. We don't need a Shaw to portray them. Pinero does that, and Henry Arthur Jones and a dozen others; but here in Joan is a great character, a heroic soul if ever there was one, and we want above all to learn how she came into being and how she was treated by men. You shirk the real problem altogether: there is more creative faculty in the first three pages of my work than in all your four hours of drama. You should have seen the effort at least in my work to realise Joan; you should have known that nothing is gained by cheap sneering.

What a curious dearth of poets in England today in comparison with the period I am writing about of my life in the [eighteen] nineties! You are, to me, the chief figure from 1895 to 1905, as Oscar Wilde was in the previous years. I shall always remember the pleasure your *Candida* gave me – much the same sort of pleasure that I had hoped to give you with my *Joan*. I have failed, it seems, but whether the failure is yours or mine is not yet easy to determine. I remember reading once how Cervantes praised Lope de Vega for his excellent comedies and sent him *Don Quixote*, and de Vega replied that he couldn't help in any way because there was no talent in the book *Don Quixote*.

Yours ever,

FRANK HARRIS

To my readers I should perhaps point out that Lope de Vega was, to Cervantes' time, what Shaw is to ours. He had written scores of plays, and was the final word of his age. Yet if he lives at all today, it's because, like Pilate, he showed enough bad judgement to get in a great man's way.

In connection with this row over Saint Joan, I am reminded of the interview Allan Dowling had with Shaw regarding our two plays. It was Dowling who carried Shaw a copy of my *Joan La Romée* from Nice to London. Shaw received him in his village retreat in Ayot St Lawrence.

'First of all, tell me about Harris! How is he? His mental condition must be close to idiocy.'

'No,' cried Dowling, 'far from it!'

'But this play of his. It is no play at all. It is rubbish. Just look what he has done. He has brought in Dunois and left out the army. He has brought in Cauchon and left out the Church. In fact, he has left out the whole Middle Ages.'

From that point on, it was a case of Shaw showing how badly I had done by Saint Joan and how well he had done by her.

A few moments of silence followed this, and then Shaw added: 'You ought to go back and write books about the United States like Sinclair Lewis. The day has gone by when the artistic section of young America could find no spiritual home but the south of Europe, and no leaders except Frank Harris and old back numbers like myself. America is at last producing an art of its own instead of merely boring Europe by returning its exports with all their charm rubbed off. Go back to your country, young man, and leave Harris and Shaw to be buried by the parish.'

Dowling was shocked to hear me spoken of in this fashion, and amazed at Shaw's audacity in coupling himself with me; for he was innocent and thought much of me and little of Shaw.

Shaw called Jesus an arrogant madman who scorned to defend Himself before Pilate and Caiaphas because He believed that when they had killed Him He would rise three days later and reign in glory over them. I agree with Dowling that humanity will think of Jesus standing dumbly before Pilate, and worship Him long after everyone has ceased to care whether George Bernard Shaw stood anywhere.

I wonder if his play would have had half the success if it had been produced at a less opportune time? French *poilus* had rallied around Saint Joan from the first shot in 1914, and by 1918 the Church was seriously getting down to the task of canonising a maid it had one time burned for heresy. Two years after France had won the war, the Vatican confirmed it by announcing to the world that Joan, the Blessed, was now standing in the communion of saints. This news timed Shaw's play perfectly.

Its immediate New York success at its first performance anywhere in the world, Christmas week, 1923, was due to Winifred Lenihan and a Press which adored this young actress. Sybil Thorndike's London performance, six months later, had an equally warm reception. After that it became known as a part for women like Hamlet for men, and revivals of it have been fairly frequent, one in London in the spring of 1931 running several weeks. But I hope I may be excused, on the basis of our amusing exchange of letters, from joining the general hysteria about it.

24

Attitude towards America

Shaw has never gone to America, and never will go now. Why should he? Half of America has come to him, and the rest supports him. He has managed to abuse the whole of it quite as well as any other English author, without going to the trouble of accepting its hospitality nor fattening at its expense on a lecture tour.

He knows all the frailties of America and its strong points too. This is not surprising, for he is more American than anything else in his point of view. Americans think you can achieve anything by publicity, and Shaw has pretty well proved their case. He, Aimée MacPherson, and Herbert Hoover could form the Trinity of the New World very nicely.

He has kept up a newspaper knowledge of contemporary America, but his literary interest died out with Mark Twain and Henry James. Before that he knew a bit of Poe, Whitman, Emerson, Longfellow, Hawthorne, and Cooper, but of Edith Wharton, Willa Cather, Zona Gale, James Branch Cabell, Sherwood Anderson, Theodore Dreiser, and such writers he hasn't the remotest idea. O. Henry he knows; Mencken, O'Neill, Upton Sinclair, too, and a bit of Sinclair Lewis.

Of course, Lewis's discourse before the Swedish Academy on being awarded the Nobel Prize was quite to Shaw's liking. It was a publicity stunt in the Shavian manner. To arouse the eager interest of Americans, Shaw believes that all there is to do is to hold them up to ridicule to the rest of the world, and he advances the idiotic theory that the reason Dickens is so much read in America is because he assailed them as windbags, swindlers, and assassins. Now, I am sure that not one American in a thousand who has read Dickens has ever read him for any such reason, or, indeed, has ever read his diatribes against America. Most American readers stop short of *Martin Chuzzlewit* and never dream of reading *American Notes*. In any case they don't accept responsibility for the manners of their great grandfathers. Why should they?

More than that, Americans are singularly clear in separating a man's talents from his limitations. Note how they read Kipling despite his Billingsgate against them. I think this is a proof of their generosity of spirit.

It may be true that Shaw is particular never to say a civil word to the United States, but I think he is contributing nothing original by remarking that the hundred per cent American is ninety-nine per cent idiot. A hundred per cent anything is ninety-nine per cent idiot, and that particular species laughed at all over America is becoming all the vogue in England, where American advertisers in London now use it against the native to strip him further of his wealth.

Since the Britisher is ordered to 'Buy British Goods', the American gladly sells him American products under that label, and among his frequent customers I am sure is George Bernard Shaw. Yet, in the face of this proof of their shrewdness in fooling him and all the world, Shaw thinks that the Americans are a nation of copyists, and that they learned the brass band method of exploitation from him. From him! It is to be presumed, therefore, that Barnum, who applied circus tactics to grand opera-singers like Jenny Lind (buried at Malvern, where now they bury Shaw's plays) was born after Shaw, not before him.

All Shaw did was to borrow freely from America exploitation methods and apply them on a huge scale to literature, which, previously, had a little dignity about it.

He has no belief in the reality of the hustling American, as opposed to the traditional deliberating British subject, and points out that in his youth Americans were portrayed as being slow and deliberate like Mark Twain. What makes him think that the national character has not changed in this respect? You can prove the case best by talking to any Englishman who has been several years in America and who comes back to London to do business. He finds everybody taking weeks to come to the smallest decision, and, being invariably out of town, to delay things even more. That may not prove that Americans hustle, but it certainly proves that Englishmen don't. Shaw objects to Americans sending in their haste long, unnecessary telegrams. This to him is not hustling. To his Puritan sense it is an absolute waste.

But hasn't he had ample proof of their hustle in his own affairs? He never tires of telling us how much they hustled on finding out that his early novels were not copyrighted, and how 'they propagated them vigorously throughout the country at a dollar and a half a copy, free of all royalty to the flattered author'. This piece of piracy was not resented by him in the least. He made the chief pirate his legitimate publisher in recognition of his superior appreciation of Shavian literature. In his early days he accepted from Harpers the then customary ten pounds for the moral right to publish one of his non-copyright novels; but when another publisher issued a rival edition he returned the ten pounds to the astonished Harpers, who asked what on earth they were to do with it, and finally sent it to a literary charity. He upholds the Russian Soviet's right to make a present of all Russian authors to the rest of the world and to take a present of all the non-Russian authors in return. The exercise of the legal side of his mind gives him all the pleasure that Dickens and Besant clamoured for in the shape of American royalties.

American hustle and foresight gave him his first shove toward an independent income at the turn of the century, and has kept him there ever since. Since 1920, the New York Theatre Guild has been the first to produce anywhere three of Shaw's best efforts – *Heartbreak House*, *Saint Joan*, and *Back to Methuselah*. If he finds so much at fault with the place, and the place finds so much to the good about him, it can only mean that for all their minor differences they have many things in common.

He suggests that America may reconsider its break with England. It is, of course, possible that America may absorb England, using the polite term 'merge', as Shaw suggests in *The Apple Cart*, but if it does it will be for all the world like a merger of a new and forceful newspaper with one that had fine traditions which are now dead. America will not come back to England as a prodigal son, and I don't really believe it will come back at all, for the simple reason that England will not be worth the buying, not even to scrap it.

I think Shaw struck out against the worst defects of America in the preface to *Heartbreak House*. Wilson's murder of freedom amazed him. As for me, it simply broke my spirit beyond all mending. Shaw pointed out that it was in the United States of America, where nobody slept the worse for war, that war-fever went beyond all human reason.

He knew of the negro massacres during the war in East St Louis; of the brazen persecution of the Mooneys in San Francisco; the clubbing of poor women in front of the Waldorf Hotel; the lynching of the workman-agitator Little by hired assassins; the gaoling of a man in New York for publishing extracts from *The Declaration of Independence*, and the fanatical crusade against Russians and Socialists after the treaty of Brest Litovsk. All these happenings caused me to write to Shaw, saying that his opinion of such doings might have some weight.

In the reply Shaw sent me his condemnation was so outspoken it would have got him two years' imprisonment, with a ten thousand dollar fine, if he had been brought up for sedition on account of it before Federal Judge Mayer.

His card ran:

10 Adelphi Terrace, W.C.
July 31st 1917

DEAR FRANK HARRIS – That sort of thing is always going on in America. What is the use of writing at 'the angry ape'? If he won't listen to Shakespeare he won't listen to me. I have no illusions about the Golden West; probably, however, it only seems the worst place in the world politically and juridically because there is less hushing up: that is, less solidarity among the governing class than in England or Russia.

G. B. S.

Read the preface to *Heartbreak House*, which is America, really, not England: England is only Horseback Hall. You will have to go far to find a finer piece of protest-writing. If words can incite to revolution, why didn't revolution follow this preface? It didn't because you can't incite to violence: you can only record it. This should effectively answer the ruling imbeciles and their fears to the contrary. I once actually did believe the pen was mightier than the sword. I believe it no longer. This preface never caused so much as a ripple in mob-minded America of 1920.

For thirty years Shaw has received invitations to visit America, and refuses several a month to this day. Every now and then the report goes out that he actually is coming, but there certainly is no reason for that, since he has all the money he needs, and is an old man now on whom the wear and tear of platform-speaking, though he is an old hand at it, would prove a hardship. But with the Press, the radio, the talking pictures, with his interviews, his plays, his novels, and his prefaces, what possible reason is there for his making an ocean voyage, which probably would only end in killing him?

Except for the very pointed scene in *The Apple Cart*, which came at the end of his career, and most of *The Devil's Disciple*, which came very much at the beginning, the American scene has not entered into Shaw's plays much. As even these two portray an America which is dead in one instance and an America as yet unborn in another; and as the Hector Malone of *Man and Superman*, who is only a secondhand and shop-soiled provincial Englishman, is as obsolete as Henry James, it cannot be heartily argued that he has occupied himself very seriously with solving America's current day problems. Indeed, considering all the demands on his time at home, it would be going very far afield for trouble if he did.

Shaw's methods of advertising and publicity are so American that it would be labouring the point to go into them much in detail. He has simply followed the principle that if you say a thing often enough, regardless of how true or false it is, the public will eventually accept it as true. Even to this day Shaw realises that the better known he gets, the more publicity he needs. This follows so precisely the methods of advertising even a cigarette in America that I am sure I do not need to do more than point it out to have everybody agree that if you go in for advertising at all you should spend more on it the more you make.

Shaw's first efforts at publicity were conventional enough. From the beginning he cried, 'The cart and the trumpet for me,' and, now that these are out of date, he cries, 'The microphone and screen for me.' In his early debates he knew how to tie himself up to a big name so that thereafter the two should be for ever associated in the public mind. I recall his once getting up in a debate with Hyndman and remarking, 'Marx's theory of value is as dead as mutton. I, Bernard Shaw, have killed it.'

Then, too, you recall how he leaped on the shoulders of Shakespeare so that he might tell how much bigger he was.

Another medium he ceaselessly pounded was letters. He was for ever writing letters to individuals and publications, and if one addressed to *The Times* was refused, Shaw would eventually get it published if it had to keep going down the line until it finally arrived at an anti-vaccinationist weekly.

You will recall, too, how often the name Bernard Shaw appears in his plays. But this sort of publicity has no great value, since you only learn about it after you have bought the book or your theatre tickets. It doesn't, I mean, induce you to buy them.

It is certainly true that his perpetual dinning in the public ears that he is an extraordinarily witty, brilliant, and clever man, has now made that so much a part of public opinion that no power will change it while he lives. In his early years he dissembled his self love under many names, even under such absurd ones as 'Redbarn Wash', but in time he learned the value of the single impression, though he never quite got it down to such a simple formula as merely referring to himself as Shaw.

In only this instance do I find him a poor Press agent. Most of them know from the beginning that you must try for a single effect, that you must set down what you want to sell and try then to arrive at as many possible variations, short of boredom, as the thing permits.

The belligerent, rapid-thinking features of his public character he watched always like a hawk. Anybody submitting an interview to him, however accurate (and accuracy is by no means limited to Shaw), found the interview returned as if it had been through six major campaigns. It was scarred and marred and blue-pencilled and red-inked and otherwise arranged to suit, not the point of view of the writer, but the public character of Shaw.

Let me give you an instance in this: in George Sylvester Viereck's *Glimpses of the Great* you will find a photostatic copy of a page of Viereck's interview corrected by Shaw, in Shaw's own handwriting. It reveals how Shaw is ever alert to keep alive his newspaper character.

There Viereck, taking the lead in the conversation, finds, in his altered interview, that Shaw has changed things so that he might appear to better public advantage himself. At one point of the interview Viereck quoted Shaw as saying: ' "This problem," Shaw replied, after *pondering* the question.' Shaw changed this to read: ' "They do now," Shaw replied *promptly*.'

The italics are mine.

Now it may be argued, and probably will be, that Shaw was not trying to present himself to the public as a man of quick mind, but that in this particular instance the question was of a sort that required no great thinking or pondering, since it happened to be a subject (the subject was easy divorces) about which Shaw already had given much thought. Still, I maintain the change was more to keep his public character than to correct a minor detail of an interview.

The chief difference between him and any other public performer is that Shaw is capable of living up to his public character, whereas most such persons have to hire a director of public relations to do it for them. Many great personalities have been built up in this manner. The only difference between such mountebanks and Shaw is that Shaw was shrewd enough to do his own building.

In the early days he would talk on twelve topics, but these were in time reduced to one lecture, to which the secretary of the Fabian Society was good enough to invent four or five different names. But he did not confine himself long to the platform. As other mediums of publicity were discovered, Shaw was early in appraising their value and bending them to his purpose. Nor was he above ridiculing some well-known person or work in order to gain popular attention.

One time in Paris, when Shaw was sitting to Rodin, a photographer caught him coming out of his bath, and, on being asked to look pleasant, Shaw tried to assume the pose of Rodin's *Le Penseur* and immediately proved its impossibility by falling on his nose on the bathroom floor. He reseated himself in a more practicable attitude; but this proved in the print highly suggestive of costiveness, and not at all of pensiveness. It is the only photograph of Shaw that has never been published.

His trick of refusing prize money on occasion and therefore getting no end of publicity has been practised often. *Collier's Weekly* and the Nobel Prize are among his better-known surprises of this sort. He has long known also how to play one publicist against another and so sit on their head while they struggled to hold Shaw aloft.

But print alone was never the limit of Shaw's genius for publicity. He was among the first to see the value of talking pictures as such a medium, and, indeed, did more to launch movietone as a popular medium of cinema entertainment than anybody else. Here a lifetime's work as a lecturer served him beautifully. He gave an imitation of Mussolini, and even an imitation of Shaw, which places him among the greatest actors: the last word in sham; and sham was I believe what he cried out most against in the middle years of his life as a dramatist. He even appraised his acting talents critically, and saw from his movietones that he was getting old and his mouth was losing its shape. After that he turned to the radio, which can carry the voice around the world and not bring up issues of personal pulchritude.

But before that arrived he had managed to have a movietone made of his Malvern Festival in which he urged all people to go to see his shows there! This was distributed free of charge (free of charge, that is, to Shaw) in all cinemas – a competing form of entertainment!

When you reproach Shaw for advertising himself he tells you a story of a Christian Socialist parson's attempt to reclaim the village drunkard, who was a carpenter.

'Do you know, my friend,' said the clergyman, 'that there was once a carpenter who gave His life to redeem the world?'

'Was there?' replied the reprobate. 'Then you bet he did it to get his name up.'

Ask Shaw why his name is always conspicuous in the papers, and he will say, 'Why is the sun always rather noticeable in the heavens?'

25

Summer of Success

If Shaw had died, like Keats, at twenty-six, he would never have been heard of, but, living on beyond three score and ten, he saw every form of recognition come to him before age began to wither and custom stale his infinite waggeries.

Wealth poured in on him; honours were heaped on his shoulders. By 1929 Sir Barry Jackson and Captain Roy Limbert even staged a festival of his plays at Malvern, attempting to rival the festival of Wagner's operas at Bayreuth. Short of bringing on a revolution in England and giving Shaw the dictator's whip to snap, everything had been done for him that human hand could do.

People even sat through a play of his that took three nights to perform. As a test of endurance this may go down in history along with those interminable tree-sitting enterprises and marathon dances which marked the post-war years. For Shaw at sixty-six to have accomplished such a colossal task, surpassing in drama what Wagner's writing does in music, was in itself an achievement that might well have stumped a genius. Its completion did more to strengthen the suspicion that the superman had arrived than all his or any other Nietzschean writings on the subject.

Beginning a play with Adam and Eve and ending it thirty thousand years in the future ought to have assured Shaw's immortality, if anything could. Unfortunately, mere length cannot assure anything but contemporary comment, like any other test of endurance, and so Shaw may have to be satisfied with that and a full purse.

Speaking of his purse, here he is a miracle of miracles, a writer who has not only made plenty of money, but saved it. I shall presently quote his own rough estimate, which represents a tidy sum for a man to make by writing. I found out very early in my career that the only way for a writer to be free from financial troubles is to be on the inside of the Stock Exchange; and in my early years in London I never gave a thought to what my books would bring in royalties. Instead, I trailed along with the manipulators in the City and lived in luxury. But Shaw has never done anything so simple as that. He has written his way to every penny he has.

Shaw has told us that his failure was so complete at first that in nine years he had made by his pen a total of £5 9s. 6d. I paid him £312 a year for his work on *The Saturday Review*; and this was the top of his market as a feuilletonist. Not until his first serious box office success with *The Devil's Disciple* in America had run his bank balance up to four figures did he cease living from hand to mouth. He then married a wife who had a considerable independent income. Since then he has been a well-to-do man. For the last twenty years he has been classed as a rich author.

He has no children, and his wife is well provided for. Viewed in terms of the two thousand pounds that D. H. Lawrence left or even the forty thousand of Arnold Bennett, Shaw's fortune may seem enormous: but it really isn't anywhere nearly so big today as it would have been thirty years ago. Wanting to satisfy the reader's desire to know how it felt to be a rich man, I wrote Shaw, and received the following reply:

Malvern
September 18th 1930

DEAR FRANK HARRIS – You want to know what it feels like to be a rich man. Well, you should know, for if you are not a millionaire at this moment, you have been one for an afternoon, or for a week, or, if rumour be true, for perhaps a year, when you married a lady in Park Lane and spent all her money consorting with Randolph Churchill and Edouard Sept. As a matter of fact, I am not rich as money goes nowadays. My professional income is taxed and surtaxed both in America and England. When from time to time I make, say, twenty thousand pounds, what does that come to when it is invested, and the tax and surtax comes off both the capital and the income it produces? Between my wife's settled property and my own we are in the class that has between five and ten thousand a year, and doesn't spend it all. I am far too busy to enjoy money: I have more than I want, and I have had nothing; and the difference in happiness has been negligible. I am one of those to whom money means security and exemption from petty tyrannies: if society would only provide me with both, I should throw my money out of the window, because it is troublesome to take care of and attracts parasites and hatred. I loathe charity and bountifulness and patronising and so forth: I repeat that when I have to relieve people financially I hate them as heartily as they hate me.

Faithfully,

G. BERNARD SHAW

He loathes charity and bountifulness, because he believes that the only trouble with the poor is poverty; therefore naturally he infers that the socialisation of production and exchange would tend to make poor persons the sporadic exception rather than the most numerous class.

Indeed, I know of no one else in modern days who condemns alms-givings and all organised philanthropy so unconditionally. His attitude in this is well illustrated by his answer to a correspondent who was planning some philanthropic work. In his best vein Shaw advised him: 'By all means give "every penny you can spare to those who are most in need of monetary help". If you will be kind enough to send it to the Treasurer of the Fabian Society, 11 Dartmouth St, London, SW1, you may depend upon its being wanted and well used. If you prefer relieving needy persons, I can give you the names and addresses of several fathers of families who can be depended on to absorb all your superfluous resources, however vast they may be. By making yourself poor for their sakes you will have the satisfaction of adding one more poor family to the existing mass of poverty and contributing your utmost to the ransom which perpetuates the existing social system. You will go through life consoled by an inexhaustible sense of moral superiority to bishops and other inconsistent Christians. And you will never be at a loss for friends. Where the carcass is, there will the eagles be gathered. You are not a prig – only a damned fool. A month's experience will cure you.'

His indignant correspondent naturally resented Shaw's manner and attitude. But his resentment could not sway Shaw from his position. He emphasised it by writing the aspiring philanthropist again: 'Yes: you are an ass; and nothing will help you until you get over that.

' "A has money, B is without. If A doesn't share with B he is – well, I call him a thief." Just what an ass would do. Pray what do you call B if he accepts A's bounty? I strongly recommend you to become a stock-broker. You believe that doing good means giving money; and you fancy yourself in the character of Lord Bountiful with a touch of

St Francis. Yes, a hopeless ass. No matter: embrace your destiny and become a philanthropist. It is not a bad life for people who are built that way.'

But do not make the mistake of taking Shaw's apparent callousness for a lack of sympathy for those who suffer. It is the callousness of conviction rather than of selfishness. I must admit, however, that Shaw is more successful in living up to his convictions on poverty than to any other phase of his Socialist *credo*. Still, I could cite certain examples of Shaw's kindness, but I cannot stress it too emphatically that Shaw does hate to have his kindnesses get abroad. And not because such publicity shocks his sense of good taste, but because he fears that if it does get about that he's a pretty decent fellow at heart, beggars will make it a world of outstretched palms for him from London to Cairo every time he takes a holiday.

Where he errs so badly is in his publicity values. Beggars there are by thousands who never heard of him. Do I exaggerate? Then stop the first tramp you meet, or go several steps farther up or down the social and economic ladder and ask a truck-driver, policeman, or farm-hand. Ask who is Ford? Rockefeller? Edison? Rothschild? You will get approximately correct answers. Ask about Shaw, and nine times out of ten they will tell you it's just a sissy expression meaning, 'Oh, hell!'

Now, if these millionaires who are every bit as generous as Shaw have not been reduced to poverty, just how well founded is his fear? Obviously not well founded at all. He isn't well known enough. He's as secure in his riches from anything but a united attack by all the income tax assessors of the Governments of the world as, say, the manufacturer of Nuxated Iron.

In the light of such knowledge, the following letter seems to be drawing the long bow a bit:

The Metropole Hotel, Minehead, Somerset
April 5th 1923

DEAR FRANK HARRIS – I can't afford it. Your letter declaring that X must have five hundred pounds on Sunday or perish, fortunately (for me) did not overtake me here until yesterday; and I did not read it, being tired with the journey and confronted with a mountain of letters, until today.

All I can do is to write to Grant Richards to say that if he will take up the book I will throw in my contributions as in America. If that fails, X must drive a taxi; for he has come to a Europe where men of high academic and literary distinction are trying to keep body and soul together by writing the most piteous begging letters, and mostly failing. I cannot describe to you what this side of my correspondence is like: the poor wretches are like crying children: they pour out everything in desperate protest against the cruelty of their situation; and we who have escaped only by the skin of our teeth have to harden our hearts and let them perish, as all we have would be only a drop in the ocean of their needs. As to the unfortunate students . . . !

Meanwhile I am a multi-millionaire. In Vienna my bank balance (I have never drawn a farthing since the war) is 30,090,000 kronen. In Berlin I have masses of marks on which I have paid income tax at 240. Their valuta is now 100,000! I have a couple of million roubles in Moscow which cannot be sent to me because they are not sufficient to pay for a draft and a registered letter. In London my plays draw receipts undreamt-of for highbrow stuff before the war, and un-common then even for popular stuff; but theatre expenses have been doubled, and left me economically impossible except in the provincial repertory companies. The net result is that, since the war, every January 1st and July 1st, when my taxes have to be met, has been a squeeze to avoid selling out. I have had to resort to journalism in the Hearst papers to save the situation more than once. In short, I am one of the fortunate ones; and I am personally comfortable and keep two cars; but I have not a penny to spare. Some time ago the wife of one of the richest men in England, with God knows how many times my income, said to me what I have just written to you: 'I have not a penny to spend.'

That is what we are up against over here: culture penniless and profiteers rolling in money but indifferent to culture. Appeal to humanity, generosity, good nature; and it is the kindest man who meets you with the hollowest laugh. From starving millions in Russia and Austria, starving authors, professors, and boot-blacking students in Germany, to starving relatives at home, he has had his feelings so harrowed since 1918 that he is like Macbeth, past caring for anybody in distress.

I could draw a cheque for five hundred pounds; but here is a letter from my cousin's daughter, destitute and despairing; and here is another from an Irish gentleman, whose friendship dates from the eighteen-seventies, begging me to advise him as to where he can sell his pictures. Here, too, is Nansen, vainly trying to feed multitudes with five loaves and two small fishes. And my own hotel bill is about four guineas a day even here on the mud of the British Channel. There is only one chance for me: to give nothing. So X starves; the cousin starves; and the old friend may eat his pictures; and the multitudes may perish whilst I overeat and deplore the shocking condition of the others. My Viennese translator, a Jew, would not take money. I had to translate one of his plays and get it produced in New York for him. It took me longer than an original play, and drew only ten thousand pounds. We got each four hundred pounds: a heavy loss for me; but for him the delirious sum of forty million marks pure surcroit.

Yours,

G. B. S.

It is this attitude of his toward charity and philanthropy that causes him to be generally considered as lacking feelings and heart. But he expresses abhorrence for 'those abominable bastard Utopias of genteel charity, in which the poor are first robbed and then pauperised by way of compensation, in order that the rich man may combine the idle luxury of the protected thief with the unctuous self-satisfaction of the pious philanthropist'.

It is evident that Shaw is ungenerous and uncharitable 'on principle'. And here again I am reminded of his castigation of the Englishman who exploits other nations, robs and murders them 'on principle'. It is wonderful and great to live up to one's convictions, provided they are worth living up to. Shaw's Socialism is certainly worth it, but, as I have shown in the previous pages, he has not lived up to a single one of his Socialist creeds – with the sole exception of not indulging in anti-Socialist philanthropy.

This Scotch strain has him even claiming that he has helped Germany pay its indemnity! Witness: 'The money with which they paid my theatre fees,' he says, 'became so worthless that I can show you a note for ten million marks which I could not lodge to my credit in Berlin because the bankers would not take account of anything less than billions – real billions, not American billions. In other words, the Germans have paid the indemnity largely with my money and that of their other victorious foreign creditors. So much for the method of your financial experts. The laugh is with Germany as far as I am concerned.'

He refuses to share his riches even for the benefit of hospitals. Yet surely he knows that the sick and maimed cannot wait till the Shavian social panacea will bring them relief. I cannot characterise Shaw's anti-philanthropic stand 'on principle' better than by quoting this letter:

10 Adelphi Terrace, W.C.
June 12th 1908

DEAR MARRIOTT – The Honourable Sydney So and So is a tremendous swell, being the son and heir of Lord Somebody and married to the daughter of the Earl of Elsewhere. He is a jolly energetic sort of chap. He was a great swimmer and rowing man twenty years ago, and now he is on all sorts of companies and public bodies. But the main point for you to remember is that he is a Chairman of the London Hospital, the Poplar Hospital for Accidents, and the Tilbury Cottage Hospital. Just consider what this means. When the docks are very busy an accident case comes in to the City of London Hospital every twenty minutes or thereabouts, and no doubt it is the same at Poplar. Every one of these accidents should be treated at the expense of the dock companies. If they were, the dock companies would take a good deal more care to prevent them happening; but as they can hand them on to the hospitals, which are supported by public subscriptions, they are practically using those subscriptions to pay the cost of their own operations. Everybody who subscribes to these hospitals is subscribing something to the dividends of the dock companies. Now you may ask me why the Honourable Sydney So and So is an indefatigable collector of hospital subscriptions – why he writes such stirring appeals to *The Times* – why he is chairman of three riverside hospitals and of none others. The explanation is very simple. He is Deputy-Chairman of the London and India Docks Company.

He once wrote me a private letter telling me that he had noticed that I was not subscribing to the hospitals and that it was my duty to do so. I replied, explaining the position exactly as I have explained it to you. He took it with the greatest possible good humour; and the correspondence ended in quite a friendly way.

If he calls you hysterical idiots, I think you may fairly reply that at all events there is nothing hysterical and nothing idiotic about him, and that he is quite the best man of business in London, as nobody else has succeeded in getting half so much out of the public for the benefit of his dock company as he has. Don't be indignant about it.

Keep your temper and pay him compliments on his smartness; and you will knock him into a cocked hat.

Yours faithfully,

G. BERNARD SHAW

But the crosses of greatness are not only spiked with the miseries of money: fame also has her agonies. Perhaps the thought of all the besieging, begging letters he would have to read drove Shaw into accepting the Nobel award but not the money. When the Swedish Academy voted him the Nobel Prize for Literature in 1925 it was worth nearly eight thousand pounds.

Shaw didn't even understand why they had picked him that particular year.

'It must be,' he said, 'to reward me for not having written anything then.'

Of course, recognition by the Swedish Academy, or by any other academy for that matter, never includes striving authors. Discovering real genius is not the Academy's field. The prize committee is always guided by a 'reasonably dignified' popularity, and, as Shaw has remarked, 'The Nobel business is a lottery open to all who have achieved a minimum of celebrity.'

Receiving the prize gave Shaw a chance for a grand gesture. People were asking what a millionaire author would do with eight thousand pounds in prize money. Well, lover of surprises that he is, Shaw handed one to the world. The man who wouldn't give a penny to help an injured dock-worker gave his Nobel Prize to the poor writers of Sweden, thus telling the prize-giving committee in effect that charity should begin at home.

It was a fine piece of Shawmanship, yet strangely out of keeping with his denunciation of charity and bountifulness. At such moments Shaw reminds me of that other champion of humanity, Andrew Carnegie, who had proclaimed that it is not disgraceful to die rich, and proved it by dying a multi-millionaire.

To what degree affluence and publicity had raised Shaw can best be illustrated by the Malvern Festival. It was to be the crowning moment of his career, and all preparations in the summer of 1929 seemed to indicate that the festival, which would open with a new play of Shaw, would be England's answer to the German festivals at Salzburg, Bayreuth, and such places.

Early on a Sunday morning in August, a trainload of critics was despatched from London to Malvern, a four-hours' trip, to see *The Apple Cart*. As plays are opening every day all the way from Birmingham to Glasgow, with London as their ultimate destination, and no critic ever bothers to leave the West End to see them, this pilgrimage to Malvern indicated either one of two things: that Shaw had the Press eating out of his hand or that the play was his best ever and no journalist should miss it for anything.

For weeks before, Malvern was magically interested in the drama. Previously it had been a Worcestershire resort, a hill town, the last resting-place of Jenny Lind, the Swedish Nightingale, surrounded by historical monuments and a beautiful countryside, but no more interested in the theatre than any such resort is likely to be. Shaw liked it because it had no trams, and because Sir Edward Elgar lived near by.

Everybody agreed that Shaw was magnificent. He climbed over the hills, amazing the young men with his agility, swam in the pool of the town, to the delight of the flappers, and otherwise had a wonderful time.

I have no doubt that Shaw, on realising that Malvern was just over the hills from Stratford-on-Avon, thought his own festival might effectively close the Shakespearean controversy for all time. He even invited the Stratford players to come over on the opening Sunday afternoon to view *The Apple Cart*.

The Apple Cart itself in its actual writing took him six weeks. He writes in shorthand, you know, and, once started, he soon finishes a play. But here at least was a play that might better have been finished the first day. Never were things staged so impressively and never was the labour so little worth it. A house full of critics sat through the first act, which took one hour and twenty minutes, one speech alone running quarter of an hour and, when they went out in the garden for fresh air, most of them wondered why they ever had to go into the theatre again. But back they went for an interlude that had nothing to do with the play, and then some more fresh air, only to be thrust back into the chattering prison until in the end they staggered out of one of the feeblest plays Bernard Shaw had ever written.

The plot is simply told. About the year 1962 a King of England is confronted with a Cabinet ultimatum. If he signs this ultimatum he must henceforth never speak in public, never by even indirect methods present his ideas to the Press, and never use his royal veto on an Act of

Parliament. Rather than acquiesce in this, the King says he will ab-dicate, and, while the Cabinet is welcoming his idea, he adds that he will abdicate in favour of his son, divest himself of all titles, and stand for Parliament as a commoner for Windsor. As the new King will have to call somebody to head the Cabinet, who knows but what he may call the ex-King Magnus himself? The Prime Minister sees in this an even worse condition than he has to endure at present, and so tears up the ultimatum, giving the King the victory.

So ends Shaw's career where Shakespeare began, playing up the princes of the blood against the mass of mankind. Except for two parts, both violently exaggerated – a thundering ribald leader dressed in a Russian red smock and black trousers tucked into high boots, and an American ambassador who was like an Uncle Sam cartoon done in three colours by Winsor McKay – there was nothing in this play to impel a critic to walk across the street to see, let alone travel more than a hundred miles on his day off.

Since Aristotle tutored Alexander in the vain hope of producing a philosopher-king to replace the warriors that had ruled the world since history began, others have looked for such leaders and have created them out of their own dreams when they didn't exist. England has not had such a ruler since King Arthur's time, and he was a legend. Yet in *The Apple Cart* Shaw saw such a king ruling in England after all of us now living are dead.

Who was the most civilised King in Shaw's own time? King Edward VII, unquestionably. Yet imagine placing him against Asquith, Balfour, or Lloyd George in a play of wits. The fact is that kings, almost without exception, whether in apple carts or royal carriages, are spoilt children. Great nobles and sons of millionaires suffer under similar disadvantages. Why they suffer this way is because every path is made easy for them.

In King Edward's case, because his mother always spoke German he talked with a strong German accent all his life. This was because he was not subjected to criticism when a boy between the ages of fourteen and eighteen. Any other boy would have been laughed at, and this would have quickly corrected the fault. He was no judge of men except by the title they bore, and would have been patronising toward Shaw, though he would have received a duke, who might have been next door to an imbecile, with utmost consideration.

For a king in these times, then, to outwit a Prime Minister when in point of fact most of the kings have lost their jobs because of incompetence, shows Shaw as far removed from realism as Sir Walter Scott. Shaw could only do it by making the Prime Minister a fool, and, in fact, all the characters fools but his King Magnus.

In a subsequent preface Shaw denied that the play was an attack on democracy, but his denial only makes his play more addled, not less. For all the things one may say against democracy, it is more competent than any monarchy. You can prove that quickly by illustrating the superior merits of French officers in the World War where the leaders came up from the *bourgeois* or peasant classes. The English and German armies, for all their marvellous resources, were inefficient precisely because the commanders were of the aristocracy and had never earned their jobs.

In industry the reverse is true. Here the Germans were more competent than the French, because the aristocracy confined themselves to the Court and the army and left industry to the people. That is why Germany forged ahead so rapidly after the war. She is far more efficient in industry than in war, far superior to all her rivals in the arts of peace. Where this law of the survival of the fittest operates freely in war, industry, or politics it is unbeatable, and all the charming manners in the world go out like a candle in the wind when placed against it.

For Shaw to miss this obvious truth showed, indeed, that the pre-seventy part of him was dead.

The next year he had no new play, and the honours of his own festival were filched from him by Rudolf Besier's *The Barretts of Wimpole Street*.

By 1931 the Malvern Festival had moved far from an all-Shavian programme. Five centuries of English drama formed its programme, with no Shaw play mentioned anywhere in the five centuries. That was quite a drop for Shakespeare's superior; from the whole programme to no place on the programme whatever in two years – a fair index of his lack of staying-power.

26

Future

Shaw shares a widely established opinion that the biography of a living man can't be finished till he's dead. This means that my Life of him ought to have ended with the dispute over *Saint Joan*, for surely *The Apple Cart* was written by a dead man.

But long before he died, Shaw took the precaution to assure his immortality by prevailing upon Rodin to cast his features in bronze. He expected to be mentioned in biographic dictionaries a thousand years hence as: 'Shaw, Bernard: subject of a bust by Rodin: otherwise unknown.'

I don't think this is funny. I only wish it were, for Shaw has tried hard and deserves a better fate.

On re-examining Shaw's forty odd volumes – on every subject in the world and beyond it – I find only one consistently persistent idea throughout all of his works and life, and that is improvement. However contradictory his writings, views, and opinions, he always wanted things to be better than they were. Never mind that he was a scoffer and religious at the same time; an atheist and pew renter, a Socialistic supporter of war, a peace-loving Fabian favouring a strong Army, a libertarian eulogising Mussolini, a zealous champion of State control fighting the Government censor, a believer in freedom advocating compulsory equalisation of incomes, a zealot of 'the true joy of life' scoffing at love and sex, and a man of many other parts like a crazy-quilt.

These things happen in all of us, and a day's indigestion can destroy the consistency of a whole year's effort.

For that reason I have no quarrel with him because of his inconsistencies and contradictions. But discussing his chances of survival, I conclude that here is too much confusion, too much sound and fury signifying nothing, to mean much to posterity. Our children's critics will have no patience going through all that maze which is his mind.

I wish with all my heart I could say, as Shelley said of Keats:

> Till the future dare forget the past
> His name and fate shall be
> An echo and a light unto eternity.

But I cannot find it in me to praise him beyond all men. He will not live. His rhetoric is racy, intuitively good, but it lacks inspiration; and though often fine, never reaches genius. A play here and there may be ranked with Sheridan, Congreve, and Wilde, but certainly not above them.

Though he remains a writer of importance, his plays on re-reading are dull. Only a few seem to me likely to live. The others will be as out of date before Shaw is dead twenty years as Ibsen is out of date today. And what's worse, Shaw has no imitators. His own aping of Ibsen kept Ibsen alive for another generation, but nobody seems to be doing as much for him.

One usually has a good time in the theatre with him, but no better than at a circus or a cinema. An hour later you need a strong effort to remember what the thing was about. This is significant; it is the very essence of what Shaw lacks to make him live. He is the wittiest author of our time; he may even be the wittiest in English literature. But his plays, almost all of them, lack vitality.

But as a personality, Shaw will live longer. He certainly is likely to survive as have Doctor Johnson and Samuel Pepys, two men in English literature whose personalities also were bigger than their works. He has missed greatness in many ways. I only wish he had gone to gaol at least once for some big idea. It would have been something to bring before the court of heaven when asking for his immortal soul. But he has never gone to gaol, not even for contempt of court as I have, nor for poaching as Shakespeare did, nor for folly as Wilde did, nor for roguery as Villon did, nor for another man as Cervantes did.

Why such a bizarre test? Because great men are different from the general flock. They do not follow the beaten path – they wouldn't be great if they did. They are apt to feel and think differently, and – what is more important – to *act* differently.

It is not this difference that makes them great; it's their greatness that makes the difference, and makes it inevitable. That difference leads, one way or another, to condemnation and denunciation and ultimately to prison, to the gallows, or to the cross.

The great men cannot keep within the confines of an established order which is rigged against the good of this world. Shaw, however, has succeeded during his almost four score years in containing himself within the limits of good behaviour and manners. Now he is too old, I fear, ever to attain the distinction of the kind of service-stripes which are cast by shadows through prison bars.

He has been in the public eye for forty years, and yet it would be false to say that he has been an important figure. When I try to point out what he has accomplished in political or social life, I find nothing to put my finger on. His Socialism and similar lifelong propagandas have left no effect whatever. The English censorship, which he has fought throughout his public career, is stronger now than when he began. As an advocate of various cases and reforms he has been an absolute failure.

What, then, did he accomplish or give to the world that will secure him immortality? Nothing that I can see. How could he? All he had was a clear eye for seeing what the trouble was. He didn't kill, nor was he killed by it. All he did was to spit putty balls at it from his ivory tower, and laugh.

Let us briefly examine the various fields of his endeavour. In philosophy he has given us no new or vital truth; no new word in religion, no glimpse even of any great human vision. He is neither philosopher nor scientist; neither passionate prophet nor self-sacrificing martyr. How, then, hope to hold the human stage 'for generations to come'?

He thinks otherwise. 'I shall be a panjandrum of literature for the next three hundred years,' he once said to William Archer. But his own estimate, I think, is too obviously subjective and exaggerated.

He is a world dramatist, he says, simply because they play him, with or without his leave, everywhere from London to Japan, both ways round, and at all the intermediate stations. His currency is as universal as that of *Charlie's Aunt* or Charlie Chaplin. He crosses all frontiers. So does Mr Chaplin. 'But when we are inclined to feel conceited about it,' he confesses, 'we are pulled up by the fact that a good many popular entertainers, whose claims to be at the bottom of their profession are as strong as ours to be at the top of it, get round the world as easily as we.'

I sense the tone of disillusion and sadness in these words. I sense sadness in myself on reading them, for I know Shaw is right. Make people laugh, and they will rank you as successful and pay you well. All the world loves a jester, and stones the true prophet. The future forgets the jester, and immortalises the prophet.

We live in a democratic age, and Shaw has justly said: 'Democracy always prefers second-bests.' True and tragic, and Shaw is the preferred.

So mere popularity means nothing. It can turn sour like cream overnight. This fermentation in Shaw's case is taking place now. He is not nearly as popular today as he was five years ago. Before another generation grows up he will be as dead as Artemus Ward is today, and in a hundred years not even calendars of his epigrams will remain.

A philosopher may live for posterity by his arguments, but a dramatist cannot. Shaw's wisdom is too light. Those paradoxes and epigrams of his, paraphrased from the sayings of La Rochefoucauld, Schopenhauer, Strindberg, Ibsen, Nietzsche, and Samuel Butler, are rapier thrusts at the sun. They mean nothing when it's all over. The cleverness of his dialogue is stage journalism. There is not a single character in all his plays, nor a solitary line that haunts one's memory.

Not an original thinker, not a great dramatist, Shaw will live for ages as personality. He has always been a strong, marked and unique individuality. His views and opinions may have antagonised, his manner may have offended, his idiosyncrasies may have amused, yet none was able to remain indifferent to what he said and did. In this he touches genius: but this part of men dies, and when the daily stimulant comes no longer, those left behind forget quickly, or turn to new mimes to amuse them.

In all ages there have been pioneers who have lived long enough to seem conservative because the times have caught up to them and passed them. In Shaw's case the reverse is unfortunately true. The world has not advanced, but the former reformer has turned reactionary. Usually the real thinker becomes more revolutionary as he grows older, because he loses faith in conventional methods of reform. Shaw, on the contrary, has not progressed with increasing years and success. He did not grow, and that means he regressed. Take any simple point as an example.

Thirty years ago, from his very first play, the wealthy parents were pragmatic persons who knew that their wealth, whether derived from slums (*Widowers' Houses*), prostitution (*Mrs Warren's Profession*), or munitions (*Major Barbara*), was tainted. They knew, more, that everybody was tarred with the same brush (even the young reformer-heroes), and consequently nothing could be done about anything.

He still writes that way, as witness *The Apple Cart*, where again nothing can be done about anything.

So in thirty years his growth has been nil. But in thirty years his fame has circled the earth.

Such are the sweet uses of dogmatic reiteration.

For a quarter of a century I have been waiting for just one book from Shaw with the heart and guts and brains of the whole meaning of life in it: one world-shaking play, the story told once for all and told astonishingly, thrilling as from scene to scene, holding our breathless interest from act to act, burning into us unforgettable scenes and visions of men at hand-grips with Fate, leaving us finally shaken, exhausted, drained of emotion, dazzled by new vistas, throbbing with wild hopes.

But in vain I look for it. Shaw, the dramatist, was getting weaker all the time, dying. When asked how he would like to do this he once said: 'I should prefer to die in a reasonably dry ditch under the stars.'

I am afraid there is no hope for him to arrive at even that. All through his life defeated, he is doomed to be defeated even in his choice of death. He is too successful to die in a ditch, it will have to be in a comfortable bed, with the window shades down and – no stars.

The world has softened much toward him. Politicians have even been offering him a knighthood, for all the world as if he were nothing but an actor or soap-maker or speed-demon. They have done this out of compassion for a white-bearded sage with a funny twist in mind, not in any sense a man to be feared any more. So he comes to the end, a Puritan rebel who insulted his times and was well paid for it.

'Life levels all men,' he believes, 'and death reveals the eminent.' Unfortunately it is death that levels all men and time reveals their masters.

And more's the pity; for I who loved Shaw much, and knew the man he might have been, wanted him to endure until another careering planet crashes into this one and blows us all to glory.

*   *   *

Postscript by the subject of this memoir

Frank Harris, having finished this last chapter, died on the twenty-sixth of August, 1931, in his seventy-sixth year, leaving his proof sheets to be corrected for the press by me. I have had to do many odd jobs in my time; but this one is quite the oddest.

For Frank, famous for his pen-portraits, was the most impossible of biographers. He himself called the sketches of his contemporaries which form such a large part of his writings *Contemporary Portraits*. And that is exactly what they were: portraits, and very rapid impressionist portraits at that. In spite of the fame of his *Life of Oscar Wilde*, it is not really a biography: it is a series of impressions from successive personal contacts and directly observed incidents. And this book he describes always as a portrait, and never as that portentously exact result of laborious research and scrupulous verification implied by the word biography. The truth is that Frank was an exceedingly sensitive man, who reacted with such violence, not only to authentic facts, but to any sort of gossip that stirred up his always seething susceptibility to scornful indignation, that he could not stop to ask himself the first question of the professed biographer, which is, 'What is the evidence for this?' and the cognate question of the intellectually honest judicial critic, 'What else could I have done had it been my own case?'

One consequence of this was that Harris suffered deeply from repeated disillusions and disappointments. Like Hedda Gabler he was tormented by a sense of sordidness in the commonplace realities which form so much of the stuff of life, and was not only disappointed in people who did nothing splendid, but savagely contemptuous of people who did not want to have anything splendid done.

He often reminded me of a revolutionist who rose at an obscure meeting held in a cellar near Gower Street shortly after the settlement of the great London dock strike of 1889. In that struggle the champions of the dockers were Mr John Burns, Mr Tom Mann, and Cardinal Manning. Mr Burns shared with the Cardinal the credit of the settlement; and I, being the principal speaker at the meeting, gave him his due.

But this hero had been dreaming of greater things than the miserable sixpence an hour which I was claiming as a great victory for the dockers. He denounced Mr Burns in unmeasured terms; and he denounced me similarly for supporting him. He was quite beyond argument; so I put the critical question to him, 'What would you have done had you been in John Burns's place?'

He was quite equal to the occasion. 'Done!' he thundered. 'I would have taken the scarlet cardinal by the scruff of his gory neck and chucked him into the incarnadined river.'

What else could a man say when, dazzled by millennial visions, he was invited to cheer himself hoarse over sixpence an hour for a job so heavy and dangerous that accidents requiring hospital treatment occurred every twenty minutes? I sympathised with the protest, though I knew very well what an enormous effort it had cost to get the dockers that wretched sixpence, and how utterly incapable my Boanergic denouncer would have been of getting a farthing for them.

Frank, too, was a man of splendid visions, unreasonable expectations, fierce appetites which he was unable to relate to anything except to romantic literature, and especially to the impetuous rhetoric of Shakespeare. It is hardly an exaggeration to say that he ultimately quarrelled with everybody but Shakespeare; and this book contains several attempts to quarrel with me. But I bear no malice, as he is at bottom trying to quarrel with a scheme of things in which fellows like me crawl between earth and heaven and snatch little successes in which there is no sort of justice and fundamentally no reality. Many of those spirits, who, like Frank, can by no means learn to live in the real world and suffer fools and humbugs gladly, have nobility of soul, though for want of adequate secular faculties – economic faculty, legal faculty, mathematical faculty, business faculty, and objective faculty generally – this nobility cannot always save them from comparatively squalid adventures in the material sphere. Harris seized his opportunities with a confident audacity that carried everything before it. His resonant voice, capable of every accent of scorn, his brilliant eyes, his ready tongue, his bold individual style, imposed him, on men and women alike, as one who was his own best credential. His knowledge and capacity were assumed without evidence at first sight. He believed himself to be a strong man and a man of action; and he was taken by everyone at his own valuation from the moment when his first marriage rescued him from some very dark days of poverty in Germany, whither he had been drawn in pursuit of literary learning, and where the only thing he learnt was that unless he had money the world would have no mercy on him. But though he took the tide in his affairs unhesitatingly at the flood, he was not thick-skinned enough to hold his friendships; and the worst of it was that instead of shewing his sensitiveness he made everyone believe that he was as tough as hickory.

I remember my own surprise when the late Julia Frankau (Frank Danby) one day remonstrated with me very earnestly for treating him too roughly. She urged me to remember that he was an exquisitely sensitive man. My own early experience, which included nearly ten years of apparently hopeless failure, had hardened me to such a degree that I had lost all sensitiveness to any criticism but my self-criticism. It is impossible to acquire this hardness and retain a sympathetic understanding of how something that falls on you with the weight of a fly's foot can sting apparently tougher men like the lash of a whip. So I was somewhat incredulous at first; but I soon saw that Mrs Frankau was right, and that Harris could not bear the spurns that patient merit from the unworthy takes with any sort of equanimity. He accumulated quarrels and tired of all his enterprises. It was at last apparent that in any concern which depended on his co-operation with and management of colleagues he would never get anywhere because he always stopped to fight somebody, and imagined every position that occurred instead of studying it. He blazed through London like a comet, leaving a trail of deeply annoyed persons behind him, and like a meteor through America, where the war betrayed him into backing the loser in his generous indignation against the Allied ambush. Then he retired to Nice and became a sort of literary sage to whom all high-souled young Americans with literary ambitions made pilgrimages in their wander years, and at last died there peacefully enough.

He really had not one career but two, simultaneous but on different planes. On the imaginative plane the invariable generosity of his transports of indignation, scorn, pity, chivalry, and defiance of snobberies, powers, and principalities enabled him to retain the regard of people who had the same sympathies. But on the prosaic plane of everyday life he got into difficulties and incurred maledictions from which it was not always possible to defend him.

These difficulties are not worth bothering about now. They were all made worse by his main delusion, which was an enormous one and sometimes highly comic. He was firmly persuaded that the human race consisted entirely of Frank Harrises and women of the sort Frank Harris idealised. Any departure from this standard was in his eyes delinquency, cretinism, unforgivable sin, diabolism. As there was only one Frank Harris in the world, and the sort of woman he idealised never completely existed except in his imagination, the effect on his social manners was often disastrous. And the matter was complicated further by his manifold nature; for his scope ranged from depths of materialism to heights of spirituality; and his ideal of womanhood varied accordingly.

As a result his dinner-table conversation was often of the most disconcerting inappropriateness. If he took in a quiet deaconess he would entertain her on the assumption that her personal morals and religious views were those of our post-war night clubs. If, knowing this, you took care to put him beside the most abandoned lady present, he would discourse to her on his favourite subject of the beauty of the character of Jesus, and his intention of writing a great book about it. And as all his conversation was uttered in a resonant and arresting voice that reached the farthest corners of the room, he was apt to produce the situation which was in Oscar Wilde's mind when he said, 'Frank Harris has been received in all the great houses – *once.*' In the end it was inevitable that he should establish himself in a retreat where he could be approached only on his own terms; and this, after making London and New York too hot to hold him, he found in Nice as aforesaid. He impressed many young bloods in revolt against *bourgeois* civilisation as a great man, as I have reason to know; for when they came my way afterwards I had to be careful not to shock them by the slightest levity in discussing him. He was no solitary prophet either: he could inspire and hold the devotion of his wife, who was much younger than he, and knew quite well what she was sacrificing for him. When he was editor of *The Saturday Review* he chose and held together for a while a team of contributors whom no one else had the gumption to choose or the courage to back with a free hand. I think I know pretty well all the grievances his detractors had against him; but if I had to write his epitaph it should run, *'Here lies a man of letters who hated cruelty and injustice and bad art, and never spared them in his own interest. R.I.P.'*

It remains for me only to explain the extent to which I have had to revise this book in order to make its publication possible. Frank knew very little of the facts of my life, and, having no patience for the very dull work of investigation, or even for a look at Professor Archibald Henderson's monumental biography of me, put in a good deal of guesswork. His guesses were not always successful: some of them were miles off the mark. Even when he had obtained information from me directly he could not jettison the guesses that conflicted with it, and continued to write with the information and the imaginative conjecture running in his head concurrently, and coming uppermost alternately, thereby landing himself in obvious contradictions. I have got rid of the contradictions on the objective plane by simply supplying or correcting the facts, so that future writers using the work as a book of reference will not be misled. But I have made no attempt to reconcile the subjective contradictions, even when these have arisen through his slips backwards and forwards between conjectural fiction and accurate information. Many of these contradictions and inconsistencies are between the mood of one day and another as he wrote, and are none the worse for that. Nothing can be more unnatural and biographically worthless than a rigid single estimate with everything else forced into harmony with it: it is like an instantaneous photograph of a horse transfixed by the camera in the act of galloping. In one or two places, where a criticism was attached to some fable that had to be deleted, I have transposed it to a context which saved its coherence. All the criticisms, jibes, explosions of passing ill humour, and condemnations have been piously preserved; and I have taken care that they have lost nothing by a few inevitable displacements.

I could not, however, save Frank Harris from doing himself some injustice in this book. His list of the passions that life offers to the dramatic poet: 'love, jealousy, envy, the will to power: passions as primitive as they are enduring', would put him out of court in dealing with humanity in its highest stage of evolution, or with society in its highest stage of civilisation. If you are to rule out religious ecstasy, political utopianism, the pursuit of knowledge and of power over matter and circumstances as distinguished from vulgar ambition, the struggle in that pursuit to extend mental faculty, especially mathematical faculty, and the fixation in language, music, colour and form of imaginative conceptions, thereby making their inspiration communicable, you have nothing left but savagery; and if Harris had been really limited, as he implies, to love, jealousy, envy and ambition, he would obviously have been no more competent to write a book about my work than a Hollywood scenario inventor to write a book about Einstein. His own work clears him of any such disqualification. He was a cold-blooded writer, even when his theme was sex, like the French 'realist' writers who pleased him most. His impatience with artistic graces of expression, which sometimes extended to quite harmless and convenient decencies of conversation, was at bottom a scientific matter-of-factness. He rails at me for not writing like Swinburne and D'Annunzio; but you have only to turn to his stories to see that in his own work he is a hard and austere dissector of humanity, and that the only heroine who has moved him to an outstanding and touching feminine creation is not Cleopatra, but Perovskiaia (Sonia) who sacrificed herself and assassinated a Tsar in a passion of pure political *Weltverbesserungswahn* (world-betterment-craze) which, as he rightly

points out, is my own devouring malady. Note also his contemporary
portraits, every one of which is of some quite hard-headed celebrity
without twopennorth of love story. Evidently Cleopatra no more
satisfied his soul than she satisfies mine, in spite of the thundering
luxuriance of literary power with which her story is told by
Shakespeare.

I think that in every case where Frank Harris does not understand
me, or any other of his contemporaries, the real difficulty always is that
he does not understand himself. It is an old rule in business not to
throw out dirty water until you get in fresh; but the extent to which
men muddle themselves by applying this to affairs of the mind is disastrous. To change the metaphor, they take their loaded guns and put
in a fresh charge without carefully taking out the old, with the result
that at the first fire they scatter their own brains instead of those of their
opponents. Frank's gun was originally loaded, one guesses, by a very
old-fashioned Welsh family with Irish Catholic servants. When he rams
down a supercharge of the latest high explosive on top of their ancient
black gunpowder and lets fly at me – or anyone else – he blows himself
to bits and leaves his adversary amazed but unharmed. But the incident
is always entertaining, and sometimes more instructive than an accurate
shot would have been. In truth this book is valuable, not in the least
as an explanation of my works (for anyone who looks for such an
explanation at second hand when my works are there to tell him all
about it at first hand must be an idiot) but as a demonstration of my
reactions on Harris, who was interesting enough to make his reactions
very readable. Now, to produce a sufficiently strong reaction there
must be some incompatibility; and I find this book amusing (in the best
French sense of the word) in proportion to the clash made by our two
temperaments as they collide.

Naturally, then, I do not endorse all the judgements in this book. Its
scale of values, on which my sociological work appears so insignificant,
and the most negligible sex episodes – or absence of episodes – appear
of supreme importance, could be justified only in a book avowedly
dealing with my sex history solely. I never discussed sex with Frank
Harris, because his intolerant Irish-American prudery – the last quality
he ever suspected in himself – made complete and dispassionate discussion impossible. He never could understand why I insisted that his
autobiographical *Life and Loves*, which he believed to be the last word
in outspoken self-revelation, told us nothing about him that was dis-

tinctively Frank Harrisian, and showed, in one amusingly significant passage, that there is a Joseph somewhere in every Casanova.

This much I am obliged to say, lest it should be held that in passing the proofs for press as corrected by me I am endorsing everything that he says about me. I am not. But no man is a good judge of his own portrait; and if it be well painted he has no right to prevent the artist exhibiting it, or even, when the artist is a deceased friend, to refuse to varnish it before the show opens. I hope this makes my part in the matter clear.

Ayot St Lawrence
October 5th 1931